HOW TO BECOME AN EXPAT

And Move Out of the U.S.

Second Edition

By Ann Fourt

Northoak Books

Northoak Books/Ann Fourt
514 Americas Way #8034
Box Elder, SD 57719
northoakbooks@gmail.com

ISBN 9798743849574
Printed in the United States of America

Acknowledgements

Thank you to all who have given me such positive feedback on the first edition of this book. Since information of this type tends to go out of date quickly, the second edition has updates for every chapter. I have also added an index to this print edition.

I would like to acknowledge the support and encouragement of the Cuenca Writers Collective of Cuenca, Ecuador in reviewing the manuscript for this book and making many valuable suggestions and corrections.

I would particularly like to thank Frances Hogg Lochow, founder of the Cuenca Writers Collective, for all the work she does in volunteering her time to helping other writers improve their craft in all genres.

Special thanks to Betty Alderete, medical facilitator formerly of Cuenca, Ecuador, for providing her insights into obtaining healthcare in a foreign country, and to Canadian IT expert Tim Williams for his insights into IT security and privacy issues for expats. Thanks also to J.T. Neira for his unique insights into American vs. Ecuadorian culture and politics.

I would also like to thank all of the expats, too numerous to mention by name, whom I have come across in my journeys outside the U.S. for their experiences that have been incorporated into this book. There is nothing like the school of hard knocks to teach important lessons.

Ann Fourt
Cuenca, Ecuador
September 2022

To Dorothy Perkins Fourt

I wish you were here to come along for the ride.

Table of Contents

Chapter 1
Introduction

Welcome! So, you're thinking of moving and living somewhere outside the U.S.?

Life can be a challenge when there is ever-increasing rent, out-of-pocket health care costs that your health insurance won't pay, student loan debt, car repairs, family emergencies, job layoffs, or maybe some bad choices that you made along the way.

Maybe you've had enough of the corporate rat race: the endless overtime, the ever-increasing workload without any increase in pay or title, the office politics, the lengthy round trip commute every day. You've gained 40 pounds in the last year but don't have time to exercise, and your health is going downhill.

Maybe you're considering becoming a digital nomad, doing the same work that you're now doing but from outside the U.S. with a far lower cost of living, with the additional attraction of getting to know different cultures and people.

Are you already a remote worker but ready to live somewhere more permanently outside the U.S.?

Has the coronavirus pandemic completely wrecked your finances and turned your life upside down?

Are you sick of paying $2,000 per month (or more) for health insurance that has a $7,000 annual deductible?

Are you ready for a different adventure, living outside of the U.S.?

Married or single, there's no reason why you can't prepare yourself to take the plunge.

Chapter 1 – Introduction

Are you just plain tired of living in the U.S.?

This book is for you.

I went through all the steps that you are probably now asking about when I left the U.S. in mid-2017. I did a lot of research about how to move abroad. I found plenty of books about 'Retire to Costa Rica' or 'Move to Thailand' or 'Run Away from the U.S.' but none of them seemed to address the nuts-and-bolts details of how do you actually accomplish this from a practical standpoint. So, I'm going to share with you what I have learned about *how to do it*.

Deciding to move out of the U.S. is a big decision. **You should not make it lightly or quickly.**

I have noticed that when one is mulling over a big decision – job or career change, divorce, a move across the country – it usually takes some time to "ripen." You first start thinking about the idea for some months (or years), then maybe you do some research to look into the details, then you start planning, and eventually you're ready to take the leap.

What at first seems like a terrifying idea then becomes "maybe," and you say to yourself, "hmmm," and after more time it starts to seem like a real possibility. You then start reading more about it, like this book, and then maybe you're ready to use some of your vacation time (assuming you still have a job) to go visit various places and do some research on the ground.

Don't rush the process. You may ultimately decide that you're not ready for such a dramatic change, or that it's not right for you.

My goal is to make this the best value for the dollar that you've ever spent on a book. I wish I had had this information *before* I moved abroad. Learn from the experiences of others who have gone before you.

This book will show you how, step by step, to move out of the U.S. and become an expat, and what issues you will face in doing so. It deals generally with issues faced by all U.S. expats, and is **not specific** to any particular country or continent.

I'm going to assume that you:

- Have enough funds stashed away to live on,
- Have some sort of steady income stream from investments, a pension or annuity, disability payments, Social Security or the like, **or**
- Have some plan to generate income to live on while living outside of the U.S. such as a business or working remotely via the internet.

If you will need to generate income to live on, part of your homework in researching your move abroad will be to investigate ways to do that, which will vary depending upon your individual situation, skill set/work history, where you choose to live, and what kind of work that country allows you to do with the type of visa you have.

Chapter 3**, *"How to Decide Where to Go,"*** discusses factors to consider in deciding on a location. Cost of living is only one factor and while it's important, it should not be the only deciding factor. **You should not rush the location decision** or get locked into only one choice.

This book is written for U.S. readers, whether still working, thinking of becoming digital nomads, or hoping to retire abroad, and focuses on issues common to all U.S. citizens or residents such as worldwide income taxation, banking, receiving Social Security benefits abroad, etc.

Because many people from the U.S. will be interested in Latin America, and that is where I have been living thus far, most of the anecdotes and stories about being an expat will be from Latin America. However, my goal is to make this book relevant to anyone thinking of moving abroad, anywhere in the world; *it is not location-specific in any way*.

I lived in Germany for over a year in the 1980s while attending the University of Heidelberg and became a fluent German speaker. More recently I have lived in Mexico (a year and a half) and Ecuador (over three years) and have also spent time in Colombia, Guatemala, Nicaragua, and Costa Rica.

This book will, in detail, help you how to:

- Decide whether you're a good candidate for living abroad
- Research and make the decision where to go
- Decide what to keep and what to ship to your new home overseas
- Keep U.S. bank and brokerage accounts while living abroad
- Receive Social Security benefits while living abroad
- Stream your favorite U.S. TV shows, movies and live sports events
- Decide whether to keep Medicare or not
- Get your mail and packages
- Decide where to have a U.S. driver's license and register to vote
- Safeguard your computer and stay safe on the internet
- Reduce the chances of identity theft and financial fraud
- Plan for and deal with U.S. and state income tax issues
- Have a U.S. phone number while living abroad & why you should have one
- Select a smart phone for use abroad
- Adjust to your new home abroad

In other words, 'How do I do this?' in granular detail.

Note: things change rapidly in our modern world, so the information contained in this book can become out-of-date. It was current when written as of June 2022.

Let's get started!

Chapter 2
Am I a Good Candidate for Living Abroad?

Questions to Ask Yourself
Will You Be an Unhappy Economic Refugee?
Language Difficulties
Psychological & Social Issues
Friends and Family
Aging Outside the U.S.
Interacting with Locals
Single Women Expats
Male Expats & Female Companionship
Illegal Activities

Let's face it, not everyone is cut out to move and live abroad.

In other countries the residents may have wildly different ideas about what is an acceptable level of noise from parties at 3 a.m., home improvement projects, or barking dogs. There may not be any zoning regulations (or they're not enforced), resulting in a noisy or smelly industrial factory being in the middle of a residential block.

Sometimes the resources available online and in books about moving and living abroad or being a virtual nomad, working online from a remote location, make it sound exotic or romantic. And yes, it's very do-able.

But realize that some of these sources may have a vested interest in *downplaying* the negative aspects of living abroad to sell their books and seminars. I can attest firsthand that some of these expat publications have actual guidelines that prohibit their writers from mentioning anything negative about the place. Personally, I think that misleads your readers.

Questions to Ask Yourself

Ask yourself some hard questions before deciding to move out of the U.S.:

- How adaptable are you to a strange new environment?
- How do you handle feeling lonely and isolated?
- Have you ever traveled to a foreign country?
- How do you feel about having to learn a new language?
- How savvy and "street smart" do you consider yourself to be?
- Do you have an independent personality with a spirit of adventure?
- Can you be assertive without being obnoxious or demanding?
- Do you like to experience new things and explore new places?
- How many times have you moved to a new city in the U.S.?
- How easily do you get frustrated or impatient?
- How flexible or adaptable are you to new situations?
- Is your spouse or significant other on board with moving abroad?
- How resilient are you in dealing with setbacks and disappointments?
- How judgmental do you tend to be of people who are different from you?

Do not jump into this decision with rose-colored glasses, thinking that everything will be fantastic and exciting and an adventure. You don't want to be returning to the U.S. in a year, regretting your decision to move overseas.

Will You Be an Unhappy Economic Refugee?

More and more of the spots around the world that are popular with U.S. expats are seeing a new type of arrival – I'll call them economic refugees. In contrast with earlier arrivals from the U.S., these folks have been wiped out financially by unemployment or health problems, or never earned much during their lifetime to be able to save, and do not have pensions. The prospect of living on a Social Security check of $950 a month isn't very attractive in the U.S.

There absolutely are folks who are happily living abroad solely on their monthly Social Security check, but there are many more who are miserable and bitch and moan about everything and spend most of their time online posting nasty messages as "trolls." You don't want to be one of them.

Now, I am **not** saying that if you are in a situation of limited income, do not move abroad. Your money will definitely go a lot further in many places outside of the U.S. But you do not want to be one of the unfortunates who move abroad, hate where they live and are totally miserable, but don't have enough money to move anywhere else. They're stuck.

Language Difficulties

> *Do not underestimate the frustration of being unable to communicate or express yourself; it is the number one reason why people leave a foreign country and return to the U.S. Are you willing to learn at least a little of the local language?*

If you don't speak the local language very well, it is likely that you will need assistance in accomplishing certain tasks, such as local banking, finding a dentist, accessing healthcare, making phone calls, dealing with your internet provider, etc. If you're on a really limited budget, can you afford to pay for this assistance?

Additionally, you can feel very isolated if you are not able to speak, read or write the local language. Your social circle may be limited to other foreigners or locals who speak English. You may be fine with this, but **realize this** before you make the leap. Expat communities can sometimes be very gossipy or clique-y. What if you don't like the expats in the area where you are living?

If you're not able to speak, read or write the local language, you can also be more susceptible to fraud.

Psychological and Social Issues

Some people are more psychologically fragile than others. Some people prop up their low self-esteem by endlessly attacking others; some seek attention from outrageous behavior. Other expats are so filled with resentment, bitterness or anger that it poisons their relationships. Expat "cliques" can make you feel as if you're back in junior high school.

If you're lucky, you might only encounter expats complaining about being bored or lonely, but sometimes, places popular with expats have a few seriously disturbed individuals who make everyone else miserable with their behavior. Other expats may be intent upon revenge for imagined grudges.

If you have existing psychological issues, are prone to depression or are not fully functioning in a social, psychological, or mental sense, please don't move abroad thinking that a new location will solve all your problems. *It won't*.

All your existing issues will still be with you, plus you will have the additional stress of living in a foreign country and social isolation. Some people find themselves less than welcome in expat groups due to needy or inappropriate behavior, which can breed yet more resentment. It's not a pleasant situation for anyone.

What about Friends and Family?

How Does Your Spouse or Partner Feel About Moving Abroad?
If you have a spouse or partner, is he/she on board with this move? Many divorces or breakups result from a move outside of the U.S.

Typically, one person is enthusiastic about the move and the other is reluctant. After living in the new country, the reluctant spouse hates it and wants to leave. Sometimes it's the opposite: the one who wanted to move abroad hates it, and the reluctant spouse loves it – with the same resultant conflict.

> *Any existing problems in the relationship are magnified by the stress and isolation of living in a new country far away from a support system. Moving abroad will not "solve" any existing relationship problems, but will only magnify them.*

Will You Miss Your Family?

Do you have children or grandchildren that you will miss seeing? Maybe you have no grandchildren currently, but how will you feel in ten years when there *are* grandchildren? What about nieces, nephews, and cousins?

> *Various surveys and studies consistently list the top reasons for returning home to the U.S. as frustration with the language or culture, missing children and grandchildren or other family members, a new serious health condition that can't be treated in the new country, or elderly relatives back in the U.S. (such as aging parents) who need help.*

During the coronavirus pandemic, a significant number of expats living abroad moved back to the U.S. out of concern that they might never see loved ones again if they should die from coronavirus.

Aging Outside the U.S.

What may be fine for you in your 60s or 70s may be completely different as you age into your 80s or 90s.

If you are part of a couple, what will you do if one of you becomes seriously ill or incapacitated and needs round-the-clock care? If your partner or spouse dies, what will you do? Are you prepared to remain in the foreign country, or would you want to return home to the U.S.? How do you feel about dying in a foreign country far from family?

If you plan to live outside of the U.S. indefinitely or permanently, what are your plans for when you can no longer manage on your own? What if you have a serious illness and need assistance with the "activities of daily living"? What if, God forbid, you develop Alzheimer's or dementia?

> *Remember that you will be a foreign resident; there may not be any Medicaid-equivalent safety net to pay for nursing home care. If you become a citizen, there may be some indigent care available but you almost certainly will not like the standard of living.*

That said, it is entirely possible to plan for old age (it's not like we don't know it's coming), and the cost of caregivers, cooks and housekeepers is *far lower* outside of the U.S. Every country has elder care facilities, often at far lower cost with higher quality (due to better staffing levels) than in the U.S.

When I fractured my ankle in Cuenca, I was able to hire a local who had a business cooking for expats. A week's worth of meals - customized to my choices and gluten-free since I have to avoid gluten - cost $45 plus the cost of the ingredients.

Plan on getting old eventually; nobody gets out alive in the end.

Will You Interact with the Locals?

When some expats first arrive in a new city, after getting settled in their new apartment or house, they go for walks every day to learn about the neighborhood. Then they get on a city bus just to see where it goes and see the sights along the way -- of course, before you get on a city bus, you should have some idea of whether there are any bad parts of town that you as a foreigner shouldn't go.

This is the right attitude to have: a sense of adventure, along with the appropriate level of common sense and caution.

A fair number of expats only interact with other expats. Whether this is from an inability to speak the local language, fear of crime, physical infirmities or just shyness or timidity, I can't say. I have been surprised to find expats who have lived in a city for four or five years and still don't know major boulevards, parks or landmarks.

If you stay home 90% of the time, watch only U.S. TV and sports programs, and only interact with other expats, you are missing out on a lot of the benefits of living in a foreign country. Your adopted home is a fascinating place with many interesting people and a different perspective on many aspects of life.

The more you venture out from home, the more familiar you will be with the community and the more comfortable it will feel. Give it some time and it will seem less foreign.

The local grade school, junior high or high school would be thrilled to have a native English speaker volunteer as an assistant in their English classes, and universities would be happy to have a volunteer as well. By interacting with locals, you will have a much better understanding of the place you call home.

I find politics interesting around the world; I enjoy observing how different countries conduct elections. In Mexico I observed presidential election campaigning, watched political analysts on TV discussing the candidates and issues, and watched televised debates between the candidates. Ecuador held presidential elections in 2021, and I did the same thing. It's all very interesting and gives me a better understanding of the culture. It's a fun way to improve my Spanish, too.

Recognize that in some countries, expats are an important part of the local economy because they may have more purchasing power than most locals. Some expats mistake this appreciation for purchasing power with genuine friendliness, when it is more likely to be a reflection of locals' need to survive and feed their families.

I am not saying that many locals do not feel warmly towards expats; many do, but it is more likely that they are appreciative that your presence enables them to earn a living. I have heard expats say how "friendly" everyone is, but unless you speak the language well and understand the cultural contexts, don't jump to conclusions.

Can Single Women Live Abroad Successfully?

Absolutely! I know many single, independent women who are thriving as expats, able to pursue long-deferred dreams. Financially it can be so much cheaper to live abroad that single women find that they can have a superior standard of living to what they would have had in the U.S. with many more options to travel or pursue other interests. Divorcees, widows or never-married all are living full, rich lives as expats.

There are many places around the world with expat communities that have a good number of single older women, who often create their own social groups based upon mutual interests – a rotating dinner club, quilting, bridge, golf, writing, you name it.

Male Expats & Female Companionship

For you fellas out there seeking female companionship, you should know that the local gals already have your number. There are women who specifically target foreign men to get money out of them, and some of these men are foolish enough to spend thousands of dollars on their "girlfriend" only to find out that she's only interested in their money.

Some (but not all) foreign women view U.S. expats as a meal ticket, and if they can snag one, they expect to be taken care of from head to toe, and may be "high maintenance." You have been warned. That said, there are cases of genuine romance and affection that result in long, happy marriages.

For some reason, Colombia seems to have more of these situations than other places, although Vietnam and the Philippines are also places to watch yourself. A British expat in Vietnam lost his life savings in a scheme involving a forged deed and a crooked notary (his girlfriend ended up owning his house).

> *If you are moving abroad to join your "soul mate," whom you've only ever dealt with online, and have already "helped" her pay for family or health emergency expenses, be prepared to be disappointed. She probably has multiple online "soul mates" and might even already be married. "She" may not even be a she. If she's fifty years younger than you, do you **seriously** think that she's head over heels in love with you, having never even met you?*

Illegal Activities

Needless to say, if you're into pedophilia, narcotics or other illegal activities, you're upping your risk profile big time. If you don't get killed, you risk being deported for criminal activities, after a prison sentence with, shall we say, less than comfortable accommodations.

> *The U.S. government's Homeland Securities Investigations (HSI) unit has 10,400-plus employees in 73 offices in 47 foreign countries who actively investigate, in conjunction with local country authorities, transnational narcotics trafficking, money laundering, financial fraud, cybercrime, human rights violations and war crimes as well as child pornography, child sex tourism and child sex abuse crimes committed abroad by U.S. citizens.*

Some expats specifically move abroad **because** they want to be able to have sex with children more easily, due to lax local laws. Colombia had an expat who was a notorious pedophile who always avoided prosecution every time he was arrested. He even gave a media interview from his yacht boasting about how he was untouchable. Shortly thereafter, he was found murdered (gee, what a surprise).

A newspaper in Medellin, Colombia in 2017 had a very interesting article of two full pages that analyzed every single murder of a foreigner in the city in the past two years. About 95% of them were involved in some sort of illegal activity, including poaching upon the territory of locals in selling drugs or booking sex tours to foreigners. The locals didn't appreciate the competition.

The state police of Baja California, Mexico have a 12-officer unit dedicated solely to catching U.S. citizen fugitives who are wanted in the U.S. for various crimes.

When you move to a new country, things that are not a crime in the U.S. may well be criminal in your new home, so take time to find out what is prohibited locally. Ecuador has a criminal statute against slander and libel; publicly maligning the reputation of a person or business can land you in prison. In other countries, same-sex relationships may be illegal.

Follow all local laws and avoid illegal activities

Chapter 3
How to Decide Where to Go

What is my Financial Situation?
What would my Ideal Place to Live Look Like?
LGBTQ Issues
Country Financial Stability
Political Climate
Expat Conferences & Tours
Research and Visit Countries
Local Cost of Living & Health Care
Residency Visas for Expats
Digital Nomad-Friendly Places
Online Resources for Researching Destinations

There is no right or wrong answer as to a destination; what is perfect for one person will be wrong for another. If you are part of a couple, deciding where to go may be more complicated if one person wants very different things than the other person. Compromises will likely be involved.

This chapter will offer observations, comments and advice about deciding where to go. See the end of this chapter for a list of resources that may help you learn more about various locations, about residency requirements abroad and about options for working or volunteering abroad.

What is my Financial Situation?

If you will need to generate income to live on, then start with that – where you pick to move to will need to include options to legally earn a living. Do you have a skill that you can do online, that won't require getting local permission to work? Then you will need somewhere with reliable high-speed internet. See the section later in this chapter about digital nomads and working remotely.

If you have only USD $1,000 a month to live on, obviously you will have fewer choices (from both a cost of living and a residency visa standpoint) than if you have an income of USD $3,000 a month.

Once you've determined what your monthly living allowance in USD will be, the question to ask when looking at potential places abroad is not "how much does it cost to live here?" but rather **"how would I be able to live on X dollars per month?"** *Even in an expensive place, there are ways to live inexpensively, but you might not be willing to live that way.*

Everyone has different preferences in how they want to live. Someone who wants to eat out in restaurants every day (or wants to have a cook or chef prepare the meals at home), have a maid and gardener, will play golf every day or own a car etc. will obviously need a different budget from someone who is content to live more simply in a simple house, do their own food shopping, meal preparation and house cleaning, and use public transportation.

You will need to decide upon a budget that you can live within and have (by your standards) an acceptable standard of living. **Only you can decide what that means, and for each person the answer will be different.**

The cost of living can vary widely within a given country or even the same city. How much will you need for health care? What about future caregivers? How much do you want to travel? What about hobbies? This will be part of your homework in researching where you want to live.

Leave some room in your operating budget for future inflation and caregivers as you age. If the currency in your new home is not the USD, it's also best to allow some room for exchange rate fluctuations as well. The dollar can and does lose value against other currencies, although currently (2022) it has been performing well.

You should also have a capital reserve to cover larger, less frequent expenses such as surgeries or hospital bills that your health insurance (if you have any) doesn't cover, hearing aids, dental work, eyeglasses etc. as well as repairs and maintenance of real estate that you own or the purchase or replacement of furniture or appliances.

> *Check out the income tax laws in your intended country of residence – does it tax income earned outside of the country (many countries do not)? What level of in-country income can you earn before you will be subject to local income tax? Are there any wealth taxes on net worth?*

What would my Ideal Place to Live Look Like?

- Do you want to live where people speak English?
- Are you willing to learn a foreign language?
- Is crime a problem in the country?
- How well does the government function?
- How is the local health care system?
- Can you obtain needed medications?
- What current (and future) health care needs might you have?
- What are the health care capabilities of the place you are considering?
- What health insurance options are available? Is paying out-of-pocket a viable option?
- What would you do in case of a catastrophic health problem?
- How difficult (or impossible) is it for a U.S. citizen to open a local bank account?
- What kind of climate do you prefer? Hot, humid temperatures or cooler, dryer climate?
- Do gray, cloudy skies and rain affect you?
- How's the air quality? The water?
- How do you expect climate change to affect this location in the future?
- Do you want to be near the beach? Would a lake or river work instead?
- Do you want other expats around, or would you rather "go native"?

- Do you want to be near lots of restaurants or bars?
- How much does noise bother you, and what kind of noise?
- Do you want to attend live opera or symphonies? Art galleries?
- How important is it that family and friends visit you from the U.S.?
- How far are you willing to live from a major airport?
- What is the maximum travel time you would like to have to travel to the U.S.?
- Are there natural hazards such as earthquakes, volcanoes, flooding or tsunamis?
- How much of the food supply is produced locally vs. imported?
- What is the source of the local water supply, and how secure is it?
- Do you want an active literary scene in your community?
- Does the educational level of expats and locals matter to you?
- Do you want to have local universities nearby?
- Do you have a preference regarding the expat community's political leanings and philosophies?
- Would it bother you if U.S. expats were liberal Democrats or ultra-conservative Republicans?
- How much nasty gossip and back-biting are you willing to tolerate among expats?
- Do you want to explore the arts such as painting, pottery, textile fiber arts, sculpting, etc.?
- Are you a sports fan who needs a local bar with NFL and Major League Baseball games?
- Do you want to play golf every day (or week)?
- Do you want to go sailing or deep-sea fishing?
- Do you want to play poker/bridge/chess every week?
- What's your budget and what lifestyle will that get you in this location?

You get the idea. Answering these questions **honestly** and **realistically** will help you narrow down a list of possible places that might work for you outside of the U.S.

> *Make sure that any area facilities that you plan to use will be available to you. In Colombia, an avid golf-playing expat purchased a condo with an excellent golf club and course not far away, only to learn that to become a member, one had to be invited. The club didn't want any U.S. persons as members, so he was out of luck. He sold the condo and moved to Portugal.*

Are Mosquitos an Issue for You?

Check into whether immunizations are recommended for the areas you are considering. Many tropical or warm, humid areas are in yellow fever zones and you will want to receive a vaccination for yellow fever. Is malaria endemic to the area? What about chikungunya? Dengue fever? West Nile virus? Zika?

I myself get bitten by mosquitoes all the time if they are around. I therefore knew that I did not want to live in an area where there were mosquitoes. Even living above 2,500 meters as I do, I still get bitten whenever the weather warms up for any period of time.

Narrowing Down the Possibilities

After you've defined what you want in a location, then start researching which places might meet your criteria. Don't just jump at the first place you come across; compile a list of five to ten countries and then rank them.

You might be surprised to learn that the best choice is a place that you've never heard of or considered, so **keep an open mind** to the process. Start doing further research on the first three or four places on your list.

Even if you've decided on a single country, there can be a great deal of variety in conditions **within** that country, so you may end up with four or five possibilities within a single country. That's OK too.

People can have serious misconceptions about places. I had a brief conversation with someone several years ago, mentioning that I had just returned from several months in Medellin, Colombia. This person replied that "Oh, I could never live that far from the U.S." I responded that I didn't know what their definition of "distant" from the U.S. was, but that

Medellin was only a three-hour flight from Miami, shorter than a flight from the East Coast to the West Coast within the U.S.

LGBTQ Issues

If the LGBTQ-friendliness of a place is of importance to you, then definitely some on-the-ground research is advisable. Some places are very LGBTQ-friendly, some only tolerant, and others downright hostile. Within a single country, conditions can vary dramatically.

In Mexico, for example, Mexico City, Cancun, Guadalajara, Puerto Vallarta and Acapulco are very gay-friendly, whereas other cities and states are more conservative. Guanajuato, where I spent almost two years, is very conservative but even there, it is possible for LGBTQ persons to live (cautiously) in peace.

Are you looking for more of an LGBTQ party scene? A quieter, lower key community? Just somewhere non-judgmental? If you're part of an established couple, then looking for a partner may be less important, but isolation can put additional stress on relationships.

While there are ratings of countries by international LGBTQ groups, these may reflect the purported status of laws and not the actual on-the-ground reality. Ecuador, for example, has statutes on the books and in the constitution granting full equal rights, but enforcement is almost non-existent and LGBTQ persons face daily discrimination with no legal recourse. The police, prosecutors and courts are unsympathetic to LGBTQ crime victims and frequently refuse to investigate hate crimes.

You as a foreigner may be granted more latitude than locals would be in this area, especially if you have money. Here in Ecuador, it is quite common for married Ecuadorian family men to have some action on the side ("on the down low") as long as they are married and have children and outwardly conform to expectations.
Consult Google using "gay friendly" and the country you are considering and see what comes up.

Country Financial Stability

You should consider the financial stability of a country for personal and financial security reasons. While there are many measures, one simple one is the *country risk index*, which is used by international investors to measure the risk of default on government (sovereign) debt.

Why look at the country risk score? It's a quick-and-dirty proxy for possible turmoil resulting from financial problems. What might happen if the government suddenly has to curtail sharply spending on education and health care, or raise taxes? How well is the country managing its financial affairs? What might happen if its access to international credit markets were to be cut off?

It's also useful to compare one country's risk score against other countries that you are considering, to give yourself a benchmark.

There are two factors evaluated in the country risk score: one is a country's **ability** to repay its debts when due and the other its willingness or **political will** to do so.

Below is a graph of Ecuador's country risk for the years 2018-2020. You can see the impact that the coronavirus pandemic has had on the country's finances.

In 2021 Ecuador was running an operating deficit of 50% and was dependent upon funding from international organizations, other countries and any other sources it could find, because it cannot print its own currency as it uses the U.S. dollar. In March and April of 2020 in Latin America, Ecuador's risk score was *worse* than Argentina's, and behind only Venezuela. By 2022 the situation was much improved, although the government is still in financial difficulty due to the pandemic's impact on its budget.

Country risk scores are published by major international banks and ratings services such as JP Morgan Chase, Standard & Poor's and Fitch Ratings and generally capture the difference in yields between the U.S.'s sovereign debt and a foreign country's debt.

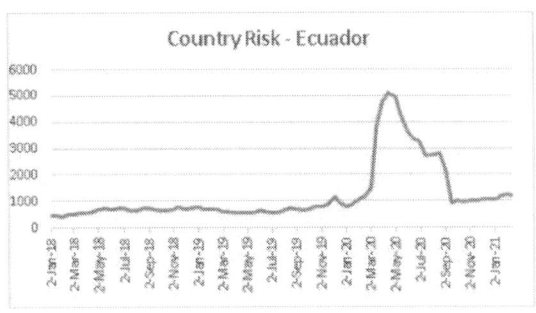

U.S. Dollar/Local Currency Exchange Issues
If a country you are considering has its own currency, consider that your budget could be negatively impacted if the exchange rate to the U.S. dollar moves significantly against the dollar.

Conversely, if the U.S. dollar appreciates against the local currency, you would enjoy an increase in purchasing power upon converting dollars to the local currency.

Even if a country uses the U.S. dollar (Panama, Ecuador etc.), there is no guarantee that in a significant financial crisis the country will continue using the U.S. dollar, in which case USD-denominated local bank accounts could be forcibly converted to the local currency. In other situations, individual banks might limit the amount of cash (in USD) that can be withdrawn per day.

In some countries it may be possible to keep a local bank account in U.S. dollars (much of Europe, Mexico), but in a financial crisis access to these dollars might be restricted.

See more on this topic in **Chapter 7**, ***Banking and Finances***.

Political Climate

In addition to financial stability, you should inquire into political stability. You wouldn't want to move to a country only to see the previously middle-of-the-road government replaced by a far-right or far-left extreme regime. Anti-American or anti-western sentiments could make things uncomfortable, although frequently locals differentiate between U.S. government policies and U.S. citizens' beliefs and actions.

- Can the government provide basic services to its citizens and guarantee the rule of law?
- Is the government unstable or in danger of collapsing?
- Is there high turnover among government ministers and vice presidents?
- After resigning from office, is it customary for a senior minister to be on the next flight out of the country?
- Do wealthy citizens keep their funds outside the country?

Nicaragua, for example, even though having much antipathy towards the U.S. government, up to 2018 still welcomed U.S. tourists as well as U.S. citizens interested in living there permanently. Its current political instability probably means it's a good idea to stay away for now.

In 2022, Sri Lanka is experiencing the worst financial crisis since its independence from Britain in 1948, with food, fuel, medicine and other essentials either skyrocketing in price or unobtainable at any price. Widespread rioting and protests can make the situation pretty iffy for expats.

China has acted aggressively against U.S. citizens of Chinese ethnicity, accusing them of espionage or anti-government activities. You don't want to get caught up in that.

Cuba and Iran are examples of countries hostile to the U.S. where it's not feasible for most Americans to consider living as residents, due to the many U.S. government restrictions imposed upon U.S. citizens.

Expat Conferences & Tours

One way for prospective U.S. expats to learn about potential locations and residency requirements is through expat conferences and tours.

Some offer multi-day conferences in U.S. cities once or twice a year (often over a weekend or holiday period) that present information for five or ten different countries. Live, in-person conferences are starting to be held again after several years of being only online, although this may vary depending upon current circumstances of the coronavirus pandemic.

This can be one way to get a high-level introductory overview to the whole idea of moving out of the U.S. **without having to travel outside of the U.S.**, and also connect with other like-minded people considering the same thing.

Some companies also put on "prospective expat" conferences or tours specific to a single country in locations popular with retirees such as Mexico, Colombia, the Dominican Republic, Panama, Belize, Portugal, or Spain. These country-specific events are usually held in the country in question to allow you to visit the country in person but may or may not be conducted online due to the coronavirus pandemic.

Some conferences are held in a hotel, others are tours where you visit different parts of the country you are considering. Usually, they have presentations by immigration attorneys, health insurance brokers, realtors, and shipping brokers. These conferences and tours can be a good way of getting a lot of information in a short period of time.

My personal experience? In one of these conferences, *half* of the presentations were geared towards selling us investments and had nothing to do with becoming an expat; the presenters had **PAID** the organizers to make their presentations. The presenters weren't able to answer some of my questions, either.

In a different seven-day "prospective expat" tour (different country) that I took, the country expat "expert" didn't seem to be very familiar with the country. Was there good information from the tour? Yes (from the various local professionals). Was it helpful to see different parts of the country? Yes. Was it worth the $1,600 plus airfare? No.

Remember that these conferences and tours are money-making ventures with a vested interest in making a place look as enticing as possible, and may omit important but less attractive information about a place. *You want the unvarnished truth, not something through rose-colored glasses.*

See the sample list of resources regarding expat tours and conferences at the end of this chapter.

Relocation Consultants

If price is no object, there are independent consultants who will be happy to help you choose a place and introduce you to immigration attorneys, real estate agents and health care brokers for a fee of USD $5,000 to $10,000. You don't necessarily want a relocation service, which comes into play once you've decided upon a specific location for your move. I see no reason to pay such fees, but if you're interested, you can find them with a Google search.

Research and Visit Countries

It's fine to take advantage of organized "prospective expat" tours and seminars, but don't stop there.

Visits to Prospective Countries

I **strongly urge you** to spend at least a month, two or more if possible, living in a place, preferably during the *most uncomfortable* part of the year. Take some language classes and get to know the place. Wander around the neighborhoods and markets. Talk to other expats who have been living in the place for a while (not recent arrivals). Find out why expats have left the country, as this can be very revealing of the less attractive aspects of a place.

> *I would even go so far as to say do not just pick up and move to a country that you have never visited; you may regret your decision. I have seen a number of expats who moved out of the U.S. without ever having **even once** visited their destination, and it often is not a happy ending.*

You may find YouTube videos online made by English speakers about various places. Be aware that many of these people may not really know what they're talking about, based on my observations. They may provide some information, but if they don't speak the local language, how much do they really know?

They are looking to earn an income from their videos. The videos will let you see what a place looks like, but take the information offered with a grain of salt unless you know the source is well-informed. The expats who really know a place well probably aren't going to be making videos on YouTube.

Familiarize yourself with the possible downsides to a place:

- Are there income tax or wealth/net worth tax traps for the unwary?
- Is the place unlivable for three months of the year due to heat and humidity?
- Are there earthquakes?
- Is there periodic flooding? Wildfires?
- Is there an active volcano nearby? Volcanic ash in the air?
- What's the crime situation?
- How stable is the country politically?
- Is there an exit tax on capital exiting the country (even if it's your own money that you brought in to the country)?

If your budget is limited but you still want to visit different places to see what they're like, one inexpensive way to do this is to work as a volunteer via cultural exchanges or working holidays.

> *The website **Workaway.info** lists short-term volunteer opportunities in 170 countries around the world. Volunteers **of any age** live in a place for free room and board in exchange for two to four hours a day of volunteer work (usually in a business); the rest of the day is free to do what you want. The type of work varies from helping out at a hostel, to working on an organic coffee farm in Colombia or specialty vineyard in Chile, to teaching English to a family's teen-ager in Europe. Time commitments vary from one week to a month or two.*

During your visit to a country that is a candidate for your relocation, do some homework regarding the reality on the ground. **You're not there as a tourist**; you are there to investigate the location as a place to live.

> *I actually prefer to visit a place when I can see it at its **worst** – you can get a false impression if you're only seeing a place at its best. When is it coldest/hottest/rainiest/most unpleasant in the place you're considering? Go visit during that time at least once before deciding to move there.*

I lived in Medellin, Colombia for almost three months, and during that time they had a number of "red alert" smog days where the air quality was really terrible, but I didn't notice any ill effects. It was helpful to know that. I am sensitive to air pollution but Medellin's never caused me any obvious problems.

Conversely, I have been in Mexico City when the smog was so bad that it affected my vision, making everything blurry, and I had to cut short my visit. Once I got back to cleaner air, my vision was fine again almost immediately.

During a month-long stay in Quetzaltenango, Guatemala, the exhaust from the diesel city buses was so bad that one of my eyes swelled completely shut and I could not see at all out of that eye. I was pretty sure this was an allergic reaction, so I bought antihistamine eye drops at a pharmacy, and I was soon able to see again.

I have a location-related issue that I never could have anticipated. Volcanic ash seems to trigger really bad spells of vertigo for me. Something about the volcanic ash causes problems in my inner ear. The first time this happened to me, there was so much ash in the air that the local airport was closed for three days, which I spent vomiting due to severe vertigo. I have no respiratory symptoms, just the vertigo. It's weird as hell.

Evaluate the Local Cost of Living & Health Care

In the U.S., the "Big Three" living expense categories are housing, health care and education, especially university. In many parts of the world, you will pay far less for these three categories, so even if other things cost more than in the U.S., you will still come out ahead financially.

Many of us are seeking a lower cost of living, so keep in mind that some things cost MORE in other countries than in the U.S. This can be determined by visiting stores and checking out the prices during your research visits there before you move to a country.

In Ecuador, I was astonished at the high prices for kitchen gadgets. A KitchenAid mixer identical to one that sells for USD $250 in the U.S. retails for USD $600 in Ecuador. Even washing machines and dryers cost twice what they cost in Mexico.

Some countries must import everyday items, making them more expensive. A box of Kleenex in Ecuador will run you $3.00 to $4.00 (imported from Colombia), and may not be available at all in Guatemala or Nicaragua.

What's Available Locally?
If there is something important to you, you want to make sure it is available in the foreign country. Examples to consider include:

- Do you need gluten-free flour?
- Can you get peanut butter or sharp cheddar cheese locally if they are important to you?
- Is your favorite brand of scotch, whiskey, beer etc. available? At what price?
- How difficult is it to eat a vegetarian/vegan diet in the country?

Availability and Cost of Health Care
Many readers of this book will be near or at retirement age, and health care looms large as a terrifying expense in the U.S. Housing and education may be weighted less if you are in this age group.

You will want to closely examine the local health care system of a potential place to live. Even if you're healthy now and fit as a fiddle, if you plan to stay long term, at some point you will need medical attention; health in your 60s can be vastly different from health in your 80s. What is the availability of medications? Are there shortages of certain specialists, resulting in long wait times to see one (although it's not like we don't have this problem in the U.S.)?

- Prescription medications – are they available and at what cost?
- Are there hearing aid providers?
- How is the dental care?
- Which vitamins and supplements are available locally? How expensive are they?
- Do you need special orthopedic shoes?
- Can you get regular chiropractic treatments for a bad back?
- Can you use the public health care system? Would you want to?
- Should you buy private health insurance? Are you *required* to do so?

See **Chapter 10, *Healthcare, Medicare and End of Life Planning***, for more information about how to identify locations that have above-average quality of health care.

Residency Visas for Expats

Once you've identified what features you're looking for in climate, cultural amenities, educational institutions etc., have thought about what health care services you want to have on hand, and have identified the budget you have to work with for living expenses, investigate which countries have visa programs that would fit your circumstances. Some countries are more welcoming of expats than are others.

> *Exercise extra caution if you are planning on acquiring a residency visa by investing in a business or by purchasing real estate – the locals (and some expats) know all about this and some are waiting with open arms to overcharge you or even rip you off.*

The paperwork needed in applying for residency can vary widely. Some countries make it super easy for someone from North America to become a resident – all you need is your passport, maybe a copy of your birth certificate, and that's it.

Other countries will want to see more documents, including birth certificates, proof of income and criminal background checks at the federal and state level, and you may have to go through the process of getting your documents **apostilled**. I confess, I hadn't heard of apostilles until I was applying for residency to Ecuador, when I had to get *scads* of documents apostilled.

What the Heck is an Apostille?
It's the international version of notarization and is used by signatory nations to the Hague Convention to authenticate legal documents for use in another signatory country.

Note that the United States is a signatory to the Hague Convention regarding apostilling of documents, but *Canada is not.*

---

*Most countries want the issue date of the documents **and** the apostille to be **no more than 90 days old** when you present the documents to the immigration office.*

Plan carefully to have everything done within the required time frame, otherwise you may have to start all over again with the document collection, notarization and apostille process.

In the U.S., each of the fifty states will apostille a document *issued by that state*, and the U.S. Department of State will apostille federally-issued documents. A birth certificate will be apostilled by the state that issued it. An FBI criminal background check or Social Security statement of benefits must be apostilled by the U.S. government, because it's a federally-issued document. A state criminal background check has to be apostilled by that state.

Be prepared for headaches if your name has changed from what is on your birth certificate for any reason (you've been married or divorced; you fellas too, if you've hyphenated your name). You may have to get your marriage or divorce record notarized and then apostilled, depending upon the country's residency visa application requirements.

It is possible to get apostilles done by mail, and there are private businesses that will be happy to assist you with this for a fee. In my experience, *if you're still in the U.S.*, you can do it yourself and obtain most apostilles by mail or FedEx/DHL in an acceptable amount of time and save money. Most states have an expedited service fee by mail that's worth paying.

The only service that I paid to get an apostille for me was for the U.S. Department of State, because their mail service can take 4-6 weeks (pre-coronavirus pandemic; longer now) unless you use the in-person counter service in Washington D.C. That cost me $60 including return express mail.

For state apostilles, usually you get the state-issued document notarized first (many issuing agencies can notarize it for an additional fee). The state apostille is then attesting to the authenticity of the notary's signature.

Check to see if government offices are operating during the coronavirus pandemic and what their processing times are, or if they are shut down. Additionally, in this age of budget shortfalls and political gridlock, from time to time state and federal government offices will shut down over funding or political disputes, which could really mess up your timeline for getting needed documents, the notarizations and the apostilles.

Non-Hague Signatory Countries (Canada)
For countries that are not signatories to the Hague Convention (such as Canada), the process of authenticating documents is called *legalization*. The foreign ministry of the country where the document originated will certify the document, and then the foreign ministry of the receiving country must do the same.

This means that the document must be certified twice before it can have legal effect in the receiving country. As you can imagine, this can sometimes cause problems with time limits if one or the other of the foreign ministries takes too long to certify documents or loses them in processing.

A few highlights about residency visas

A general observation regarding residency visas: it seems that the income or asset requirements to qualify for residency as well as fees paid to governments become higher each year, so you might want to keep that in mind if you're thinking of waiting another ten years before deciding to move abroad.

Getting Residency in European Countries
In general, for non-residents of the European Union, it is more difficult to get residency in EU countries than in other parts of the world.

- Portugal's most accessible visa, the D7, issued for a two-year period (renewable), has requirements based on either income or savings: for a single individual, at least €705 a month of income (€1,000 recommended), OR savings of at least €16,920, OR a combination of the two (income and savings). Having more than the minimum monthly income or savings is generally a good idea. Its Golden Visa program requires investments of €280,000 to €500,000 in exchange for a visa. Starting in 2022, real estate purchases in Lisbon or the Algarve area no longer qualify.

- Spain's retirement (non-lucrative) visa, no employment allowed, requires you to have at least €27,800 in a bank account (for a single person; higher amounts for a couple or with children). Depending upon the consulate processing your application, they may double these amounts at their discretion. A balance of €35,000 or higher is recommended.

- Italy has an elective residency visa if you have annual passive income of at least €31,160 (singles) or €38,000 (married couple). Alternatively, you may be able to apply for citizenship if you have a grandparent born in Italy.

- If you have a grandparent born in Ireland, you can qualify for Irish citizenship without too much difficulty or cost; it's a matter of rounding up the documents proving your descent and applying. Pre-coronavirus pandemic, this process took about nine months; plan on it taking longer now.

- If you can prove descent from Jews expelled from Spain during the Spanish Inquisition of the 1490s, you may be able to obtain

Spanish citizenship. Many U.S. citizens with roots in New Mexico dating back centuries have Jewish ancestry from Spain but do not know it; it might be worthwhile to research your genealogy. Anecdotally, there are stories of people's well-documented applications being rejected by Spain, but it might still be worth investigating.

- Similarly, Austria recently passed a law granting citizenship to children, grandchildren and great-grandchildren of Jews who were forced to leave Austria before or during World War II due to Nazi persecution.

- Austria has a different visa for "residency by independent means" (pensions, annuities or private investment funds) for those with regular income; it does not permit you to work in Austria. Minimum monthly regular income must be at least €1,000 per month in 2022.

- Germany passed a law in mid-2021 that eliminated provisions that prevented victims of Nazi persecution and their descendants from applying for citizenship. The new law allows persons descended from groups persecuted by the Nazis to apply for citizenship. There is no deadline to apply for citizenship.

Getting Residency in Latin America
Countries in Latin America vary widely in their requirements for residency.

Persons eighteen or older can apply for the *pensionado* (retired) residency visa in **Panama** if they have unearned income of at least USD $1,000 per month ($750 if they buy property of at least $100,000). You are not allowed to work. The requirement that you *must* use an attorney (USD $1,500 or more) to apply for residency substantially raises the cost of acquiring residency.

Colombia is another option that can be a do-it-yourself proposition if you have some knowledge of Spanish. The government **requires** you to apply for residency online; what they have on their official web site as the requirements *are* the requirements, with no surprises or drama. The M-11 retirement visa in 2022 requires a monthly income of at least USD $750 (varies with the Colombian peso's exchange rate).

Ecuador will give you residency and the right to work legally if you are a graduate of a specified U.S. university (there's a lengthy list - with no online courses in your transcripts). This option does require you to show some means of support in terms of income or savings. Alternatively, if you have monthly income of USD $1,275 or more, can deposit USD $42,500 into an Ecuadorian bank CD, **or** purchase real estate you can also qualify for residency (no work permitted) in Ecuador.

Digital Nomad-Friendly Places

A number of countries, wanting to diversify their economies away from tourism, have come to appreciate the positive aspects of digital nomads, who up to now have generally been forced to work somewhat clandestinely using tourist visas, able to remain in one country for only a limited period of time.

Pre-pandemic, many digital nomads were forced to relocate every few months to destinations with an international airport and good internet such as Chiang Mai (Thailand), Bali, Barcelona, Berlin, or Medellin (Colombia).

There are predictions that more countries will create specific "digital nomad" visas tailored to remote workers to create a more sustainable, long-term diverse economy. There are sure to be more countries adding this option, so do an online search to see what new options are available.

As a personal observation, I would start with countries that have lower application costs for their digital nomad programs – why pay thousands of dollars for permission to work remotely when other countries' applications are low- or no-cost?

Countries that have a digital visa program as of June 2022 include the following:

- **Antigua and Barbuda** has a program for remote earners who earn at least USD $50,000 per year; qualifying digital nomads can live and work for up to two years under the "Nomad Digital Residence" program. Costs for a single applicant are USD $1,500, for a couple USD $2,000 and USD $3,000 for a family of three or more.

- **Argentina**'s *rentista* visa allows self-employed work for one year if you have income of at least USD $2,000 a month (in practice; the amount per the statute is less but widely ignored by authorities); application costs are about USD $250 plus an additional USD $600 immigration fee if you are from a non-Mercosur country. One year visa, renewable for up to three years. After two years you may apply for Argentine citizenship.

- **Aruba** began its "One Happy Workstation" program in September 2020, which allows U.S. persons to remain up to 90 days by booking a stay with a participating property ranging from hotel rooms to apartments; all have internet. No visa needed.

- **Bali** (Indonesia) is proposing a new *five-year* digital nomad visa that would exclude income earned abroad from taxation. Plans are in the very early stages and it's iffy as to whether anything will be finalized in 2022. Check online for new developments.

- **Barbados**' "Welcome Stamp" allows remote workers to stay in the country visa-free for up to one year without being subject to local income taxes. Apply online; fees are USD $2,000 for an individual and USD $3,000 for families. Applicants must have an annual income of USD $50,000 or more or be able to have resources to support themselves.

- **Bermuda** has a one-year residential certificate with digital nomads in mind; you must provide proof of employment sufficient to support yourself and proof of health insurance. The visa fee is USD $263. Note that Bermuda is not the cheapest place to live, but if you can afford it can be quite lovely.

- The **Cayman Islands** is targeting high-earning remote workers with its Global Citizen Concierge Visa. Remote workers who make over USD $100,000 annually (couples USD $150,000 or families with children USD $180,000) can remain in the country for up to two years. Applicants must have a bank reference, letter of employment and proof of health insurance. The application fee is $1,469.

- **Costa Rica** in July 2022 issued regulations for its digital nomad visa that allows remote workers to remain in Costa Rica for one year, with extensions available. This is not a residency visa and *cannot* be converted into permanent residency. You must have at least USD $3,000 per month income ($4,000/month for a family), plus health insurance. The visa costs USD $250 with a $90 processing fee.

- **Croatia** started a digital nomad visa program in 2021, with a maximum stay of one year. You must provide proof of income (minimum of USD $2,600 per month) or savings of USD $31,000 plus proof of accommodation and a criminal background check. Application fee of $110.

- **Dubai** issues *Remote Work Nomad Visas* to digital nomads who earn at least USD $5,000 per month to live and work remotely in Dubai for up to one year. The visa fee is USD $290.

- **Estonia** in the summer of 2020 rolled out a digital nomad visa, part of Estonia's *e-Residency* program to attract entrepreneurs, which allows remote workers to remain legally for up to a year in the country. Applicants must have gross monthly income of €3,504 or more from outside the country. The application fee is €100 for the one-year visa.

- The country of **Georgia** (formerly part of the USSR) announced its ***Remotely from Georgia*** program tailored to foreigners who work remotely; applicants must provide proof of employment and must earn at least USD $2,000 per month. Citizens of 94 countries may enter Georgia without a visa and remain for one full year.

- **Iceland's *Work in Iceland*** program lets remote workers work from Iceland for up to six months, as long as they earn at least USD $8,000 a month; USD $60 application fee.

- **Italy**'s digital nomad visa was approved at the end of March 2022 but is not yet in operation. It's a one-year renewable visa designed for non-EU professionals who carry out highly qualified work activities remotely for non-Italian companies. As of June 2022, not many details have been released, so do an online search to see more details.

- **Mauritius** now has a Premium Visa that will allow you to remain in the island nation for one year. You must provide proof of your employment, accommodation during your stay, and health insurance. *There is no processing fee for the visa application*.

- **Mexico** lets U.S. and Canadian citizens remain on a tourist visa for 180 days. While there is no digital nomad visa, it may be possible to do "border runs" and go to another country and then return and get another 180-day tourist visa without much fuss (subject to change). The temporary residency visa (USD $35) is valid for six months to four years; monthly income must be at least USD $2,100 or savings of USD $104,000.

- **Panama** allows remote workers a nine-month visa, renewable for another nine months (total 18 months) if they earn at least USD $36,000 per year. The visa application costs USD $250 and the visa itself USD $50.

- **Portugal** offers the D-7 residency visa for independent workers and entrepreneurs for up to two years (renewable). It is recommended to submit proof of monthly income of at least €1,000 plus mandated proof of business ownership or other financial means, health insurance, and a criminal background check.

Further online resources to research possible destinations for your move abroad:

- Retire Early Lifestyle (Billy & Aikasha Kaderli) - https://www.retireearlylifestyle.com/
- No Particular Place to Go (blog of expat retirees) - https://noparticularplacetogo.net
- Live & Invest Overseas - https://www.liveandinvestoverseas.com/
- International Living - https://internationalliving.com/
- InterNations (networking group for expats still working) – https://www.internations.org
- Panama Relocation Tours (Jackie Lange) - https://panamarelocationtours.com/
- Panama Retirement Tours (Louis O'Connor) - https://panamaretirementtours.org/
- Live in Costa Rica Relocation Tours - https://www.liveincostarica.com/
- Retirement Services International (tours) - http://retirementservicesinternational.com/
- Portugal Senior Living (Algarve tours) - https://www.algarveseniorliving.com
- Transitions Abroad - https://www.transitionsabroad.com/
- Workaway.info – volunteer visiting opportunities www.workaway.info
- Expatistan (cost of living data by country) – https://www.expatistan.com/
- Association of Americans Resident Overseas – https://www.aaro.org/
- American Citizens Abroad - https://www.americansabroad.org/
- Expat Forum (region and country specific info) - https://www.expatforum.com/forums/
- Transparency International (corruption index) - https://www.transparency.org

Chapter 4
What Do I Do with My Stuff?

M oving abroad means you will have to decide which of your possessions you cannot live without, and which things you will leave behind.

This is often an area of disagreement for couples. One person absolutely must bring the woodworking shop with him/her while another cannot live without the wine or cheese-making equipment kept in the basement. You alone as a couple can decide what's a deal-breaker. Compromise is key to any relationship.

What Should I Take with Me?

You will want to research during an on-the-ground visit *before your move* what items are difficult to obtain in your new home, or which items cost twice as much, and perhaps bring those items with you. Is locally made furniture going to work for you if you're 6'10" tall?

The traditional advice is to move with as few possessions as possible, but this can vary greatly depending upon where you are moving to, shipping costs, and the cost and availability of things locally. Do your homework. If you have an employer, the U.S. government or military paying the cost of shipping household belongings, then the decision is much easier. I will assume that most readers of this book are paying their own freight (literally).

Can You Get Spare Parts Abroad for U.S. Domestic Appliances?
If you bring appliances (refrigerators, stove/ovens, washing machines etc.) from the U.S., and they need repairs, you may not be able to get replacement parts for them. You may have to order the part from the U.S., which could take time. Local appliance repairmen may not be familiar with working on U.S. brands or models; it will most likely be easier, faster and less expensive to repair locally purchased appliances.

Don't Forget the Local Electrical System
Be sure to investigate the electrical system in use in your new intended home. Some countries use different voltage and plug size, so your household appliances may not be suitable for use in the new country. It may be advisable to bring an electrical converter and set of international plugs (that you'll use anyway for international travel) until you get settled into your new residence.

Mexico, Central America and the northern parts of South America (Colombia, Ecuador) use the same voltage and plug outlets as North America, so you needn't bother with a voltage converter and plug adaptors. Argentina and many other countries, on the other hand, use 220 volts and have different plug formats.

Most laptop computer power chargers (that bulky box in the middle of the power cord) will automatically adjust the voltage; if the country's voltage is 220 and the laptop uses 110, you may not need a converter. You may still need a plug adapter. Check your laptop's user manual before plugging in.

Are There Items Difficult to Get or More Expensive Where You Are Going?

Do a Google search for "what items are hard to find for expats in XYZ country?" and put in the name of the country to where you'll be moving. Results will vary depending upon the country and the item.

Smart phones may be cheaper in Asia than in the U.S. (because they are manufactured there), but in Latin America can cost up to twice the price of what they are in the U.S. Laptop computers and Apple brand electronics may be less expensive in the U.S. than in other countries.

The following is a list of items that **might** *be* more expensive or unobtainable outside the U.S. (this varies by foreign country):

Clothing and shoes in larger sizes (particularly for men)
Electric blankets
Higher quality cotton bedsheet and comforter sets
Flannel or fleece bedsheet sets
Good quality bath towels
Consumer electronics (flat screen TVs etc.)
Laptop computers
High end smart phones
Peanut butter
Gluten-free products and flours
Vitamins and nutritional supplements
Specialty spices and seasonings
High end kitchen appliances (KitchenAid, Vitamix etc.)
Silicon baking mats for cookie sheets
Oven mitts or hot pads for baking
Specialty power tools (drills, compound miter saws etc.)
Better quality running shoes and athletic gear
Hiking boots and camping gear
Amazon Fire Stick for streaming TV and movies

Should I Sell My Home?

This topic would fill an entire book in and of itself, but I will mention a few points. You may want to keep your U.S. house or condo for a while until you are 100% sure that living overseas is for you.

Renting Out Your Home

If you decide to keep your property for now and rent it out to tenants, know that being an absentee landlord is never easy, and even with a property management company it can be a headache. It is a good idea to pay a visit to your property at least once a year to check up on the property management company. If they don't think anyone is monitoring them, they may start to get lazy or overcharge you.

If you have trustworthy family or friends who can live in your property and take care of it (and pay rent), that may be the best option.

Current U.S. tax laws (as of 2022) allow you to exclude up to $500,000 of capital gain on the sale of a principal residence (for married couples) or $250,000 for other taxpayers. You must have lived in the home as your principal residence for at least two of the last five years in order to claim this tax break; otherwise, the sale will be fully taxable.

If you rent out your property, you will be taking (mandatory) depreciation and will probably need assistance with preparing your income tax return. When you sell, even if you qualify for the principal residence capital gain exclusion, the depreciation will be recaptured and generate tax.

"What if I rent it out for ten years and then move back into it as my principal residence for two years?" I hear you asking. In that situation, you take the period of ownership during which it was your principal residence and divide that into the total period of ownership, and use that ratio to calculate the portion of gain that can be excluded. *You cannot exclude the entire gain in this situation.*

Additionally, the tax laws may change in the future and all your well-laid plans may be for naught. Weigh the carrying costs of keeping a U.S. home (mortgage, property taxes, homeowner's association dues, repairs and maintenance) before deciding what to do with your home.

Options for Moving Your Stuff Abroad

Your choices generally come down to variations on two extremes: you can fill a shipping container with furniture, appliances and household goods (or share a container with another shipper), or else really minimize what you're bringing to what will fit in *X* number of suitcases.

The Container Option
If you go with a container, you will want to use a shipping broker to handle the details of your shipment, from the U.S. to your final destination in the country of your new residence. Many countries allow people applying for residency to bring in a certain quantity of household goods, which will vary by country.

Your shipping broker should be able to advise you on what the restrictions and limitations are – and if he cannot, then find another broker. Many soon-to-be expats use a shipping broker affiliated with or recommended by whomever is advising them on their residency visa (often an attorney but not always) to coordinate the two services, since they are interrelated.

A standard 40-foot container (just under 2,400 cubic feet) will likely cost at least $10,000 or more in shipping costs, depending upon the destination, but can hold a lot of stuff. Shipping by container is done in **cubic feet**, which means units of space one foot by one foot by one foot.

As an illustration, household goods that take up a space of ten feet by ten feet by twenty feet would be 2,000 cubic feet, almost filling a 40-foot container (which holds around 2,400 cubic feet); you would have 300-400 cubic feet left unused. This situation can lead you to find someone moving to your destination and share the container (see below).

Usually, weight does not enter into the equation unless you've got something extremely heavy (in the tons), in which case a surcharge may apply. The weight capacity of the truck is the limiting factor.

> *A cubic foot is one foot by one foot by one foot. As an example, goods that measure five feet by five feet by five feet would equal **125 cubic feet** (5 x 5 x 5).*

With a container, the shipper will come to your location or storage unit with the empty container, the trailer will be loaded with your belongings, and then placed on a trailer bed of an 18-wheeler truck. *I recommend that you hire someone with experience in packing a container with household goods* to avoid things shifting while in transit and getting damaged.

The shipper then drives the container on the truck trailer to a designated port where it is processed as outgoing cargo, and it's on its way to its destination (usually by ship). In the destination port the contents will have to clear a customs inspection.

Note: *Every country will require a detailed inventory or manifest of the contents – appliances, electronics, clothing, shoes, books, furniture, dishes and glassware, artwork, whatever. Most countries will allow someone applying for residency to link the container to their pending visa application so as to avoid paying duty.* **Be sure to accurately list everything in your container and don't leave anything out.**

Items left off your inventory, especially something significant like a refrigerator, washing machine or dryer, or electronics, will cause major problems. Your entire container can be subject to seizure if the authorities think you're trying to pull a fast one on them. At a minimum, there will be a significant delay as they inspect everything thoroughly, and sizable penalties may be assessed (plus a possible under-the-table payment).

The principal concern of countries is that you are bringing in items with the intent to sell them for profit once in the country without having paid the applicable duty or tariff. Countries may have limitations on the number or types of items that you can bring in, such as televisions, electronics or clothing. Abide by all the regulations and you'll have a much better experience with the customs inspection.

Since the container will hold all your worldly goods, it is a good idea to purchase insurance for the contents. The shipping broker should be able to assist you with this.

Sharing a Container with another Expat
If you are moving to a place popular with other expats from the U.S., it may be possible to share a container with other expats moving to the

same country and city as you; that way you could bring, say, 216 cubic feet of stuff (6 feet by 6 feet by 6 feet) for a fairly reasonable cost (maybe one or two thousand dollars).

The other expat-to-be shipper may not have enough goods to completely fill a container, and by letting you use their excess space for your belongings, can reduce their total cost of bringing in their household goods. This method requires that all your belongings be included in the shipper's bill of lading, *under that person's name. Your name will not appear anywhere* on the shipment.

One complication of sharing a container with another expat is a shipping coordinator who does not accurately allocate shared costs and overcharges/undercharges one of the parties. You may have limited recourse to taking action in this situation.

Other issues that can arise are when either the shipper or sharer does not prepare an accurate inventory of contents, does not label their boxes correctly, or over- or underestimates the cubic feet of their shipment.

With a shared shipment all under one person's name, there is no guarantee that your items will not be "lost" in transit or on arrival. Once the container gets to its final destination in the foreign country, the contents must be divided up among the rightful owners.

Ideally you share a container in this manner with someone you know, but there are entities who will match up people with less-than-full container loads to make a full container. ***Don't ship anything irreplaceable, terribly valuable or susceptible to theft in a shared container.***

Pallets in Containerized Freight
A variation on the shared container scenario is using *pallets*. Pallets are those wooden, slatted transport bases that you've probably seen in warehouses that forklifts lift and move with cargo stacked on them from place to place. While there is no one standardized size, often pallets are 48" by 40" and can handle various weights depending upon the design of the pallet. Goods are generally stacked up to five or six feet high.

This is more of a do-it-yourself option for the more adventurous, but can be substantially cheaper. Your goods must be in boxes that can be stacked and you must deliver the goods to the U.S. port city yourself (or hire someone to do it), so it is probably best for those who live near a port. After placing your goods on the pallet, the shipping broker then shrink wraps the entire pallet in heavyweight clear plastic.

Your shipment is physically segregated from other contents of the container. While the pallet will be placed in a container with other shippers' goods going to the same port city, it has a separate bill of lading with your name on it and is not commingled in any way with other goods.

The shipping broker typically will only deal with the pallet at its offices on the sending (U.S.) end. At the destination country's port, after the customs authorities have inspected your cargo, you will need to pick up your pallet at the port and then get it to your final destination; you can hire a trucking company to do this. There likely will be additional paperwork at the receiving port, and you may need to get documents notarized locally before you can pick up your belongings.

Confidential Paper Records (Financial and Tax)

Copies of income tax returns, bank, brokerage and credit card statements should be scanned in to your computer (and backed up – see **Chapter 11, Computer Security for Expats**), and then shredded along with anything else remotely confidential.

I burned out the motor of my paper shredder and had to buy a new one during this process, because I had two full-size file cabinets of documents. It was fun to look at my federal income tax return from 1978, but I really had no reason to keep it after all these years, so into the shredder it went.

If you have a large number of paper documents to shred, there are commercial shredding services available that will come to you and shred your documents while you watch for a fee; this is much faster because industrial shredders can shred a high volume of documents quickly. Alternatively, banks sometimes offer free shredding as a promotion if you bring your documents to them.

If you have sold real estate, a business or other high value assets in the U.S. as part of your move abroad, be sure to keep copies of all closing statements and scan them into digital form. You may be asked to prove the source of funds in your new country of residence if you will be transferring significant funds overseas.

What Do I Do with Family Papers and Photos?

You will have to decide what you want to do with family papers and photos. Are there children, grandchildren, cousins, nieces or nephews who would be interested in having these items?

One option is to digitally scan as many of these things as possible, and then find a family member interested in having the physical papers and photos. That way, you can still refer to the photos and papers whenever you like without the burden of safeguarding the physical items. Keep in mind that younger family members may not develop an interest in genealogy or family history until later in life, decades later.

If you have a collection of family letters, photos and other items that are of historical, geographical, religious, social, cultural or genealogical interest, you may be able to find a special collections department of a university library interested in them. The advantage to doing this is that they are archived in a safe place but remain accessible to later generations or researchers.

For example, one of my grandfathers was head of the dairy science department at the University of Idaho from the early 1930s until 1960. I asked the University of Idaho if they would be interested in a donation of family documents and photos from that side of the family; because of my grandfather's long connection with the university, the library was happy to receive the collection as a donation.

If you have letters or memoirs written by a U.S. veteran who served in the military from World War I to the present, the Library of Congress in Washington DC is a wonderful option. The Veterans History Project (part of the American Folklife Center) gladly accepts such items as well as diaries, maps, original photographs and recorded audio or video interviews. With your permission, letters will be digitized and transcribed, making them searchable online for researchers and the public, including future generations of your own family.

The Library of Congress also welcomes portraits of soldiers, letters and other artifacts from the Civil War and Spanish-American War for their collection.

Aside from the Library of Congress, many military museums collect GI letters and memorabilia for their archives and would likely be interested in a donation. Consult Google and take your pick of where to donate your artifacts.

Sorting Through Your Belongings

Regardless of whether you're going to ship a 40-foot container or arrive in your new home with just suitcases, you will want to go through all your belongings and decide what to get rid of and what you want to keep. *Give yourself adequate time to do this*; I recommend three to six months for an average-size household.

Many people will find this purging to be psychologically difficult. You may want to recruit friends or family to help with the process. Give yourself more time than you think it will take, because it **will** take longer than you expect.

It can get emotional to part from long-held belongings, and you may come across items that you haven't seen in years or belonged to loved ones who have passed away. Give yourself time to process the emotions as you sort through things. Tears may be involved.

Some would-be expats may be unable to agree on what to get rid of, and as a result keep their house in the U.S. when they move overseas. Keeping your house for several years while you "try out" living overseas may not be a bad idea, but in the long run it is expensive to maintain two completely separate households, and can have tax implications as outlined above.

Family heirlooms are a particular challenge. Give some thought as to whether you want to pass that special item onto someone in the family now, or take it with you to your new home abroad. It may make more sense to find a home for it now instead of later.

I had a highboy dresser made in 1820 for my 2X-great grandparents' wedding that had been passed down through the generations. I wanted it to stay in the family, and fortunately my brother said he would take it. My Plan B was to seek out cousins from this line of the family and offer it to them.

Go through all your possessions and group them into four categories:

(1) Keep
(2) Sell in one way or another
(3) Donate to charity; or
(4) Throw into the trash or take to the dump.

You should do several iterations of this because the first pass may still leave you with too many things to ship to your new home. **If you are part of a couple, there may be disagreements** about what to keep or to purge, so *allow plenty of time*.

Selling Your Stuff

There are a variety of ways to sell secondhand belongings.

Garage sales are the traditional way to sell household articles; try to pick a time of year when the weather is pleasant in your region. Put up signs around the neighborhood with the day and time of your sale. For a quick sale, price your items at 10-15% of what the items cost new at retail, unless they are close to new, in which case you can price them a little higher. Don't obsess about getting the best price possible; *your objective is to get rid of stuff.*

If you live in an urban or rural area where it's not practical to have a garage sale, keep an eye out for churches or synagogues having rummage sales, and pay for a table. Post "Moving Sale" signs in your apartment building lobby listing some of the items you wish to dispose of.   As a last resort, pawn shops might buy items such as a bicycle if you have no other option.

Consignment or secondhand stores may be interested in purchasing some of your better clothing, jewelry and other items. Ask friends, neighbors and co-workers if they're interested in buying your household items.

Craigslist can be a good option to find buyers for your household items; place an ad and see if you get any nibbles. You may also be able to sell items on Facebook.

If you have specialty collectibles or antiques and there is an antique mall near you, renting a booth to sell items can be a good option. The antique mall will staff the store and handle the sale for a cut of your sales proceeds (often 30%), and you can re-stock your booth with more items as you make sales.

Items can also be sold online via eBay or similar marketplaces, depending upon the nature of what you have. Sometimes you never know what collectors will clamor for; a friend once had an ugly 1970s lamp that buyers went crazy for and the bidding on eBay went sky high, to her amusement.

For other collectibles, check whether there is anyone online who specializes in selling similar items. I had a collection of original early 1970s TV scripts and found an online resource to sell it, and five years later am still receiving occasional payments as items are sold.

If you have valuable collectibles or antiques, check with auction houses to see if it would be worthwhile to have your items included in their next auction catalog. If you are uncertain of the value of items that you have, have a knowledgeable appraiser look them over for you.

What Should I Do with My Car?

In many cases, it will not be advisable to ship an automobile to a foreign country. Even if you can import a car from the U.S. to the foreign country (which is not always permitted), will you be able to get parts for it? Will mechanics be familiar with the make and model? Buying a car locally is usually the better idea.

For example, Nicaragua allows you to import a car tax-free in the first months of your residency, or buy a car in Nicaragua without the sales tax. Nicaraguan immigration attorneys strongly advise against importing a foreign car that will stick out and advertise you as a foreigner. Additionally, it may be impossible to get spare parts. It's much better to obtain the same benefit by buying a new or used car locally.

So, if the old (or not so old) girl still has some value left in her, by all means sell your car. I had an older car that was still in very good condition and very reliable, but not worth much, so I gave it to family friends with a recent college graduate who needed a car.

If you decide to donate a car to a charity, read through **IRS Publication 526, *Charitable Contributions***, for the latest rules about donating a vehicle, boat or airplane; they are beyond the scope of this book.

You may need to file **Form 8283** with your income tax return for the year of the donation. Usually, the charity will need to furnish you with Form 1098-C for you to take a tax deduction, but there are some exceptions. Some charities may pick up the car from your location or offer an airport drop-off service for a donated car.

> *For any transfer of ownership of a vehicle (whether to a friend, family member or to a charity) verify that the title and registration is changed to the new owner. Signing the transfer of title form is only the first step; the Department of Motor Vehicles must receive and process the paperwork. If you are still the owner of record on the title, and the vehicle is involved in an accident, you could face legal liability. Once the transfer of ownership is confirmed with the DMV, notify your insurance company that you no longer own the vehicle.*

Charitable Donations

If you're able to itemize deductions on your income tax return, be sure to get tax receipts for your donations to charities for items that you donate to them. I took several hundred books to the local public library in multiple trips, and listed each book in an Excel spreadsheet along with the original cost and the value I was claiming as a deduction (thrift store value).

Donations of property (as opposed to cash) may need a special donor acknowledgement to comply with IRS requirements. Consult **IRS Publication 526, *Charitable Contributions*,** for the latest requirements.

> *If you have a number of old eyeglasses (with or without cases), these can be donated to a local Lions Club; they specialize in eye care and vision as one of their missions, and rehabilitate old eyeglasses for re-use among the indigent. I found eight old pairs of eyeglasses with cases when I was going through my things.*

Large kitchen or laundry appliances in decent condition and good, working order that you are unable to sell can be donated to organizations such as Habitat for Humanity, Salvation Army or Goodwill. They may be willing to pick them up from your home.

Bedding and mattresses are almost impossible to donate, so see if any friends, family or neighbors can use them if you will not be keeping them.

Items to Put in the Trash or Send to the Dump
Items that are not salable nor can be donated to charity (Goodwill and Salvation Army are becoming ever more picky in what they will accept), have no realistic prospect of being repaired or renovated, and can't be re-purposed for a different use are candidates for the trash. You may have to pay to have large items hauled away to the dump, such as furniture or appliances.

Renting a Storage Space, Truck or Trailer

As part of your moving process, you may need to rent temporarily a storage space.

If you will need to rent a U-Haul trailer or truck, keep in mind that late May is one of the busiest times of the year for trailer and truck rentals due to high school and college graduations, and it may be difficult to get one. Late August/early September are also busy periods due to college students moving into dorms or apartments, so plan accordingly.

Additional Resources

Any move, let alone an international one, is a lot of work. Many experts say that the single most common mistake made in a move is underestimating the amount of time it will take to sort through your belongings and pack everything.

Ali Wenzke, a Chicago real estate broker who has moved ten times in eleven years, has a blog about moving, "The Art of Happy Moving" at https://www.artofhappymoving.com. The blog goes into topics such as decluttering, moving with kids, and packing and has checklists and moving tips.

There are any number of books about the process of moving. While the books below aren't specific to international moves, some of the better reviewed ones include:

- *"The Art of Happy Moving: How to Declutter, Pack and Start Over While Maintaining Your Sanity and Finding Happiness"* by Ali Wenzke (Kindle/hardback 2019, paperback in 2023)
- *"Get It Together: Organize Your Records so Your Family Won't Have To,"* by Melanie Cullen (10th edition September 2022)
- *"Organizing Your Move: Moving Checklists, Worksheets and Timeline"* by Jenny Cogan (2020)
- *"Organize Pack Move! Strategies and Money-Saving Ideas to Simplify Your Move,"* by Nancy Giehl (2009)

Conclusion

With all of the above to be accomplished before leaving the U.S., you really need to allow yourself sufficient time. ***Don't underestimate*** how long it will take you to deal with your personal possessions.

Consult the free "to do" checklists and timelines available for download at my website, https://sites.google.com/view/northoak-books.

Chapter 5
Keeping in Touch with the U.S.

Choosing a Smart Phone Model
Backing up your Smart Phone's Apps and Data
Why Receiving Text Messages from the U.S. is Critical
Virtual U.S. Phone Number with Text Messaging
Ways to Make Voice or Video Calls for Free
Sending Faxes to the U.S.
If Internet is Essential for Working Remotely

The internet has made global communication almost instantaneous, and keeping in touch anywhere in the world is a whole lot easier nowadays than it used to be. For tips about local cell phone service in foreign countries, see *Chapter 16, Settling into Your New Home*.

Most people have a smart phone these days, so I will assume that you are familiar with the basic functionality. If not, there are online YouTube tutorials aplenty, or you can hire a tutor to give you lessons. *I recommend that you have a smart phone and that you know how to use it.*

Why Do I Need to Have a Smart Phone?
You will want to keep in touch with family and friends back home, unless you wish to completely sever contact with that ex-spouse, your parents passed away decades ago, your adult kid is a meth head, and your siblings are all sociopaths. OK, I'm exaggerating a little bit here, but you get the idea.

A smart phone is *critical* to expats because often banks, credit card companies, brokerage firms, Amazon etc. will insist on sending you a text code before giving you access to your account. *You must be able to receive verification codes sent by text message* if you want to be able to access your accounts online. See below for more about the importance of receiving text codes by phone.

Choosing a Smart Phone Model

Until recently, the U.S. used two kinds of cell phone technology, CDMA and GSM, but for the most part has ended the use of CDMA. GSM is the technology that nearly all of the world uses. **You want a GSM phone.** Don't even think about bringing your CDMA phone abroad with you; it just plain won't work anywhere.

Different countries use different *bandwidths* for wireless communications, and you want to make sure that your cell phone is compatible with your destination. There are multi-bandwidth phones on the market as well, if you haven't yet decided where you want to go.

Before leaving the U.S., check on what cell phone technology is in use in the country that you're considering. There are online resources that will tell you countries' cell phone bandwidths, such as:

- https://www.worldtimezone.com/gsm.html or
- https://www.frequencycheck.com/countries

The second web site listed, frequencycheck.com, will also let you run a compatibility check on an individual phone for a specific country, using the phone's model number or IMEI (International Mobile Equipment Identity) number. The IMEI will also tell you other information about the phone, including the maximum storage size for a micro-SD card, if it has a slot for one.

> *A **sim** card is the thumbnail-size card that identifies the phone to the cellular carrier with the assigned phone number; the carrier issues it to you. A **micro-SD** card is the same size as a sim card but provides additional storage for photos, videos or other files.*

Buying a GSM Smart Phone

Amazon sells a huge variety of cell phones, some of which are clearly labeled "international." Local retailers may also sell unlocked international phones, but an online seller may have a greater choice of models and bandwidths.

As a personal observation, I would stay away from lesser-known brands or models as you may not be able get spare parts for repairs. It's hard to go wrong with a newer iPhone or Samsung smart phone model anywhere in the world.

> *U.S. carriers are notorious for locking their phones, meaning that you can only use it on that carrier's network. Once you have finished paying for the phone, the carrier is now required by law to unlock it for you if you ask. You want to buy an* **unlocked phone** *that uses GSM technology in the correct bandwidths.*

Be aware that if you buy a smart phone with limited internal storage, you will not be able to install very many apps on it. 8 GB of internal memory may sound like a lot, but in reality you will only be able to install four or five apps because there may be other programs installed on the phone that you cannot remove (*bloatware*).

> *I recommend getting a phone with at least 64 GB (even better, 128 GB) of internal memory. A phone with two sim slots is also handy as it gives you the flexibility to use two physical sim cards or one sim card with a micro-SD memory card. Some phones with an extra sim slot will take a 256 GB micro-SD card, which will hold a* **whole lot** *of stuff.*

Note that in Asia the price of smart phones, including dual sim phones, may be lower than in the U.S. If you're heading to that part of the world, you might want to buy your phone there instead of in the U.S. or Canada.

Google Fi Phone
You can purchase a phone or global cell phone service from Google Fi (a service from Google) which gives you a U.S. phone number with a physical sim card that will work in over 200 countries around the world. Google Fi must be activated while you are in the U.S. and should be used in the U.S. occasionally to keep Google from deactivating your account.

You might want to start off with Google Fi if you are a free-roaming "digital nomad" (online worker) traveling to different countries, if you haven't yet decided where you will end up, or if you travel back and forth a lot between the U.S. and foreign countries.

You may be able to use your existing phone (Android or iOS; not all are compatible), or you can purchase a new phone from Google if it's time for a new one anyway. There are reports of poor customer service from people who purchased a new phone from Google; the phone I purchased from Google for my Fi service died in less than 18 months. There may be a trade-in credit for your old phone depending upon the model (but you could just sell your old phone yourself). Google Fi has an online tool that walks you through which phones will work with their network.

The main disadvantage is that if people in a foreign country want to call you, it's a U.S. phone number. If you use a phone with two sim card slots, you can use one for Google Fi and one for a local sim card (for a local country phone number) as you travel the world.

There is an eSIM option for Google Fi if your phone is a newer model compatible with eSIM (see below for more about eSIMs).

If you already have a U.S. phone number, you can port over the number to Google Fi and Google Fi becomes your U.S. carrier. If you want a new number, you can pick from dozens of different U.S. area codes. Google Fi is intended to be a permanent U.S. phone number.

Google Fi's base rates start at $20 a month for a single user plus $10 per gigabyte for data. After you've used six gigabytes of data, further data is free, albeit subject to slower speeds. There are discounts for multiple-user plans. Calls over Wi-Fi are free but international calls to the U.S. using a local cell phone network (using data) are 20 cents per minute. **Text messages work worldwide with Google Fi.**

Google reserves the right to terminate service if data use over local cell phone networks is "excessive," defined at their discretion. I imagine that this means that lots of video streaming over data (not using Wi-Fi) will get you kicked out. **Use Google Fi over Wi-Fi as much as possible to avoid issues (and save money).**

Their website is located at https://fi.google.com/about/ which explains how it works in detail.

Backing up your Smart Phone

Once you have a phone that will function in your country of planned residence, it is prudent to back up the apps and data from time to time.

If your smart phone should be damaged, lost or stolen, you may have to buy a new phone. Having apps and data backed up will enable a much easier and faster recovery, although you'll still have to re-install everything.

It's easier than you think to drop your phone or spill liquids on it. On a regular basis, expats accidentally leave their phone in a taxi; it's not likely that they will ever see it again.

The good news is that it's now easier than ever to back up your smart phone, and Google and Apple have automated the process once you set things up.

Android Phones
With an Android phone, you probably registered it with your Google account when you purchased it. Under Setup there are options to automate a backup using the built-in Android Backup Service. Go first to "Accounts and Backup" and then select "Copy and Restore."

If you have a Samsung phone, there will be an option for a Samsung account as well as a Google account, because Samsung offers its own cloud storage. It's probably simpler to just stick with Google's account features because they are synchronized across the Google environment.

Select the "Backup copy of data" and "Automatic restoration" options and check that the registered Google account for the phone is correct. Then tap on "Google account" and select "Create backup copy in Google Drive." You can also select whether you want to restrict backups to only Wi-Fi, or whether using data is OK.

Your phone data such as Wi-Fi passwords and call history, list of installed applications and files will be backed up automatically to the cloud. You can configure which videos, if any, you want backed up to your Google account under "Backup Copies and Synchronization" as well as select the quality of photos (original, high quality or express) to conserve space.

Google gives you 15 GB of free space across its various storage platforms such as Google Photos, Google Drive and Gmail. When you have used 80% of your free storage space, you should get an email from Google. You can purchase additional storage space with Google that will apply to Google Drive, Google Photos and Gmail as follows:

- 100 GB is $1.99 a month or $19.99 a year if paid annually
- 200 GB is $2.99 a month or $29.99 a year if paid annually
- 2 terabytes is $9.99 a month or $99.99 a year if paid annually, includes VPN (Android only)
- 5 terabytes is $24.99 a month or $249.99 a year if paid annually

Google's Android cell phone app One Drive uses this same 15 GB free allowance but allows you to manage your storage options and synchronizes cloud storage, letting you free up space. The VPN bundled into the 2 terabytes plan is unlikely to work with pay streaming services like Netflix, however. You can download One Drive for free from the Google Play Store.

Most Android phones come pre-loaded with Google Photos which is integrated with the phone's camera. By using the built-in Android Backup Service, you can have your photos automatically backed up to Google.

Google's free Play Music app allows you to import your MP3 collection to your phone, up to 50,000 songs, and then access your collection from any Android device or PC via a web browser once it's been backed up to your Google account.

There are third party Android phone apps that will do comprehensive backups to the cloud, where you will need to specify where you want everything stored (Microsoft OneDrive, Amazon Drive, to a laptop or desktop computer, or other location), but in my opinion the built-in Android Backup Service does an adequate job for free.

Resilio Sync is an interesting free Android phone backup up that will back up your phone to your desktop computer, not to the cloud. There are paid versions for business users.

Apple/iPhones
The easiest option for iPhones is of course to use Apple's iCloud service. The first five GB of storage is free, but note that the 5 GB is *per iCloud account* and not per device, so that 5 GB can start to look pretty stingy if you have multiple devices registered to the same account. Additional storage space can be purchased (billed monthly). 50 GB of extra storage capacity is billed at 99 cents per month, 200 GB of additional storage is $2.99 a month, and 2 terabytes is $9.99 per month.

If you subscribe to the Apple One bundle subscription plan with four to six services, it comes with additional storage. Apple One has individual ($14.95 per month and 50 GB of extra storage), family ($19.95 per month and 200 GB of extra storage) and premier ($29.95 per month and 2 terabytes of extra storage) tiers. The family and premier tiers permit content sharing with up to five family members.

To use iCloud Backup, go to iOS settings, select your name, iCloud and then finally iCloud Backup; your phone will be backed up periodically and automatically to Apple's iCloud.

iCloud backups include data, device settings and home screen layouts, but exactly what gets backed up depends upon your configuration of each individual app. Go through each of your apps and see how you have them configured and what data is involved.

> *An alternative to iCloud is Google's new free app for iPhone, Google One. It's more of a storage app that will back up photos, videos, music, text messages, apps, other files and Contacts and Calendar apps. You can manage your files across Google Drive, Gmail and Google Photos and the app's included Storage Manager lets you see how you're using your storage and free up space. The cost to purchase additional Google storage space is the same as listed above under Android phones.*

Why Receiving Text Messages from the U.S. is Critical

It is **vital** to be able to receive text messages when living outside the U.S., but many people don't realize that (or that they might have problems receiving U.S.-based text messages) until they've already moved abroad.

Banks, credit card companies or brokerage firms often use **two factor authentication** (2FA) to allow online access. This means they send a text code to your cell phone number of record or (sometimes) to an e-mail address already on record. Even Amazon or other retailers sometimes use two factor authentication to prevent fraud.

You then enter the code into the site that you are trying to access; if you are unable to do this, *you will be denied access to your account*. Some companies let you choose between e-mail or text messages, but some banks (and PayPal) will insist on a cell phone number, and then what are you going to do?

Even if your U.S. cell phone is on roaming and registered for travel, you may not be able to receive text messages. If you're living permanently outside the U.S., this is not a viable option due to the exorbitant cost of roaming (up to $10 a day). It is also desirable to keep a low profile about the fact that you're living overseas permanently (see **Chapter 7, Banking and Finances**, for why this is so).

Note that some senders of SMS text messages (some banks, the IRS, etc.) may block text messages sent to a VOIP phone number. This is beyond the control of the U.S. virtual phone carrier.

If you have a laptop computer that was previously used to access your online account (before you left the U.S.), you might be able to continue accessing your U.S. account online for a while. But what happens if your hard drive crashes? Or you have to buy a new laptop? If you don't have a smart phone or U.S. phone number, you will not be able to receive a text code from the bank, and you may be restricted to doing all transactions by voice over the phone. You won't even be able to download monthly statements. Not a good situation.

Why do companies require two factor authentication?

In a nutshell, fraud prevention. In addition to verifying your contact information that is on file, banks and others also use two-factor authentication for two other reasons:

(1) **Location Checks** - When a banks or others send you a code by text message, they're able to get a general idea of the current location for that device; not an exact location, but they're able to see which mobile network and country you're currently roaming on.

I normally keep my data turned off on my phone (to conserve data) and access things only via Wi-Fi, but according to my techie sources, companies can *still* see where your phone is connecting to the internet unless you are using a virtual private network, or VPN (see **Chapter 11, *Computer Security for Expats*,** for further details about VPNs). Use a VPN with your phone or computer when accessing U.S. online accounts.

(2) **SIM Identification** – Sending a text message involves providing basic sim card information to the sender. The sender (bank, credit card company or brokerage firm) can compare this information to see if the sim card has physically changed from earlier transactions, which could be a fraud indicator (especially if in conjunction with a location outside the U.S.). Google "sim swapping" if you want to know more.

That said, *SMS text messaging is not secure.* Although it was never designed to be a verification of identity, banks, credit card companies and brokerage firms treat it as if it were a secure method.

For more information on the security problems with SMS text messages, see **Chapter 11, Computer Security for Expats**.

Options for a Virtual U.S. Phone Number with Text Messaging

What we expats want is an internet phone provider that will:

(1) Give us a U.S. phone number without a physical sim card ("virtual" sim);
(2) Let us make and receive phone calls to/from the U.S.;
(3) Receive all-important text messages from the U.S.; and
(4) Use an app that resides on our smart phone

Installing a "virtual sim card" app on your phone will enable you to have both a local phone number (with a sim card) and a U.S. phone number (via an app) on your physical phone. Note that this is different from an eSIM, which is discussed later in this chapter.

The app functions as a second phone number in conjunction with an U.S.-based internet phone provider. You will be able to receive voice and text messages **without** having to tote around two physical phones.

How Do I Find a VOIP (Voice Over Internet Protocol) Provider That Does All of the above?
There are any number of U.S. VOIP providers who can provide the above functionality; below is a list of some options.

This is by no means an exhaustive list. Do your own search for other providers and see what you can find. I am not recommending any of the below options, and with the exception of Google Voice, have not used them.

The internet phone providers below provide both voice and texting internationally.   I'm going to list them in order of *least to most expensive*.

This information is subject to change at any time, so do an online search for reviews and the latest information about these kinds of services before deciding on which one to use.

> *All U.S. internet phone providers are required by law to allow you to "port" an existing phone number to them from your current landline or cell phone carrier, or you can pick a new number from dozens of area codes. Your choice.*

Google Voice

Google Voice is a telephone service that provides call forwarding and voicemail services, voice and text messaging for Google customers. The service was launched in 2009, so it's been around for a while. Google could decide to discontinue the service at any time, but it is free for incoming calls (for now anyway).

You must have a U.S. telephone number to establish service. Google Voice lets you choose a U.S. telephone number from available numbers in selected area codes free of charge. Once this number is assigned, you associate it with one or several cell phone or land line numbers for call, message and voice mail forwarding. ***Text messaging is not supported in all foreign markets, so check first.***

Google Voice is integrated with Gmail and for each call received you also receive an e-mail notification with transcription (if you have a Gmail account) and a recording that can be played back on your phone or computer.

You get unlimited incoming calls (up to three hours in length each) and texts to and from numbers in the U.S. and Canada. Users in the U.S. can place outbound calls to other U.S. numbers for free. Users in foreign countries can place outbound calls to the U.S. and other destinations for a small per minute charge.

Google Voice is usable over Wi-Fi or over a local cell network using data, but be warned that if you take a call over a local cellular network outside of the U.S., the data charges may add up fast. I once answered a call from a friend using my local in-country mobile network and burned through $10 worth of data on a brief call. It's best to let calls go to voicemail if you're not connected to Wi-Fi and talk later.

Here's the thing: if you first have Google Fi and then move to Google Voice, you don't have to configure any of the call forwarding features, just let the calls come directly to your Google Voice phone number via the app on your phone.

People or companies in the U.S. can call or text (or leave a voice mail) at any time to your U.S. phone number.

I use Google Voice mostly to receive text messages or phone calls to my U.S. phone number from credit card companies, banks, brokerage accounts or when ordering from Amazon. Friends and family can call me on the U.S. number as well.

TextNow
TextNow offers a "virtual" U.S. phone number with free calling and texting over Wi-Fi within the U.S. and Canada. The service offers voicemail and conference calling as well, and with the optional sim card activation kit you can purchase access to Sprint's nationwide U.S. network (now part of T-Mobile).

The TextNow smart phone app lets you talk and text for free with ads on the app. TextNow is available in 33 countries (some are iOS-only, some Android-only); as long as you have Wi-Fi, you can get a free U.S. phone number and call North American numbers for free (with ads). If you want to call a local number outside the U.S., you will have to purchase international long distance credits.

You can enter your phone's IMEI number to see if it is compatible for use with TextNow, or you can purchase a phone from TextNow. If you want to remove the ads from the Wi-Fi calling in the app, it's $9.99 a month without a data add-on. You can add data for when you can't access Wi-Fi, from USD $8.99 a month (1 GB) up to $27.9 a month for 5 GB. All but the 1GB option get rid of the ads. Once the data runs out, you get unlimited 2G (basically usable only for email or texting) data access. https://www.textnow.com/

GrooVe IP
GrooVe IP is a VOIP calling and texting app that lets you receive calls and texts (except for verification texts) for free from anywhere in the world, and call any number in the U.S. or Canada. It is designed for use with an Android or Apple smart phone with native apps from the Google Play store, the Apple store, or the Amazon app store. The free app contains ads; there is a paid app version without advertising that costs $6.99.

You purchase credits when you want to make *outgoing* phone calls. Each month you get 16 credits free, which is enough for 10 minutes of phone calls or 45 text messages. Additional credits start at 200 credits for $1.99 (125 minutes), with further discounts for 550 credits ($4.99) or 1,000 credits ($8.49). Currently outgoing phone calls are 1.6 credits per minute, or about one and a half cents per minute (less if you purchase more credits at one time).

The app "strongly discourages" signing up to use primarily for receiving verification codes, and charges 100 credits (about $1.00) for *verification code* texts; the free credits *cannot be used* for them. If they determine that your account was opened *solely* to receive verification texts (no other activity), it will be closed and your phone number released. If you have not placed or received calls or sent or received text messages for more than thirty days, they have the right to terminate your phone number.

You can receive calls with GrooVe IP from anywhere in the world, but you can only make calls to a U.S. or Canadian phone number.

If you already have a Google Voice number (see above), GrooVe IP has a Google Voice integration feature where GrooVe IP will display your Google Voice number as your outgoing call phone number. This involves configuring both your Google Voice settings and your GrooVe IP settings.

GrooVe IP may not be a bad option if you primarily want to be able to receive phone calls and text messages from the U.S., though they clearly will be happier if you make the occasional outgoing phone call for one and a half cents a minute. For general information, go to **https://snrblabs.com/GrooVeIP/**.

NumberBarn

This is a phone number porting service that allows you to move an existing U.S. or Canadian phone number to a virtual number. For $2 a month it will park calls and notify you that you have a voicemail. The $2 a month plan includes text messaging.

The NumberBarn app can be used on your smart phone for incoming and outgoing calls, and will show a caller ID number corresponding to the ported number and not to the cell phone number. Callers will hear a message that the phone call is being parked with NumberBarn (which you as an expat won't want), or you can record your own custom outgoing message instead (a better idea).

For $6 a month it will give you 300 minutes for incoming and outgoing calls and incoming caller ID. Additional minutes over the limit are three cents each. With the $6 a month plan it will also forward the voicemail as a .wav attachment to an e-mail account and send text messages to e-mail. https://www.numberbarn.com/

Skype

Skype, owned by Microsoft, lets you sign up for a "virtual" U.S. phone number or one in over 20 foreign countries for a monthly fee. As long as you have Wi-Fi, you can make and receive phone calls and text messages throughout the world.

There is no charge to call U.S. or Canada 1-800 numbers but you do have to deposit at least $10 to open your account with Skype before you can make phone calls. I use Skype to call banks, credit card companies, LL Bean etc. I have had troubleshooting calls to 1-800 numbers for computer and software issues that lasted over an hour and a half, so free is good.

The free Skype software is available for Android or Apple smart phones, and also for Windows, Mac OS and Linux desktops. If all you want to do is make outgoing calls, you can use the Skype software without having a Skype phone number.

> *Skype-to-Skype calls are free, so if you just want to be able to chat with friends or family anywhere in the world and they have Skype on their smart phone or computer, this is a good, economical option.*

If you want a U.S. phone number, Skype has a <u>subscription model</u> and a <u>credit model</u>. The subscription model starts at $2.99 a month for "unlimited" calling to Guam, Puerto Rico and the U.S. The "unlimited" is in quotation marks because there are some exceptions, such as special and premium numbers as well as for certain geographic areas. There are other plans that go up to $16.79 per month for calls to anywhere in the world. If Microsoft deems your usage to be "excessive," they can terminate your account or charge you extra.

The credit model is a pay-as-you-go model for $5 a month, with outgoing calls charged at 2.83 cents (and on up) a minute, depending upon to where you're calling. Charges are determined by the destination country, not where you're calling FROM, but calls from a U.S. number to a U.S. number incur a fee of several cents a minute, which can vary by type of call (cell phone vs. land line). https://www.skype.com/en/

> *Skype has a nifty option called **Skype to Go** that lets you "provision" up to thirty different U.S. numbers to a foreign local number (or vice-versa) so that you can call a specific number and it will be treated (and charged) as if it were a local number.*
>
> *For calls from outside the U.S. to the U.S., using **Skype to GO** you will be charged only as if you were making a local phone call within the country where you're living (using Wi-Fi or minutes from your local cell phone plan). This feature is available in over 22 foreign countries plus the U.S. and Canada.*
>
> *For calls from the U.S. to foreign countries, you can call almost anywhere in the world using **Skype to Go** except to Egypt, Morocco and Nigeria (due*

> *to high levels of fraud and abuse). For example, if you're in Milwaukee and call someone in Berlin regularly, with **Skype to Go** you would call a U.S. number and be charged as if it were a domestic Skype call.*

Hushed

Although its name sounds like a plan for people cheating on their spouse, Hushed is a virtual private phone number app that does not require that your phone have a sim card so long as you have Wi-Fi. You can choose a number from over 60 countries, including the U.S.

Using Wi-Fi, your virtual phone number can make and receive calls and receive texts. You can have multiple phone numbers on a single Hushed account, and you can select which caller ID number that a recipient will see when you call them. Free apps are available for both Android and Apple smart phones.

The prepaid plan is $1.99 a month for bundled minutes and texting. Unlimited calling is $3.99 a month for U.S., Canada or UK numbers. The international plan is $4.99 a month and includes texting and international calls at a per minute rate. https://hushed.com/

CallCentric

The residential plan offers calls and text messaging to and from your U.S. phone number. They have multiple tiers of plans; you can select inbound calls only or outbound calls only, or both. Rates start from $1.95 a month for 120 minutes for outbound calls to a U.S. number and $5.95 a month for unlimited inbound calls from a U.S. number.

Text messaging on the basic plan is $1.00 a month plus one cent per message. Some senders of SMS authentication messages may block codes sent to "virtual" VOIP numbers. In order to make and receive calls directly over VOIP you need to install a mobile phone app for iPhone or Android, available from the Apple App or Google Play Stores. https://www.callcentric.com/

iPlum

Plans start from $5.99 a month for a U.S. phone number using Wi-Fi VOIP calls with 200 credits, reload 500 credits for $5 (airtime over cell network starts at 1 cent (1 credit = 1 cent) per minute, higher for international use). Free calling to toll-free numbers in U.S. and Canada. SMS text messaging works internationally.

Downloadable apps for iOS and Android, no sim card. Encrypted voice and messaging, HIPAA compliant. **Within the U.S.**, iPlum is intended for use with a cell phone with a U.S. sim card, so it won't work without Wi-Fi if your phone has no U.S. sim card. Reviews indicate above-average customer service and troubleshooting assistance.

Sideline
$9.99 per month plus sales tax, six months for $49.99 or one year for $99.99 (plus sales tax). Sideline has mobile apps for iPhone and Android; no hardware is involved. Text messaging and calling to/from U.S. phone numbers is included. Port an existing number or pick a new phone number. You can put one phone number on multiple phones. https://www.sideline.com/

Dingtone
Dingtone is a VOIP downloadable phone app (no physical sim card) that utilizes a credit system for international phone calls. You get a U.S. phone number with voice mail and text capability. International calling over Wi-Fi costs from less than 1 credit per minute to 5 credits per minute.

Credits cost from $9.99 (550 credits) to $93.99 (5,500 credits). You can earn free credits by participating in surveys, watching videos, or "checking in."

eSIMs for U.S., Regional or Global Use While Traveling

eSIM service lets you create a temporary cell phone number and download a digital sim card; no physical sim card is used. This is ideal for traveling, including visits to the U.S., because you can install the eSIM before you leave home abroad and will have U.S. cell phone service the minute you land in the U.S.

The catch is that only newer model Apple or Android phones will work with eSIMs. If your current phone doesn't work with eSIMs, maybe your next phone purchase will?

Some eSIM providers offer regional or global service in addition to U.S.-only service, but all limit the length of time you can have the digital phone number (varies by carrier). Plans include data and minutes.

Generally, this is both more convenient and more economical than waiting until you arrive in the U.S. to obtain a physical sim card from a U.S. cell phone carrier. eSIM providers include Airalo, Truphone, Gigsky, Flexiroam, Surfroam, Ubigi, Redteago and Knowroaming.

Ways to Make Voice or Video Phone Calls for Free

The apps listed below won't get you text messaging for two-factor authentication, but are great options to make and receive economical voice or video calls over the internet with friends or family.

Gmail Video or Voice Calls
Not everyone knows about this nifty little add-on to the Google Gmail desktop app or separate smart phone app. The party originating the call must have a Gmail e-mail account (sign up for free), and you can call U.S. land line or cell phone numbers for free from Gmail.

I used this for the first time during the coronavirus pandemic and it worked quite well. You can do just a voice call or if you turn on your camera, you can make it a video call, anywhere in the world. I have used it for calls to the U.S. and to Guatemala. One hundred percent free to all parties on the call as long as you have Wi-Fi.

Both the Gmail desktop and smart phone apps let you do free video meetings; the person originating the call must have a Gmail account, and the call can be among a group or one-on-one. The organizer of the call creates a link and then sends it to the recipient(s), who then can access the video call. Calls can be scheduled ahead of time using Google Calendar. Participants can share their screen with others, and there is no time limit on calls as there is with a free Zoom account.

WhatsApp
Over two billion people worldwide use WhatsApp. It lets you place voice and video calls or send text messages over Wi-Fi or wireless data to a cell

phone number anywhere in the world. For voice or video calls, it's best to stick to Wi-Fi as data charges could get pricey.

If you find typing a WhatsApp text message to be tedious, within the text messaging function is an option to send a voice message; you record your voice message and then send it to the recipient just like a text message.

One aspect of WhatsApp that I find annoying is the fact that the person you are calling or texting must first be in your phone Contacts; you cannot just "dial" the phone number.

I have found WhatsApp to be a very useful app. Ask your friends and family in the U.S. to install the app on their smart phone and you can talk or video call all day long *for free* over Wi-Fi. It works in most countries that have internet and is not restricted to use within a single country.

WhatsApp is *banned* in the following countries:

China	Syria
North Korea	United Arab Emirates
Qatar	

Note that other countries may temporarily suspend WhatsApp during times of protest or national emergency.

FaceTime
If you're an Apple product user and the person you're calling also has an iOS device, FaceTime lets you call any Apple device for free and is synced to your Apple ID. Mac and iPhone users can set up conference calls; group video calls can include up to 32 people.

Calls can only be made while you're connected to the internet; FaceTime will not work with Android, Windows or Linux devices.

Facebook Messenger
If you're one of the more than two billion Facebook users around the world, you can use Messenger to make voice or video calls for free to other Facebook users as long as all parties on the call have an internet connection.

There are versions of the Messenger app for Android and iOS phones and tablets; there are "lite" versions of Messenger for devices without a lot of memory. Messenger has a collection of games within the app that you can play online with other Messenger users.

In Summary
It is entirely possible to mix and match the above services to minimize your cost, depending upon your needs. You have many options when it comes to keeping a U.S. phone number while living outside the U.S.

If I want to have calls with friends or family from the U.S., they can call me on my Google Voice U.S. phone number, which will ring on my smart phone. If I'm calling them, I'll try to do it using Gmail Video or Voice or WhatsApp from my laptop or phone using Wi-Fi. For 1-800 number calls to the U.S. or Canada, I use Skype.

Sending Faxes to the U.S.

Occasionally you may still get someone in the U.S. requesting an old-fashioned fax of a letter or document (title or escrow company, government agency, financial institution etc.). Rather than finding a physical fax machine in your new home abroad (which will involve an international phone call), just digitize the documents to be faxed and then use a web-based faxing service.

Most online services will let you send three to five pages for free; if you have more pages than that, then there will be a small per page (usually in the pennies) charge. Do a Google search and you'll find services such as **RingCentral, MyFax, eFax, or GotFreeFax**, which will vary in the file formats accepted.

If your printer can't scan documents, take them to a local shop and have them scanned in to the appropriate format and save them to a thumb drive.

If Internet is Essential for Working Remotely

If you REALLY need reliable internet, then you will want to have a Plan B in case the local internet service suffers from outages or has wild swings in speed. When the electricity goes out, so does your internet. If you're trying to earn a living by working remotely, it can be disastrous to have bad internet or electricity service.

A battery-powered portable Wi-Fi modem/router that accesses the local cell phone network and functions as a little modem/router all by itself will keep you connected *as long as the cell phone network is operating*, and can travel with you from place to place.

These devices do not use *tethering*, which uses your smartphone itself to use cell plan data to access the internet for other devices; tethering can get expensive if you are paying for data by the gigabyte. Tethering a cell phone also drains the phone's battery very quickly.

> *I have no personal experience with the companies listed below and am not recommending or endorsing them, simply observing that this is an option if you travel extensively or if reliable internet is critical for you.*

Skyroam
One option is a service like Skyroam (https://www.skyroam.com/) that gives you a palm-sized mobile hotspot device that will work in 135 countries using local cell phone networks. The device's battery will give you up to 16 hours of use between charges (less time if multiple devices are connected), so you can take it with you anywhere that has cell phone coverage.

Up to ten devices can connect to one Skyroam device, so it can be shared by families or work groups. *Skyroam will function only if there is available cell phone service*, so it will not work on cruise ships, airplanes or areas without cell phone coverage.

You purchase or rent the global hotspot device to create your own private Wi-Fi network over the local cellular network. Rent the little box if you'll only need a hotspot for a brief time (say for a business trip), or purchase one if you'll be using it for a longer period of time.

Prices to purchase the device are USD $120 or $180 depending upon features. Refurbished units may be available for sale from $49 from time to time. Skyroam also offers a VPN option for an additional fee. There are iOS and Android apps available for the service as well.

The first 20 GB of "unlimited" data is high speed, after which you get continued access but throttled back to 512 kbps (pretty damn slow). You can purchase ("top off") additional high-speed gigabytes in increments of 1, 5, 10 or 20 GB.

Skyroam has several different plans:

- USA subscription for $6-8 per GB per month (no speed throttling);
- Unlimited monthly European subscription for USD $49, or $6 per GB with no speed throttling;
- Unlimited monthly global subscription for $99 a month, with discounts for paying up front for three months or six months;
- GoData subscription without speed throttling, USD $9 per GB; or
- Unlimited GB global 24-hour pass for $9

According to Skyroam's website, you can purchase the little gadgets in many airports around the world; they are also available via Amazon or Best Buy in the U.S.

Ryoko – a new product
A new alternative to Skyroam is the pocket-sized Ryoko, which likewise uses available cell phone networks – so if there is no cell service, the Ryoko portable router will not work.

It functions as a portable Wi-Fi router, with a battery that will last about eight hours (less if multiple devices are connected). It is a small handheld device about the size of a pack of cigarettes. You can connect up to ten wireless devices simultaneously to the Ryoko.

The company is based in Europe and plans on building out an affiliate network in the U.S. It has U.S. customer service phone numbers but shipping currently (2022) comes from China.

It ships with a sim card that has 500 MB prepaid; you add more data by topping off your account. You can also swap out the sim card for any local sim card. It uses 4G LTE networks on down, and is capable of speeds of up to 150 Mbps (though I don't know many cell providers that will offer that speed), and comes with a built-in firewall. The Ryoko can also support a VPN.

Since it is designed to be a portable device, you download the Android or Apple smartphone app for it, register and log in, scan the device's bar code behind the included sim card, and then insert the sim card.

Currently (June 2022) it can only be purchased at the manufacturer's web site, https://getryoko.com/. All prices include free shipping. Purchase prices are:

- USD $89 for one device
- USD $138 for two devices
- USD $220 for four devices
- USD $265 for five devices (special offer)

Data plans operate via Viaota, a global mobile internet access service that works with Ryoko. Data tiers (with additional top-offs available) are:

- 3 GB (USD $14.99) per month
- 5 GB (USD $22.99) per month
- 10 GB (USD $39) per month

The manufacturer also sells accessories such as an all-in-one universal travel adapter, a shockproof travel case designed to hold a smartphone, power bank, battery case, adapter, charger and USB cable, or an ultra-durable micro-USB charger.

The Ryoko can be used in 125 countries in Europe, Asia, North and South America and Africa.

> **Note:** *be sure to change the default user name and password that ship with the Ryoko device, which are set to admin (not very secure).*

Renting a Pocket Wi-Fi Modem/Router

If you will only need a pocket Wi-Fi modem/router for a limited time, there are companies around the world that handle rentals, which usually involve a security deposit. They may offer optional insurance as well. Typically, the company mails you the device and you return it via mail as well at the end of your trip. Skyroam, mentioned above, also does rentals.

Providers such as https://www.my-webspot.com/ rent battery-operated handheld pocket Wi-Fi modem/routers for use worldwide, with a daily 4G LTE limit of 1 GB in the USA/Canada and Europe, 512 MB per day elsewhere, with data after that at 512 kpbs (note: this is so slow as to be useless except for texting). Rental prices are typically around USD $12-14 per day, which includes the device rental and data to use in 118 countries.

Do an online search for a company that can rent you a pocket Wi-Fi modem/router from your location.

Chapter 6
How Do I Get Mail or Packages?

Foreign Address vs. U.S. Address
Mail Scanning and Forwarding Services
Notifications for Change of Address
Sending Mail to the U.S.
Options for Receiving Letters & Documents Abroad
Options for Receiving Packages Abroad

A frequent question of people contemplating moving outside of the U.S. is, how do I receive my mail or packages outside of the U.S.? There are ways.

Foreign Address vs. a U.S. Address when Living Abroad

Using a foreign address has obvious drawbacks – it can take anywhere from a week (best case scenario - Western Europe) to a month or more (many other countries) to receive your mail. It may not get there at all – many countries' postal systems have problems with theft or competency. Some foreign countries don't even have a postal system.

For example, Guatemala's postal system was operated through 2016 by a contractor who wasn't half bad, but they had a falling out with the government and for several years until 2019 there was **no** governmental postal system at all. Ecuador has had no functioning government-run postal system for a number of years now.

There was a U.S. Tax Court case where a U.S. taxpayer living in Africa did not receive his notice of assessment (a tax bill in the six figures) from the IRS until after the 90-day deadline to appeal had passed. The U.S. Tax Court said tough luck – he was stuck, unable to appeal the assessment in Tax Court, as unfair as that seemed. His only option was to pay the entire assessment and then file a suit for refund.

Additionally, there may be companies or businesses where you do not want to advertise the fact that you're not living in the U.S. – see **Chapter 7, Banking and Finances**.

You will need to receive from time to time replacement U.S. ATM, debit and credit cards from banks in the U.S. as they reach their expiration dates; a U.S. address is best.

So use a U.S. address. But which address?

Using a family member's address might work for you. Not to be too morose, but what happens if Uncle Joe gets seriously ill and moves to a nursing home (or dies!) and can't get your mail for you? Or your sister/brother starts opening your mail and stealing from you to fund their oxycodone/ fentanyl/methamphetamine habit? Or your relatives move to another state?

If nothing else, it can impose a substantial burden on a loved one to be responsible for all of your mail. Do you really expect them to scan in your mail for you so that you can view it electronically, and then shred it or send it to you abroad? A mail forwarding service relieves them of that burden.

Mail Scanning & Forwarding Services

For the above reasons, many expats utilize a mail scanning or forwarding service – depending upon the amount of mail you get, it can be safer and more reliable than using a relative's address to get your mail.

Most of these mail services got their start serving the full-time RV and boating crowd, who have been wandering nomads for many decades --

but the concept is the same for expats. You pick a mailing address in one of the locations that they offer; keep in mind the state income tax issues explained in **Chapter 14, State Income Taxes**. Some of these mailing services will advise you how to transfer your driver's license to that state, if that is something you need to do. You sign a contract with the mail service, which will give you the exact address to be used by all your correspondents. You will fill out and sign a U.S. Postal Service form that notifies the post office of the change of address. The Post Office will forward mail from your old, physical address to the mail forwarding service for six months; after that, *there is no mail forwarding* and mail will be returned to the sender.

The mail forwarding service will send you an e-mail when you have new mail. Typically, the service scans in the outside of each item of mail at no charge; you log in to your online account and tell them whether to toss the mail, scan the contents, or shred it.

Once they've scanned the contents you requested, you can view the scan and decide whether to have it shredded or physically forwarded it to you. Expect to pay from $150 to $250 a year or more, depending upon the volume of mail that you receive and how much scanning or shredding you do.

> *I suggest switching your mail over to a forwarding service several months before you actually leave the U.S., to give yourself time to work out any kinks or unexpected issues with using the service. There will be a learning curve as you learn the company's way of doing things.*

If you need letters or documents physically forwarded to you in your foreign country of residence, you can have the mail forwarding service send it to you (via FedEx, DHL or whatever they use), or you can use a **"mule" service** (see below) if one's available to bring it to you. You can also have friends or family who happen to be visiting you bring you your physical mail.

If you have your mail service use FedEx or DHL or whoever they use, it's a nice option because you can check online to see where your item is in transit. The downside to this is the cost, often $50-$75 or more.

Note that some countries place restrictions on envelopes containing credit or debit cards or negotiable instruments (checks).

Private Mail Forwarding Services
Below is a list of some of the better known, well-established mail forwarding services (all have websites online). I am not endorsing any of them, but am simply noting that the companies below have been established for a while:

- American Home Base
- Passport America
- St. Brendan's Isle
- My RV Mail
- Escapees
- Texas Home Base
- America's Mailbox
- Traveling Mailbox
- Earth Class Mail

Most mail forwarding companies have offices in multiple states, so if all you need is a mail forwarding service, you can pretty much pick whichever U.S. city you'd like to use. If you'll be living outside the U.S. you may wish to pick a city with good air connections to the part of the world where you'll be living.

HOWEVER, if you also want to have a U.S. driver's license then the situation is a little more complicated. The state in which you have your driver's license has state income tax implications (see **Chapter 14, State Income Taxes**, for more on this) and there are also restrictions on getting a driver's license if you don't have an actual physical address in the state.

> You **really** need the address on your driver's license to match your mailing address. You will have no end of problems if the driver's license is in one state and your mailing address is in a different state.

As mentioned in **Chapter 14, State Income Taxes**, South Dakota (as of 2021) will give you a South Dakota driver's license with only a mail forwarding service address. Other states will want to see two pieces of proof of residence address in your name such as a utility bill, property tax bill, or a rental agreement.

Notifications for Change of Address

Notify all of your correspondents about your new address. Family and friends can be notified via e-mail. You may have a lengthy list of mail sources to notify, such as Costco, banks, credit cards, brokerage firms, etc. See the sample Excel spreadsheet available for download at my website, https://sites.google.com/view/northoak-books.

Exercise caution with banks and brokerage firms – see **Chapter 7, Banking and Finances** for further information. Many banks, brokerage firms and financial institutions will let you change your address online, which makes it very convenient and low profile.

> *One thing to keep in mind: if the day comes when you want to part company with your private mailbox service, the post office **will not** process change of address forms – you will need to notify all of your correspondents manually. These days, this can usually be done online electronically for most of your correspondents, so don't let that scare you off. Just be aware of this.*

Sending Mail to the U.S.

If you have other U.S. expats living in your area, quite often people will be happy to take an envelope with postage on it with them back to the U.S. and drop the letter in a mailbox once they arrive. This is far better than trying to send a letter through the country's postal system (if there is one) or using FedEx or DHL etc. which will likely cost $75 or more.

I once sent mail to the U.S. via Mexico's postal system using registered mail. It arrived safely after about 10 days; I was able to follow the letter's progress online with the registration code. In other countries this may not be a good idea.

In some communities where there are many expats, there is an organized volunteer system for taking mail to the U.S. to be posted. For example, in Ajijic, Mexico the Lake Chapala Society maintains an outgoing mailbox. You deposit your U.S.-postage-stamped outgoing U.S. mail and several times a week, a member traveling to the U.S. empties the box and takes the letters to be posted in the U.S.

Purchase a supply of "Forever" stamps from the U.S. Postal Service before you move abroad. These stamps will always be worth the price of a first-class letter regardless of future price increases. These stamps come in handy if you need to send correspondence to a bank, credit card company, brokerage firm or whatever. If you get someone to carry the letter back to the U.S. for you, the correspondence will have a U.S. postmark on it, too!

Options for Receiving Letters or Documents Abroad

The ability to receive letters from the U.S. varies widely around the world. Most European countries have good postal systems and a letter sent airmail from the U.S. will arrive within a week or two at the most. Letters from the U.S. to Canada, or vice versa, can take a ridiculously long time and usually cost double or triple the domestic price.

In countries without an efficiently functioning post office (or a post office at all), your options narrow down to using

- a private service such as FedEx or DHL (likely to be expensive);
- a private forwarding service (see below);
- a "mule" service (see below); or
- friends or family to bring your mail to you from the U.S.

Check into local country regulations about what is allowable in mail being brought in by FedEx, DHL or other private companies. Some countries prohibit negotiable instruments (checks), credit or debit cards, or cash. This may limit your options.

Options for Receiving Packages Abroad

Let's say you desperately want an electric blanket for cold winter nights and they just don't exist where you're living, or you want to order a set of chef-grade knives that likewise aren't available locally.
You have several options here.

First of all, check and see if Amazon has what you're looking for and operates in the country where you're living. This will avoid the need for any international packages to be shipped to you. **Amazon does in fact operate in twelve foreign countries as of 2022** with more being added all the time.

The countries that have Amazon marketplaces in 2022 are:

Australia	Germany	Japan
Canada	India	Mexico
China	Ireland	Spain
France	Italy	United Kingdom

If you live in one of these countries, then it's just a matter of ordering from the local Amazon operation and having your packages delivered domestically.

Additionally, Amazon ships to over 100 countries, but you may run into the issue of packages not being reliably delivered; shipping costs from the U.S. can be very high as well.

If you're not going to be living in one of the twelve countries where Amazon operates, then your options come down to the following:

Send Your Shipment via the U.S. Post Office
You could try having the shipment sent directly to your country via the post office, but this is likely to be iffy, may take months, and your package may never arrive. Packages from North America or Europe have a way of "disappearing" in customs before they even get to their destination. Given the current state of the U.S. Postal Service, ***not a good option***.

Private Package Forwarding Service
You can use a private package forwarding service, if one delivers to your country. Generally, you order your items online from LL Bean, eBay, U.S. Amazon or whomever, and you have it shipped to the package forwarding service's address in the U.S. (often in Florida). **You must set up an account with them in advance** and notify them of any shipments before they arrive at their U.S. address.

The package forwarding service then transports the packages to your location abroad, handles all the customs duties and makes sure that the package is tracked through each point and does not "disappear." They then arrange ground transportation to get it to your location and do home delivery. The fees vary quite a bit by country for this service, but generally you can count on lighter weight items such as clothing costing less than heavier items. *A crude rule of thumb is to double the price that you paid for the item to get it to your door in the foreign country*.

In Latin America there is a company called Aeropost (formerly Aereocasillas) that offers this service to most of the Caribbean and Latin America, including Costa Rica, Colombia, Chile, Ecuador, Peru, Guatemala, Panama, El Salvador, Trinidad & Tobago, Jamaica, British Virgin Islands, Honduras and Nicaragua. Their pricing is by weight and you can pay by credit or debit card or PayPal.

> *When you're making your scouting trips to countries of interest, ask whether there are package forwarding services that shepherd packages from the U.S. to that country – there very well could be. Check what they charge by weight or by type of item.*

Commercial Shipper (FedEx, DHL etc.)
You can use a commercial shipper such as FedEx or DHL, which should shepherd the package through customs and then deliver it to your home address. In Mexico, packages sent from the U.S. via DHL disappeared all the time and the local DHL personnel would just shrug and say that they didn't know what happened to the package.

This option can be expensive; expect to pay a lot for packages. Since these guys can charge $75 just for mailing an envelope of documents, you can imagine what they charge for packages.

> *Packages seem to be far likelier to "disappear" than an envelope of documents. Ask around about what the experience has been in the country where you're living for packages. In a particular country, DHL may be superior to FedEx, or vice-versa.*

"Mule" Service

If you live in an area where there are a number of other expats from your country, there may be one or more persons who run a "mule" service. This is an unofficial, under-the-radar service where they utilize people who regularly travel between the U.S. and the foreign country where you're living to bring in items in their carry-on or checked luggage. The items transported are not declared to customs officials and no duty is paid.

This can be an economical option if you don't have bulky or heavy items, but there is the risk that your items could be confiscated if the authorities detect the operation and shut it down. If you have something you can't afford to lose, or is valuable, this might not be a good option.

A further risk is that the "mule" could disappear with the goods or have a sudden heart attack and die (it's been known to happen). Personally, I wouldn't ship anything that couldn't be replaced.

Generally, for an envelope with documents, a "mule" service charge will be minimal, i.e., $5 or $10. Not bad to get that new ATM or credit card.

A clandestine "mule" service will charge anywhere from $10 to $100 or more for a package depending upon the weight, size and nature of the items to be transported. I used such a service once to get some silicon baking mats from the U.S. that were lightweight, foldable and not very bulky and it cost me $15.

Personal "Mules"

You can in effect have your own, personal mules if you have friends or family coming to visit you. They simply bring the items you want in their carry-on or checked luggage and deliver them to you when they arrive. This is the most secure and economical method of obtaining items but the timing may not be convenient.

Chapter 7
Banking and Finances

Online Banking
U.S. Mutual Fund & Brokerage/IRA Accounts
U.S. Banking for Expats
Tax Reporting by U.S. Banks
You've Closed Your Account – or Have You?
Dormant Accounts and Escheat
ATM and Debit Cards
Credit Cards
Foreign Bank Accounts
Transferring Money Abroad from the U.S.
U.S. Dollar/Local Currency Exchange Issues
Developments Affecting Expats

As an expat living outside of the U.S., managing your finances and doing banking can be a challenge. However, if you set things up correctly and plan ahead, it isn't too bad and can work smoothly. If you have the wrong U.S. bank or make some bad choices, you can have major problems.

This is an important topic and many of the "to do" checklist items will have to do with banking and finances. See my online website at https://sites.google.com/view/northoak-books for free checklist templates with timelines to use for banking, change of address notifications, and related matters.

Online Banking

Welcome to the world of online banking. If you haven't been using internet banking before, you will be now. It's the only way to go when you live outside the U.S. You'd better overcome any phobias about technology, because there just isn't any way around it.

For expats, the goal is to do all your transactions *electronically*. Receive deposits and make payments electronically **whenever possible**. Eliminate paper statements and sign up for electronic monthly statements. Online banking can be accomplished via a desktop computer, a laptop or your mobile smart phone.

Nearly all U.S. banks and brokerage firms (and many online merchants such as Amazon) may **require** that they send you a one-time code for authentication by text or e-mail; some will insist upon texting a code to a U.S. phone number that can receive text messages (no email option). **If you cannot receive these codes, you will not be able to access your accounts online.**

See **Chapter 5, Keeping in Touch with the U.S.**, for how to maintain communications with the U.S., including banks, and for cell phone advice – I **strongly** recommend that you have a U.S. phone number, which can be done for minimal cost without keeping a second physical cell phone. **You may be unable to do any online banking without a U.S. phone number that can receive text messages**.

One of the biggest inconveniences when living abroad is receiving, cashing or depositing a paper check. **This is to be avoided if at all possible.** It will involve physically forwarding the paper check to your location abroad, either via FedEx, DHL etc. (at a likely minimum cost of $75 or more) or finding someone trustworthy to physically bring it to you.

Once you receive the paper check, you may be able to use your bank's mobile banking app to deposit the paper check electronically by taking a photo of the check within the app, without having to endorse it and send it back to your U.S. bank – I was able to do this with my coronavirus stimulus paper check from the IRS in 2020.

If you have a local bank account in your foreign country, you may be able to deposit a U.S. check into your account, but be aware that it can take *weeks* (or longer) to clear and may involve substantial fees.

> *Review your bank and brokerage statements regularly every month. Many people don't realize this, but there is a time limit on reporting bank and brokerage account errors, after which the bank can say "Sorry, you didn't report this to us in a timely manner." The time limit varies by bank, for some it's as little as 30 days, for others it may be 90 days or even 120 days. If your bank makes an error, raise the issue with them as soon as possible to get it corrected.*

You can also transfer funds and make payments with mobile banking apps. I personally do not keep banking apps on my phone, in case I lose my phone or it is stolen. If I have a paper check to deposit, I will put the app on my phone, make the deposit, and then uninstall the app.

U.S. Mutual Fund & Brokerage/IRA Accounts

Have a conversation with your current brokerage firm, IRA/401(k) custodian, and any other financial firms with whom you have accounts no less than six months before your planned departure date (a year would be better).

If possible, have this conversation in person with an account representative as opposed to some low-level employee in a call center who may not be knowledgeable. Ask what the firm's policy is about U.S. citizens living abroad; couch it in **hypothetical terms** of "I'm thinking about moving to ..." and see what their response is.

Quite a few of these firms do not want to deal with expatriate U.S. citizens, and will **close your account** if they find out you are living outside the U.S. TD Ameritrade (subsequently acquired by Charles Schwab) told me that they would close my accounts if they found out I was living abroad – and I was a 25+ year customer of theirs with good-sized IRAs.

Fidelity, Merrill Lynch, Morgan Stanley, Ameriprise, TIAA, Edward Jones, Wells Fargo, UBS, e*Trade, Vanguard and others are likewise unwilling to have accounts with U.S. expats and will close accounts if they discover you are living abroad.

In late 2019 Charles Schwab in London notified clients living on the Continent that they would no longer be able to service those accounts from London due to Brexit and that they could either transition to U.S.-based account managers or close their accounts. U.S. citizens living in the UK who were customers of UK Schwab were not affected.

If they close an account, they might give you a week or two to make other arrangements (if you're lucky). Otherwise, they will simply liquidate all positions and send you a check. If this is an IRA or 401(k) account, it will be a taxable distribution (though you might be able to do a 60-day rollover). You will be screwed.

Why Don't U.S. Financial Institutions Want U.S. Expats as Customers?
There is certainly no prohibition against their having U.S. citizen accountholders living outside the U.S. The reason is regulatory compliance risk – a U.S. citizen residing outside the U.S. is not permitted to own U.S. mutual funds or certain other investments. Why? I have no idea.

The firms that avoid U.S. expat accountholders just don't *want to be bothered* with having to ensure that you are complying with the requirements. These requirements have been around for decades but were rarely enforced until now.

The good news is that exchange traded funds (ETFs) are now so common and diverse that they can easily fulfill the role of mutual funds, and ETFs have no restrictions on U.S. customers who live abroad (but U.S. brokerage firms may still forbid U.S. citizens living abroad from buying U.S. ETFs). Some financial advisers specialize in working with and advising U.S. expats and can help you with the re-positioning of assets if necessary.

> *There are IRA custodians and retail brokerage houses that will welcome your business as an expat. Interactive Brokers is one of those; they actually WANT U.S. expats' business and offer services and products specifically geared to overseas residents. Wherever you end up, when you meet with an account representative to explore opening an account, verbally discuss as a hypothetical what would happen if you moved overseas.*

Charles Schwab has been getting nervous about U.S. customers residing abroad and in late 2020 started notifying some U.S. TD Ameritrade customers **with foreign addresses** that accounts were going to be closed regardless of citizenship. This was foreseeable, because in recent years it closed accounts of U.S. customers living in New Zealand, Dominican Republic, United Arab Emirates, South Africa and South Korea, and in late 2019 it closed accounts of U.S. customers in France and Italy.

There are U.S. expat customers of Fidelity or Vanguard who live full-time outside the U.S. but use a U.S. address for their statements; these folks may not realize the danger of doing so, since if these firms find out that they are living outside the U.S., their accounts may be closed.

For any brokerage firm, the safest approach is to not mention in e-mails or recorded phone calls that you live outside the U.S. When they ask you for your address, give them your U.S. address of record. See **Chapter 6, *How do I get Mail and Packages?*** for more on this. I recommend that you keep a U.S. mailing address.

Keep a U.S. phone number where they can reach you whenever they want (see **Chapter 5, *Keeping in Touch with the U.S.***). When logging in to your online account, use a VPN with a U.S. location. Keep a low profile and don't advertise the fact that you live abroad. *You are "traveling extensively" outside the U.S.*

Some financial institutions will let you access your brokerage account from outside the U.S. without a VPN by using a number generator token, which is a battery-operated device the size of a small thumb drive that generates a new set of numbers every 60 seconds. You then enter these numbers when logging into your account. The numbers must match what is calculated on the institution's system internally.

European banks *require* a number generator token for electronic access of all accounts, making your account essentially hack-proof. If you use a VPN set to a U.S. location, you shouldn't need to use the number generator token. I have one just in case I need it.

> *Repeat after me:* **Thou shalt use a VPN for all online banking and financial transactions.**

U.S. Banking for Expats

Why is this an Issue?
Various anti-terrorism and money-laundering provisions have so spooked our domestic banks that some now practically demand a DNA sample when you need to change your address. Dealing with U.S. banks has become a huge headache if you live full time outside the U.S.

> *I highly recommend that you keep at least one (preferably more) U.S. bank accounts open while living abroad so that you can receive Social Security deposits, income tax refunds, etc. electronically with a minimum of fuss. You can also set credit card accounts, insurance premiums and other recurring obligations to be paid automatically and electronically.*

How Do I Choose a U.S. Bank?
In general, a smaller local bank is just not going to work if you are living outside the U.S. – they are not going to be comfortable dealing with overseas transactions or with an accountholder who lives abroad. *They are likely to close your account eventually.* You want a U.S. bank that won't freak out over international transactions.

However, being a customer of one of the bigger banks can also present problems – their customer service tends to be abysmal unless you have a robust (i.e., six figure or more) USD balance on deposit. Bank of America, Citibank, Wells Fargo, Chase etc. can definitely do international banking, but you will be one customer among millions and unlikely to get much personal attention.

I recommend that you keep bank accounts with at least two different U.S. banks, as a precaution in case one of the banks freaks out and blocks your account or refuses to allow transfers. This way you can rotate ATM withdrawals between banks as well.

Nearly all U.S. brokerage accounts also offer bank accounts, which is another option you can explore. You can have your investment and retirement accounts held along with a bank account at a brokerage firm. Shop around.

U.S. banks that may not freak out over international transactions

PenFed Credit Union
PenFed Credit Union (based in Virginia with branches in the Washington DC metro area) seems to be good at dealing with expatriates because many of their members are active-duty military or civilian contractors who are stationed all over the world. They won't necessarily freak out if you contact them from Colombia or the Philippines and ask them to wire $250,000, the way a small local bank might.

You do **not** need to be a Pentagon employee or member of the military to open an account with PenFed; a $10 membership in the U.S. Military Families Association will get you into their field of membership. Their foreign ATM fee is 1% of the amount withdrawn.

Navy Federal Credit Union
The field of membership for Navy Federal is not just for active-duty military members of all branches but includes reservists, ROTC, veterans, National Guard, retirees and their family members. Employees of the Department of Defense, employees working at a DoD installation, and employees of defense contractors are also eligible.

If you had a parent or grandparent who served in the military and can provide proof of this, that will get you into Navy FCU. If you are the roommate of a current Navy FCU member, you can also join the credit union.

State Department Federal Credit Union

If you join American Citizens Abroad (www.americansabroad.org), you are eligible to open an account with the **State Department Federal Credit Union**, which serves U.S. diplomats and employees of the U.S. State Department.

You do not need to have a U.S. mailing address or residence in the U.S. Products available include checking and saving accounts, credit and debit cards, CDs and IRAs. The account can be opened and maintained online. See **Chapter 18,** *Further Resources* for more information.

United Nations Federal Credit Union

If you join either the United Nations Association of the USA or the Kilimanjaro Initiative, you will be eligible to be a member of UNFCU, which has branch offices in New York City, Washington DC, Geneva (Switzerland), Rome (Italy), Vienna (Austria), Entebbe (Uganda) and Nairobi (Kenya). Their digital banking app allows you to deposit paper checks by taking a photo of the check.

UNFCU offers checking, savings and certificates of deposit, ATM/debit cards, credit cards, and home loans. More services are available to active or retired UN employees or contractors than to affiliated members.

Charles Schwab Bank

Charles Schwab (www.schwab.com) will give you a bank account if you have a brokerage account with them; their ATM card reimburses international ATM fees and you can apply for a Schwab Visa card as well. Don't use the ATM card abroad too frequently.

USAA Bank

USAA (www.usaa.com) regularly appears at the top of customer service ratings, but it has a limited customer base; to be eligible to open a bank account you must be:

- Active duty or retired/separated Armed Forces member (Army, Air Force, Coast Guard, Marines or Navy);
- Widow/er, un-remarried former spouse of a USAA member;
- Child of a parent who has or had a USAA account or insurance policy;
- Cadets and midshipmen at U.S. service academies;

- Those in advanced ROTC or on ROTC scholarship; or
- Officer candidates within 24 months of commissioning

USAA offers insurance (property, auto, life, flood etc.) as well as banking, mortgage loans, retirement planning, health insurance and shopping discounts, including a car buying service.   If you are eligible, it is worth looking into.

Note that USAA's investment management unit has been purchased by Charles Schwab, and its mutual funds by Victory Capital, so those services are no longer with USAA.

Tax Reporting by U.S. Banks

1099-INT Reporting
What happens if you have a CD maturing in February, you transfer the funds to a different bank at maturity, and you leave the U.S. in April? The bank or brokerage firm is going to send you a Form 1099-INT for tax reporting by January 31st of the following year. Mail is only forwarded by the post office for six months. Your 1099-INT (which you will need for your U.S. income tax return preparation) will be going to your old address, with forwarding expired.

Why Should I Care About the Mailing Address for Closed Accounts?
If the account is closed you may not be able to access the 1099-INT information online. The physical mail will be returned to the bank as undeliverable and you'll have to try calling them – but as a former customer, you may have difficulty getting the necessary information. It's simpler to make sure that they have your correct mailing address.

> *Be sure to give each U.S. bank and financial institution your new mailing address so that you can receive future Forms 1099-INT that you will need for your income tax returns. Note that some banks can be VERY difficult about a change of address, while others let you do it online with no fuss.*

True story: while still living in the U.S., I was having problems with mail delivery to my home address. When I tried to change my mailing address at my local, neighborhood bank to a P.O. Box (for security reasons), the branch (where they *knew* me!) **refused** to change an address from my street address to a P.O. Box without first seeing mail from a bank, brokerage or credit card account with the P.O. address.

---

*Make sure that all current **AND** closed accounts have your new mailing address. I actually had to travel back to my previous state of residence several months after having moved, with my new driver's license in hand, before the local bank would change my mailing address – for accounts that were already closed!*

Just imagine how difficult it would be to accomplish this if you are already living outside the U.S. Do it **before** you leave.

Form 5498 IRA Account Reporting

Your IRA custodian is not required to file *Form 5498, IRA Contribution Information* (which reports the FMV of your IRA account as of December 31st of the prior year to the IRS), until May 31st of the following year.

You as the IRA owner or beneficiary generally will not receive a copy of this form until June (for the prior calendar year). If you have closed an IRA account, give the former IRA custodian an updated mailing address for the Form 5498.

You've Closed Your Account – or Have You?

Another situation that is happening more and more is, you think that you've closed your account. Surprise! It may still be open.

Many years ago, when I worked in banking, when you closed your account, the teller would manually calculate any remaining interest due you and add it to the account balance before closing the account. Apparently, this is now too much trouble or beyond the ability of the staff, and so your "closed" account isn't really closed because some interest was posted at the end of the cycle.

This has happened to me at two different banks. Six months later I found out that the accounts were still open. I had to go back to the branch several times to ensure that they were "really" closed. Moral of the story: **check and confirm that all accounts are really closed**. They may not be.

> *If an account that you think is closed remains open, even with a nominal balance, there is potential for hanky-panky by a corrupt bank employee who could start using the account, knowing that you believe the account to be closed. The employee could easily change the mailing address and start using the account for money laundering.*

Offers from Recently (or Not so Recently) Closed Accounts

You may continue to receive pre-approved offers from banks that you used to do business with, but are no longer a customer. After closing all accounts with Capital One, **over two years later** I was STILL receiving pre-approved credit card offers and other garbage in the mail from them. Why? Because the morons still had me in their records as a customer.

> *For any credit card company, bank or other service provider who sends pre-approved offers in the mail, contact them and confirm that you are now registered with them as a NON-CUSTOMER and that you DO NOT want to receive any solicitations, pre-approved offers or marketing garbage from them. Send them a nasty letter.*

You do not want to be receiving "pre-approved" offers of credit while living abroad due to the potential for fraud. A bad guy could intercept the offer and take out credit in your name unbeknownst to you. See **Chapter 12, *Identity Theft and Medical Billing Problems***.

Dormant Accounts and Escheat

I thought I would mention this, since many people are unfamiliar with *escheat*.

Every state in the U.S. has escheat statutes, which dictate the treatment of unclaimed assets. Dormant accounts that have had no customer contact for a specified period of time (often seven years, sometimes less) must be liquidated by law and turned over to the state where the customer was resident.

Escheated funds can also include non-financial institution sources like insurance premiums from canceled homeowners or auto insurance policies or other overpayments held by companies.

Occasionally you hear about someone who opened a mutual fund account and intentionally did not look at any statements for years because they did not want to be influenced by market swings. When they did finally inquire about the account, they were dismayed to learn that the account had been liquidated years or decades earlier and escheated to their state of residence as abandoned property.

The original owner or legally entitled successor to the account balance can get the money back, but it involves a fair amount of paperwork and identity validation.

> *Keep your bank and financial accounts from going dormant by periodically logging in online and downloading statements (which you should be doing anyway).*

Financial institutions have strict internal policies about managing dormant accounts, which are accounts without any customer-initiated activity for a period of time (often one year). *Dormant accounts are susceptible to internal (employee) fraud, because employees know that the customer is not closely monitoring account activity.*

Do a nationwide search with the link below to see if there's anything under your name.

> *The National Association of Unclaimed Property Administrators is a non-profit group whose members are the governmental administrators of escheated assets. On their web site you can search for any unclaimed property that you might be entitled to claim: https://unclaimed.org/search/. This is a **free** service.*
>
> **Avoid using for-profit companies who will take a percentage of the assets that you succeed in claiming.**

ATM & Debit Cards

Many parts of the world rely more on cash than in the U.S.

Consequently, an ATM card is absolutely essential to get local cash. Getting cash advances from credit cards is a very expensive proposition and should be reserved for true emergencies.

How Many ATM Cards Should I Have?

I recommend having a minimum of two (more would be better) different U.S. bank ATM and debit cards in your foreign location, so that you have backup cards in case of a card being lost, hacked, or stolen. Additionally, your U.S. bank may update its technology from time to time and issue replacement cards with chips in them, and cancel the old card, resulting in a period of time where the cancelled card is not available for use.

I also recommend having a *local (foreign country) bank account with an ATM card* as well, to be able to access funds in case something happens that keeps you from accessing your U.S. bank account.

Think that would never happen? What about the coronavirus pandemic, where all flights to and from your country are grounded and the borders are closed? You might not be able to easily get a replacement ATM card.

> *You will always have the issue of a U.S. debit, credit or ATM card expiring and a new one being issued every two or three years or so, so plan accordingly.* ***Keep an eye on the expiration dates***.

Fraud Precautions

If your institution issues you a combination ATM/debit card, ask them to set the purchase limit at zero so that it can only be used as an ATM card. If your institution won't set the debit limit to zero (some won't do this), ask them if you can get an ATM-only card. If that is not possible, then at least sign up for e-mail or text notification whenever there is a debit purchase.

ATM Fees

If you use a U.S. credit card or ATM/debit card, you will likely incur fees for foreign use unless you have an issuer that waives those fees such as Schwab. A typical ATM fee is 3%, so a withdrawal of $300 would trigger a fee of $9. These fees can add up fast. These are the **U.S. bank's fees**; note that the local, foreign bank may have its own fees, too.

Some U.S. banks that issue ATM/debit cards waive foreign fees. As of 2022 (**subject to change**), the following U.S. banks' checking accounts let you use foreign ATMs for no fee or a low fee:

- Chase Bank (Premier Plus Checking or Chase Sapphire Checking)
- Capital One 360 Checking Account (online only – no bricks-and-mortar account)
- Schwab Bank High Yield Investor Checking Account (reimburses fees)
- First Republic Bank ATM Rebate Checking Account (minimum balances apply)
- Fidelity Cash Management Account – free ATM withdrawals worldwide (minimum balances apply)
- Portfolio by Wells Fargo Checking Account (minimum balances apply)

Some of the above banks will reimburse you for the local, foreign bank's fees, others may not. There may still be charges for foreign currency transactions, even if the U.S. bank's ATM fee itself is waived.

There may be other restrictions on the number of transactions per month. For example, Charles Schwab does not have any set limits, but says it will assess fees in the event of "excessive use" (undefined).

Banks can at any time change the terms of their fees for foreign ATMs.

Rotate your use of U.S. ATM cards among different banks. Don't be too obvious that you are living overseas if you don't want the financial institution to be aware of this fact. Officially you are "traveling abroad" extensively.

Foreign Country ATM Problems

It occasionally happens that you will use an ATM in a foreign country and not receive any cash, yet your U.S. bank account will be charged for the withdrawal. It is important to report this ***immediately*** to both the local (foreign) bank and to your U.S. bank. Both institutions will have to investigate the incident, but in most cases your U.S. bank will reimburse you. Try to avoid using problematic ATMs (other local expats may know which ATMs have a history of doing this).

Credit Cards

Why Should I Keep U.S. Credit Cards?

You will want to be able to pay U.S. service providers, do online shopping, buy airline tickets, book travel and rental cars, make online donations to U.S. charities, and of course have them to use when you're visiting the U.S. Keep two or three U.S. credit cards and run some charges on them occasionally to keep them from being canceled for inactivity. Pick cards with no annual fee, and pay off the balance every month.

Visa and MasterCard are the most accepted credit cards around the world. American Express is less widely accepted, although if you spend all your time in Davos, Switzerland or similar places, you can use your Amex card without a problem.

Credit card fees can be up to 3% for foreign purchases. Most of the credit cards with no foreign transaction fees have an annual fee, and are generally geared towards business travelers or frequent fliers. Capital One's VentureOne travel card has a no-annual-fee credit card that waives foreign transaction fees.

Similar to ATM and debit cards, keep an eye on the expiration dates of your credit cards, and expect to be sent replacement cards – which may entail using DHL or FedEx at your own expense, or finding someone to bring you the card abroad.

*Terms for credit cards change frequently; it's best to do a search online to find the best card for you. Decide what's most important – the foreign transaction fee, the annual fee, points/perks or miles you earn with the card, or the interest rate. Consult websites such as **Nerd Wallet, Credit Karma or Consumer Reports** to compare the various offerings. Offers change all the time.*

How to Cancel a Free Trial Period Automatically
Many online subscription services such as Netflix, Amazon Prime, background checks, credit reports, etc. offer a free trial period of seven to thirty days.

Usually, you must cancel two or more days ***before*** the free trial period ends to avoid being charged for the service. It is difficult to remember to cancel the service within the required time frame, resulting in you being charged for a service for which you did not intend to subscribe. Some sites continue charging you even after you have cancelled properly, or make the cancelling process so onerous that it's almost impossible to do.

There is a solution: a virtual credit card. The use of virtual credit cards is expected to exceed $1 trillion in 2022. There are companies that offer a tool that allows you to enter a valid credit card number and VCC code. You can assign a maximum limit to each card. You can set the maximum limit to zero ***when you are sure that no purchases will be made.*** This is legal as long as you do not use it to pay for goods or services, only for testing purposes (i.e., a free trial period).

Companies and individuals protect themselves against merchants' being hacked by using one virtual credit card for only one vendor, where purchases are regularly made. Employers can restrict the use of an employee credit card to specified vendors. Account numbers and data are encrypted.

One such company is New York-based **Privacy.com**, which offers several levels: **Personal** (free, up to 12 credit cards), **Pro** ($10 per month, up to 36 credit cards, 1% rewards cashback on purchases), or **Teams** ($25 per month, dedicated account management, create up to 60 cards). The company has smart phone apps for iPhone and Android phones.

Privacy suggests that you create one virtual credit card for each company with whom you regularly make purchases, to protect against hacks.

Privacy virtual credit cards are funded via direct debit of your U.S. checking account or a debit card linked to a U.S. checking account. ***Privacy.com claims to use the same security and encryption standards as U.S. banks.***

https://www.privacy.com

DoNotPay, a San Francisco-based company that describes itself as a do-it-yourself legal service for consumers (they are not a law firm, however), offers a vast suite of pro-consumer services, such as:

- Appeal parking tickets in many U.S. & U.K. cities
- Cancel any service or subscription
- Shortcut phone queues for companies
- Schedule DMV appointments
- Schedule a small claims court plaintiff action
- Analyze bank accounts for refunds of bank fees
- Assistance with insurance and warranty claims
- Temporary phone number to sign up for services
- "Robo Revenge" to combat robocallers and collect fines from them as allowed by state law
- Assistance in filing an unemployment claim online

Do Not Pay requires that you give them an email address, a phone number and either ACH bank account information or a debit card. They may take additional steps to verify your identity for some services.

You have your choice of subscription ($36 for three months, $144 per year) or paying *a la carte* for over **200 different specific services**.

Once you have signed up with Do Not Pay, when you enroll in a third-party company's free trial period service, Do Not Pay will email you to notify you of the free trial, will remind you of the approaching end of the free trial period, and give you the option to sign up for the service using the debit card or bank account number on file with them.

https://donotpay.com/

There are many other virtual credit card providers, just do an online search and see what comes up.

Foreign Bank Accounts

It's convenient to have a local bank account in the country where you're living, but it may come with some additional reporting obligations if you're a U.S. citizen. This is covered in *Chapter 13, U.S. Federal Income Taxes.*

Foreign banks are also subject to reporting obligations if they have U.S. citizen accountholders. As a result, quite a few foreign banks are now refusing to have U.S. citizens or residents as customers.

U.S. citizens with long-standing bank accounts all over the world have found their accounts suddenly closed because the foreign bank just didn't want to deal with the compliance headaches and potential liabilities involved with the required reporting to the U.S. government.

During research visits to a potential country, this is one of the things to check out – how difficult is it to open a local bank account?

In some countries it may be easy to open an account without legal residency, such as Ecuador or Belize (as of 2021). In other countries it may be virtually impossible to open a bank account even if you have residency, and you may be forced instead to use a local brokerage account in order to do local banking.

Before opening a local bank account in a foreign country, find out if there is any government deposit insurance for bank accountholders, and what the limits of coverage are for deposit insurance. If the foreign government offers only the equivalent of USD $50,000 of deposit insurance in the event that the bank fails, you may not want to deposit USD $300,000.

Keep in mind that in some countries, government "insurance" may not function very well, and even if it does cover losses up to the limits, it could take up to a year to get your money back. Investigate the financial stability of a bank before you deposit funds with it.

Shop Around for a Local (Foreign Country) Bank

Banking seems to be one of those industries where the level of service and fees varies widely, even within the same city. In Germany you are charged a fee to open an account, a fee for checking your balance, and a fee when you close the account. In Ecuador, checking your balance at the ATM incurs a 25-cent fee, whereas going to a human teller is free (go figure).

In Colombia, be prepared to spend at least half a day or more to open a simple bank account; that's just the way it is. Bring a book to read. Colombian banks are well known for their terrible customer service.

Once you are more or less established in a particular city and country, ask around about the reputation of local banks; some may be much better to deal with than others. Figure out which local banks charge ATM fees on their end with a foreign ATM card and which don't, and which have ridiculously high fees and are to be avoided.

One bank may have absurd fees, high minimum deposit requirements, and require you to purchase life insurance *(true story!)* whereas another in the same city might offer superior service with low fees and better interest rates.

Don't be swayed solely by whether the bank can directly receive wire transfers from the U.S. (see below); the wire transfer system works just fine for banks without that ability, too.

Find out if there is any withholding at source for local income taxes on interest paid to accountholders. There may be withholding on certain kinds of accounts, such as certificates of deposit with a term of less than one year, but not on others. Withholding of income taxes on interest income may be creditable against your U.S. income taxes as a foreign tax credit.

I have made domestic electronic payments within Ecuador with my bank for rent and utilities and was very impressed with the level of security used. The customer has to download an encrypted token generator app for a smart phone (separate from the mobile banking app), which must be used to confirm the authenticity of the payment request. If only U.S. banks would make this readily available technology mandatory as it is in the European Union.

If price is no object, third party information web sites such as Global Banks (https://globalbanks.com) have services to help you open a bank account worldwide and provide bank profiles, country reports, remote account opening options, detailed opening instructions, and more. Rates range from USD $297 to USD $697 per year (the $697 rate includes a personalized one-on-one service and information on U.S. banks for non-residents of the U.S.).

Transferring Money Abroad from the U.S.

I will briefly discuss several options for transferring money from the U.S. Much will depend upon the size of the transfer; for a transfer of USD $100,000 the process will be different than a transfer of USD $1,000.

Bank Wire Transfers
If you have a larger amount of money to transfer to another country, and you have a local (foreign country) bank account, the easiest thing to do is an international wire transfer. The foreign bank where you have your account will provide you, the expat, with wire instructions; **follow them exactly** and *do not deviate from them.*

Depending upon which U.S. bank you have (and whether it freaks out), initiating an outgoing international wire transfer may be a good experience or a bad experience. You will be asked validation questions to ensure that you are the authorized accountholder initiating the transfer.

Your U.S. bank will access the U.S. Federal Reserve FedWire system and the money will be transferred within a business day or two. The fee may be anywhere from $35 (on the low end) to $90 or $100, plus possible charges on the receiving bank's end to you.

Larger foreign banks may have an account directly with the U.S. Federal Reserve; if this is the case, they will be able to send and receive wire transfers directly without an intermediary (called a ***correspondent bank***). The funds will be credited to your account directly when the incoming wire (which will have your name and account number information) is received, and the process is pretty straightforward.

If your foreign bank does not have an account with the Federal Reserve (which may be the more common scenario), it will use a correspondent bank in the same foreign country to send or receive funds. The correspondent bank will have an account with the U.S. Federal Reserve.

If a correspondent bank is involved, you will be instructing your U.S. bank to wire funds to the correspondent bank, *not to your bank.* The correspondent bank will then transfer the funds to your bank according to the instructions that your local bank gave you. Typically, you must then notify your local foreign bank (where you have your account) that the wire has been initiated and provide them with the wire confirmation that your U.S. bank will send you.

The local foreign bank (where you have *your* account) will then move the funds from a general ledger suspense account to your personal account once you have notified them of the transfer.

Think of suspense accounts as parking places; banks use thousands of suspense accounts, which "park" funds until they can be moved to the correct final destination. Banks must reconcile their GL suspense accounts daily in order to keep on top of all the transactions that go in and out of them, otherwise the situation gets out of control and it becomes very difficult to identify older balances.

If you do not notify your local bank of the wire transfer execution, your money will remain sitting in the correspondent bank or in a suspense account somewhere and it won't make it to your institution or to your local bank account. ***Follow your bank's instructions.***

> *Note that if the correspondent bank used by your local (foreign) bank is a U.S. branch of the foreign (correspondent) bank, your U.S. bank (where you are initiating the wire transfer) may get a little confused because while you are making an international wire transfer, the funds go first to a U.S. branch of a foreign bank. Just explain this to them.*

U.S. Treasury anti-money laundering measures seem to get more onerous every year for ***foreign receiving banks***. Do not be surprised if your local, foreign bank asks you to document the source of funds being deposited if the amount is over USD $10,000. If you are transferring over USD $100,000 you may be asked to get documents notarized and apostilled in the U.S. Yes, seriously.

Foreign banks can decide to impose their own, stricter requirements on documenting the source of funds. This can make purchasing real estate abroad a real headache. One way around it is if the real estate seller has a U.S. bank account and is willing to receive funds from your U.S. bank account wired to the seller's U.S. bank account (a wholly domestic U.S. transfer of funds).

Dealing with your U.S. bank to initiate an international wire transfer will be easier if you keep your old U.S. phone number that the banks and credit card companies already had on file for years, which reassures them. See **Chapter 5, *Keeping in Touch with the U.S.,*** for more information about this. Choose a U.S. bank that won't freak out if you ask it to wire USD $200,000 to a foreign country (see above).

The foreign receiving bank, on the other hand, may well freak out and reject the transfer if it feels uncomfortable about the transaction. ***Be sure to talk to the foreign receiving bank first before making a wire transfer.***

Other Options for Transferring Funds

If you just want to transfer say USD $1,000 or USD $5,000, a remittance company rather than a bank is probably what you want for many parts of the world. Note that the customer service of money transferors can and does deteriorate drastically, so do your own search for current recommendations.

Online reviews have favorably mentioned TransferWise, MoneyGram, XE Money Transfer, OFX, SendFX, TorFX, Currencies Direct, WorldRemit and of course the old standby, Western Union, which usually has a maximum of around USD $5,000 (varies by country).   Remitly and Xoom seem to have garnered negative opinions. Choose your remittance company carefully; people have lost money with remittances gone bad.

Exercise caution if you'll be picking up a large amount of cash in person; in some cases, employees of banks or remittance agencies have been known to tip off robbers when a customer is leaving with a large amount of cash. You may want to arrange for an escort.

Take Note of Local Government Procedures for Wire Transfers
When deciding to transfer funds into a foreign country, pay attention to any local restrictions or taxes on incoming or outgoing funds:

- Is there a requirement to register incoming funds with the government (Colombia)?
- Is there an exit tax on funds leaving the country, even if it's your own money that you brought in (Ecuador – 5%)?
- Ae there limits or restrictions on funds leaving the country (South Africa)?

U.S. Dollar-Local Currency Exchange Issues

In some countries there may be several different currency exchange rates. In Argentina the "unofficial" exchange rate for the Argentine peso, published daily in newspapers, is *three to four times* more favorable than the official rate (even the robbers want U.S. dollars, not pesos).   Western Union and other established businesses in Buenos Aires handle these currency transactions and it's all above board.

Be sure to comply with each country's local laws regarding currency exchange, or you could end up in jail.

> *In some places, you may able to negotiate a more favorable price with contractors, hospitals or doctors, Spanish teachers, almost any kind of services if you pay with U.S. dollars. Be aware of what the various exchange rates are and take proper security precautions if you'll be exchanging dollars for local currency in cash, or paying for services using cash dollars.*

You may want to limit your local currency exposure, even if local interest rates are far higher than in the U.S. **Be aware of the risk that you might be assuming with a large bank account in local currency.** What happens to your purchasing power if the local currency suffers a major depreciation against the U.S. dollar?

Even if the account is in USD in the foreign bank, in the event of a financial crisis there might be a risk of restricting access to your funds. In a worst-case scenario, the country may stop using the dollar and forcibly convert all USD accounts to a local currency.

Developments Affecting Expats

Many new developments that affect expats have to do with banking, finances and taxation. As an expat, you will want to keep your eyes and ears open for things that could affect you – changes in income tax law, U.S. passports, FATCA, expat estate planning, and many more issues of interest to expats.

The *American Expat Financial News Journal* (https://americanexpatfinance.com) contains very useful news, podcasts, editorials, webcasts and more of vital interest to U.S. citizens living abroad.

American Citizens Abroad (https://www.americansabroad.org) is a non-profit membership organization dedicated to representing U.S. expats abroad with U.S. elected officials and assisting expats with specific issues they are confronting solely by reason of living abroad.

The Accidental American Association (https://www.americains-accidentels.fr) is an association based in Paris of almost 1,200 persons born in the U.S. but who have no connection to the U.S., often not speak any English, and have no idea that they are U.S. citizens by reason of their place of birth (or that of a parent). These persons often cannot hold foreign bank accounts solely by reason of the place of their birth.

Chapter 8
Social Security Benefits & U.S. State Department Resources

Social Security Retirement Benefits
Social Security Online Account Management
Receiving Social Security Benefits Outside the U.S.
The "Proof of Life" Procedure
Social Security Card
U.S. State Department Resources for Citizens Abroad

As a U.S. citizen or resident living abroad, you are entitled to receive government pension benefits just as if you were residing in the U.S. While this chapter will focus on receiving Social Security benefits, which will apply to most people at some point, you can also receive pension benefits from the Department of Veterans Affairs (VA), the Office of Personnel Management (OPM) or the Railroad Retirement Board.

Social Security Retirement Benefits

Social Security Retirement Basics – a Quick Overview
You as a U.S. citizen are entitled to collect Social Security retirement benefits even if you live outside the U.S. There are several countries where you cannot receive benefits (such as Cuba, Iran or North Korea) but you will still be entitled to collect these benefits once you are no longer living in a prohibited country.

If you have accumulated sufficient quarters of employment history (wages or self-employment income) to earn a retirement benefit, you may start collecting Social Security as early as age 62 or as late as age 70.

The earlier you start collecting benefits, the larger the "haircut" will be – the reduction in your monthly benefit. The full retirement age in the past was age 65 (at which you receive your full benefit without any reduction), but is now age 67 for those born in 1960 or later.

The longer you delay collecting Social Security retirement benefits, the more your monthly benefit will increase (to reflect actuarial life expectancy). There is no benefit to waiting beyond age 70 to claim Social Security benefits.

Additionally, if you are **collecting** Social Security before your full retirement age **AND** you continue to work, if you earn above a certain threshold your Social Security benefits will **be reduced**. For 2022 the amount is $19,560 (changes every year). You are not losing these benefits permanently; they will be added to your benefit once you reach full retirement age.

In the year you reach full retirement age, this earnings threshold increases; for 2022 it is $51,960 (also changes every year). In the year you reach full retirement age, you can earn up to the threshold without suffering a reduction in Social Security benefits. Once you are at your full retirement age, you can earn any amount without it affecting your Social Security benefits.

Go to www.ssa.gov for a fuller explanation of how Social Security works.

Note: while it may be possible to receive Social Security disability benefits while living abroad, it is a more complicated topic and outside the scope of this book. Consult a disability benefits attorney or other expert for further guidance.

Social Security Online Account Management

SSA's *My Social Security* web portal opened in 2012 and lets wage earners check their earnings history and interact with Social Security regarding their benefits.

Use the "My Social Security" portal to apply for retirement or disability benefits, set up direct deposit of your benefit payment, change your address or phone number, request a benefits verification letter, request a replacement Social Security card, or check the status of a pending claim.

If you haven't already done so, before you leave the U.S. create your online benefits account with Social Security. There have been cases of fraudsters creating an online account before the real beneficiary does so. There can be only one online account per Social Security number, so the best way to protect yourself is to **create your account before the bad guys do.**

If you're still working, it's a good idea to check your account every year to make sure your earnings have been correctly reported to SSA, and to get an idea of your projected future retirement benefit. You can also see what your disability benefit would be.

Go to https://www.ssa.gov/myaccount/ and click on "Create an Account" and follow the instructions. You will be asked to create a user name and password and list a second identifier, either an email address or a cell phone number. Whenever you log into your account, Social Security will text or email you a one-time code to complete the verification.

For security reasons, changing an email address with Social Security may involve receiving a physical letter in the mail with a code to be input online. Carefully choose your email address to be used with Social Security because changing it is cumbersome.

> *Note that you may not be able to set up a "My Social Security" account if you have a security freeze or fraud alert on your credit report. You may need to temporarily lift the security freeze or alert first (you can reinstate it later) or visit a Social Security office in person to open a "My Social Security" account.*

If you have been a victim of Social Security benefits fraud, in addition to contacting Social Security operations staff directly, inform the Inspector General's office for the Social Security Administration at 1-800-269-0271 or file a report online at https://oig.ssa.gov/.

Receiving Social Security Benefits Outside the U.S.

To receive U.S. Social Security benefits, generally you must receive the monthly payment deposited electronically to a **U.S. or foreign bank**. There are some restrictions on the foreign countries that can receive payments, such as Cuba, Iran or North Korea. Check the www.ssa.gov website for a complete list.

> *I recommend keeping a U.S. bank account to receive monthly Social Security payments, but you can have your benefits sent to a bank in a foreign country if you prefer.*

SSA regulations specify that Social Security beneficiaries **receiving benefits** who reside outside the U.S., *even if having their benefits deposited to a U.S. bank account*, should report their foreign address if they are outside the U.S. for more than three months.

Form SSA-21 is used to report the change to a foreign address, and also asks questions about foreign earned income and self-employment status.

*The SSA maintains a web page entitled "**Instructions for a Beneficiary Leaving the U.S.**" which requests that the change of address be reported to SSA before departing the U.S. The URL is https://www.ssa.gov/foreign/leaving_us.htm.*

*There is also a brochure addressed to persons who are ALREADY receiving Social Security payments entitled "**Social Security - Your Payments While You Are Outside the United States**" that can be downloaded from https://www.ssa.gov/pubs/EN-05-10137.pdf.*

Social Security's "Proof of Life" Procedure

The Social Security Administration maintains an index (Death Master File) of reported deaths that is widely used by banks, brokerage firms, annuities and pension plans. If your name and Social Security number gets onto this list you could find your financial accounts or pension payments suspended if financial institutions or pension plans believe you are dead.

Social Security recipients with a non-U.S. address living abroad must certify every two years (every year if age 90 or over) that they are still alive with a "proof of life" procedure (**SSA Form 7162**), to prevent payments continuing after death. The form asks recipients to answer several questions, including verifying their current mailing address.

The Social Security Administration sends out annually around 260,000 "Proof of Life" questionnaires. Beneficiaries with SSNs ending in 00-49 are sent the form in even-numbered years, and beneficiaries with SSNs ending in 50-99 receive the form in odd-numbered years.

*apt **Note**: Because of the coronavirus pandemic, the "proof of life" mailings have been suspended since 2020 until further notice. "SSA will resume mailing the forms at a later date when conditions have changed." As of mid-2022 the mailings are still suspended, but this will change; at some point the government will resume the Proof of Life Procedure.*

When the program is operating, the form is generally mailed out in May or June and a second mailing in September/October if no response is received. A final reminder notice is mailed out around November, and if no response is received, benefits are suspended in February/March of the following year.

The SSA may send questionnaires to Federal Benefits Units (FBUs) of U.S. consulates in the event of special circumstances such as no operating mail service in a foreign country.

With the lack of functioning postal systems in many countries in the world, many Social Security beneficiaries living outside the U.S. never receive their **Form 7162**. *Beneficiaries can download the form from the SSA's web site, fill it out and send it to SSA to avoid an interruption of benefits payments.*

Social Security Card

I *strongly* recommend having a physical Social Security card before leaving the U.S. You may be asked to provide a copy of it to various financial institutions, state Departments of Motor Vehicles, the U.S. State Department, or credit reporting bureaus once you are abroad.

If, like me, you couldn't find your card (I do remember last seeing mine sometime in the 1980s), you will need to request a replacement. Most people can use their online Social Security account to request a replacement card, if they are a U.S. citizen age 18 or older with a U.S. mailing address, are not requesting a name change, and have a driver's license or state-issued identification card from a participating state.

The following states are **not** currently eligible for online replacement as of 2022:

- New Hampshire
- Oklahoma
- West Virginia

Similarly, if your driver's license or identification card was issued by a U.S. territory (such as American Samoa, Guam, Northern Mariana Islands, Puerto Rico, or the U.S. Virgin Islands) this online service is also not available.

You can go to a local Social Security office with the required original documents (photocopies are not accepted) to request a replacement card. If you request a replacement card by mail, you will have to submit original documents such as your passport and birth certificate by mail. With the current state of the U.S. Postal Service, no thanks. **Get the replacement card before you leave the U.S. Keep it in a safe place.**

> *If you've had a name change,* ***get your Social Security card updated*** *(along with other identity documents) to the new name* ***before*** *you move out of the U.S. It may take a while to accomplish this. You may have to return to the U.S. to obtain the updated documents if you do not do it before departure.*

U.S. State Department Resources for Citizens Abroad

Outside of the U.S., the U.S. government is represented by ***embassies*** and ***consulates***. An ***embassy*** is a permanent diplomatic mission usually located in the capital city of a foreign country and represents the U.S. in all matters in that country and preserves the rights of U.S. citizens abroad.

A ***consulate*** is a smaller State Department establishment, usually located in tourist areas or in or near cities where a significant number of U.S. expats live. Consulates handle matters such as issuing U.S. visas to foreigners, engaging in trade relations, and assisting U.S. citizens living abroad.

Examples of services that the U.S. Citizen Services section of embassies and consulates can provide for U.S. citizens residing abroad typically include the following:

- **Notarization of documents** for use in the U.S.

- **Assistance when citizens die abroad** – the State Department can assist with notifying the next-of-kin, obtaining services for the disposition of remains, and issuing a Consular Report of U.S. Citizen Death Abroad
- **Issuance or renewal of passports** outside the U.S., or reporting a lost or stolen passport
- **In-person visits to jails or prisons** for U.S. citizens arrested abroad on criminal charges
- Assistance with **international parental child abduction**
- **Assist U.S. citizen crime victims**
- Help **arrange emergency financial assistance** from third parties
- Identify **local medical and legal resources** for U.S. citizens

The U.S. State Department **cannot act** as an attorney for a U.S. citizen arrested abroad for a crime, although it may maintain lists of local attorneys (there is no assurance of the quality of the attorneys on this list).

Nor will the U.S. State Department pay for a flight home. In the unlikely event of an emergency evacuation and no other means are available, the State Department may arrange evacuation to the nearest safe place, which usually will **not** be the U.S. *Pets are not allowed to accompany U.S. citizens being evacuated.*

If you live in an area with a substantial number of U.S. citizens that is near an embassy or consulate, a consular officer may visit your city on a regular schedule to perform routine functions (usually by appointment) such as notarizing documents or receiving applications to renew passports.

Federal Benefits and Obligations Abroad
This State Department's web page contains brief information and links to other agencies and services such as Medicare, the Affordable Care Act, registering for Selective Service, federal income taxes, and foreign bank account compliance:

https://travel.state.gov/content/travel/en/international-travel/while-abroad/federal-benefits-and-obligations-abroad.html

Criminal Record Checks

U.S. citizens may be asked to present a "certificate of good conduct" or "lack of a criminal record" for a variety of reasons for use abroad, including adoption, school attendance, employment, etc.

U.S. law enforcement authorities may not be familiar with such a procedure since it is not commonly requested in the United States. There are generally two options available to U.S. citizens prove their lack of a criminal record: *local police check* or an *FBI records check*.

The State Department web site also gives information about getting fingerprints taken and authenticating police or FBI criminal record background reports:

https://travel.state.gov/content/travel/en/international-travel/while-abroad/criminal-record-checks.html

Retirement Abroad

This State Department web page goes into such matters as:

- investigating visa and residency requirements
- acquainting yourself with local laws
- reviewing your finances
- researching medical care and costs
- understanding Social Security benefits
- paying U.S. income taxes
- voting from overseas
- preparing for emergencies; and
- being aware of scams

https://travel.state.gov/content/travel/en/international-travel/while-abroad/retirement-abroad.html

Death of U.S. Citizen Abroad

While no one likes to think about dying, it happens to all of us eventually. In the event of a U.S. citizen dying abroad, the State Department's Bureau of Consular Affairs attempts to locate and inform the next-of-kin of the U.S. citizen's death, and provides information on how to make local arrangements for burial or repatriation to the U.S.

Note that the Department of State has no funds to assist in the return of remains or ashes of U.S. citizens who die abroad.

Upon issuance of a local (foreign) death certificate, the nearest embassy or consulate can prepare a *Consular Report of U.S. Citizen Death Abroad* which can be used in lieu of a U.S. death certificate in U.S. courts to settle estate matters.

The first 20 copies of this document are included in the consular fee; depending upon the extent of the decedent's assets in the U.S., you may want to get additional copies.

The consulate will notify Social Security (and Medicare) of the death abroad.

https://travel.state.gov/content/travel/en/international-travel/while-abroad/death-abroad1.html

Smart Traveler Enrollment Program
The Smart Traveler Enrollment Program (STEP) is a free service that sends you email alerts regarding the status of embassy or consulate operations as well as advisories or warnings for U.S. citizens in the event of natural disasters, civil unrest or other events.

Enrolling will also enable the State Department to contact you on behalf of family and friends in the U.S. in case of a family emergency. https://step.state.gov/step/

Other Frequently Asked Questions (FAQs) from Expats Residing Abroad
This State Department web page addresses matters such as U.S. citizenship, foreign bank account reporting, how to apply from overseas for a Social Security card, how to renounce U.S. citizenship, and how to come into compliance with delinquent U.S. income tax obligations: https://travel.state.gov/content/travel/en/international-travel/while-abroad/Joint-Foreign-Account-Tax-Compliance-FATCA-FAQ.html

Chapter 9
Digital Entertainment, News & Sports Outside the U.S.

"Digital Rights" & Geographic Restrictions
Virtual Private Networks (VPNs)
Internet Speeds Needed to Stream Video Content
Video Streaming Devices – TV Shows, Movies & Sports
Applications to Stream Video to Your TV or Device
DVDs
Pay & Free Options for Digital Books & Audio

Would missing new episodes of your favorite TV show or major league professional or college sports games be a deal-breaker to living overseas? No worries! With today's technology there are a number of ways to get your fix.

"Digital Rights" & Geographic Restrictions

Movies, TV shows, documentaries etc. have what's known as "digital rights" owned by the rights holder. Often these rights dictate where geographically such movies and programs can be streamed from a content provider such as Netflix or Amazon Prime, or in which region a physical DVD can be played.

You can usually use your existing U.S. Netflix or Amazon Prime account in the country you're living in, but your choice of content will be different and some programs and movies may not be available. Conversely, there may be different content available that you like that is not available on U.S. Netflix. In Mexico I was able to stream "Downton Abbey" on Netflix whereas in the U.S. I could not.

> *If you find the whole topic of technology a bit overwhelming, in nearly every medium- to large-size city in the world there are computer gurus and techies who can help you configure your internet, a VPN, set up a "smart" TV or Amazon Fire Stick, install various apps for you, or help you with other technology issues.*

Virtual Private Networks (VPNs)

Using a virtual private network (VPN) will get around these geographical restrictions. By using a VPN, you can set your internet "location" to be anywhere that the VPN service has servers.

A VPN bypasses local, physical networks and the public internet "pipe" that carries the traffic and creates a private, secure virtual connection that goes end-to-end from the sending computer to the receiving computer. It uses existing connectivity but creates a virtual "pipe" of its own to carry traffic.

Sites such as Privacy Noob (https://www.privacynoob.com) can give you further information about internet privacy issues and VPNs. You download the VPN as an app to your device or computer and then configure it for the location that you want.

Let's say you want to be able to watch U.S. Netflix content in a different country. A virtual private network, or VPN, will let you log into your U.S. account and stream video content as if you were in the U.S. There are many VPNs, some of them free, but **most of them won't work with Netflix or Amazon Prime.** Check for online recommendations for one that will work with the more demanding requirements of video streaming, because the situation changes all the time.

Netflix and Amazon continually update their algorithms to block VPNs, so the premium VPNs that do work with streaming services release frequent updates to their app versions.

Sometimes, new episodes of a TV series air in other countries but are not available in the U.S. until months later. Solution? Set the VPN to the foreign location to get your fix *now*.

I was once visiting the cute medieval Belgian town of Bruges and wanted to watch the movie "In Bruges" (it seemed appropriate), but to my surprise it wasn't available on Belgian Netflix. So I fired up my VPN and watched it anyway.   Having a VPN will give you maximum flexibility to stream content, which will vary by country.

If you have an Amazon Kindle for books and video content, you may be able to continue purchasing and downloading books without a VPN (depending upon where you are in the world), but for video content *you will need a VPN set to a U.S. location.*

---

*Watch out for Amazon's not-so-friendly tactics if you have purchased video content and downloaded it to your Kindle. If you are not using an up-to-date VPN and turn on your Kindle outside the U.S., **Amazon will remove video content from your device.***

If you are going to stream content from your Amazon Prime account, **definitely** use a VPN and keep it updated, because Amazon enforces geographic restrictions on streaming or downloading content. Search online for a VPN that will work with Amazon Prime.

Note that the Amazon app store does not always keep the most current version of VPN apps, so you may have to update the app from the VPN's website instead. Bastards.

Internet Speeds Needed to Stream Video Content

The minimum speed needed to stream video depends upon the device and your TV's resolution for video; a VPN will also slow things down to some degree. If you have a large flat screen TV (60 inches or greater), something in standard definition is going to look *terrible*, and even something at 720p or 1080p won't look that great either.

Streaming at 4K resolutions is *very* demanding on internet service, and your internet provider may object to the use of so much bandwidth. You may get a lot of buffering (when the video freezes in mid-stream) unless you have really good internet service.

Streaming video content to your phone or tablet is usually less demanding of bandwidth because you can stream lower resolution content and since the screen is much smaller, even a lower resolution video will look OK.

As a general rule, the recommended *minimum* speeds are as follows:

- **6.0 Mb/s** to stream standard definition content (YouTube etc.)
- **10.0 Mb/s** to stream HD content (720p and 1080p)
- **50 Mb/s** for 4K Ultra HD videos

The above speeds are recommended *minimums*; you will still likely experience buffering at times depending upon the overall internet traffic in your neighborhood. *For a better experience, double or triple the above speeds to minimize buffering.*

Video Streaming Devices – TV Shows, Movies & Sports

You will probably have a flat-screen smart TV in your house, wherever you decide to live abroad. There are various devices designed to connect to a digital TV that allow you to stream programming to your TV on demand. Among the most popular are the Roku and the Amazon Fire Stick.

Once you've decided where you're going to be living, before leaving the U.S. check whether a streaming device is available for purchase locally. If it is not readily available, you'll need to bring one with you. For example, Mexico bans Roku and Amazon Fire Stick devices (although you may still be able to find one from private local sellers).

Roku
The Roku comes in several forms. The streaming player is a small box slightly larger than a pack of cigarettes, whereas the Roku stick is about the size of a cigarette lighter. Both types of Roku plug into your smart TV and come with a remote control (more recent Roku remote controls have a jack for earbuds) and cost from $30 to $50.

Connecting and configuring it is very simple. Roku has numerous channels of content, some of which are free and some of which are subscription (such as cable channels like HGTV or ESPN). You can only add channels that are in the Roku system, so something not sanctioned by Roku is out. If you are already a Netflix subscriber, for example, you would simply enter your user name and password into the Netflix channel login.

To access U.S. programming via the Roku, you will need to use a VPN set to the U.S. If you can "borrow" the cable subscriber info of a friend or family member in the U.S., you may be able to stream cable TV channels and programs via Roku without paying an additional subscription fee per channel.

Amazon Fire Stick

You've probably heard of the Amazon Fire Stick, which is a gadget about the size of a cigarette lighter that comes with a remote control and connects to your digital TV and lets you stream content. Since it's an Amazon product, it's designed to access Amazon Prime videos.

Note: *You do not need to have an account with Amazon to use the Fire Stick to stream video content. You **do** need to have good high-speed internet.*

What's different about the Fire Stick is that it runs the Android programming language and (unlike the Roku device) lets you download various apps (see below), including a VPN. This makes it very easy to configure the VPN right from the TV using the remote control to select the location desired.

The Fire Stick generally has about 8 GB of memory and ships with default apps that cannot be deleted and take up space (gee, thanks, Amazon). **It does not have enough memory to download content**, but it can hold around 20 apps depending upon their size.

---

*Remember: **never** download content to the Fire Stick because by design, it does not have space for ANY content, only for apps. A single movie can be several gigabytes in size.*

If you lose your Fire Stick remote control or if it stops working for some reason, there is a downloadable app for iOS or Android that will let you use your smart phone as a remote control, including a keyboard on your phone's screen.

The coolest part of the Fire Stick: you can download and install various Android apps to it, giving you access to a wide array of content from different sources.

The website Fire Stick Tricks (https://www.firesticktricks.com) has extensive information about all the things you can do with your Fire Stick, including tips to prevent buffering of videos while viewing, common mistakes made when configuring a Fire Stick, and how to install a VPN.

Ready to become a couch potato?

Applications to Stream Video to Your TV or Device

Pay TV Streaming Apps
Many streaming apps will work with Apple, Roku, Android and other devices. Monthly charges range from around $6 to $85 or more; some have a free trial of seven days or so for you to test the service.

If all you want to do is take advantage of the free trial period to "binge watch" a TV series, for example, it is possible to automatically cancel a free trial period for video streaming or other services. See **Chapter 7, Banking and Finances** under the credit card section.

You will need to use a VPN set to a U.S. location to access U.S. content. Among the pay TV apps with a subscription model are the following:

- **Netflix** (movies & TV shows, rotating content, from $9/month; Netflix may be offering a cheaper tier with advertising in the near future)
- **Amazon Prime** (movies & TV shows, $139 per year)
- **Disney+** (movies & TV shows including Hulu, $139 per year)
- **YouTube TV** (85+ channels of programming, about $65/month)

- **HBO Max** (TV shows and movies, $14.99 per month or $9.99 with ads, downloadable with ad-free plan)
- **DirecTV Stream Choice** (64-140 channels depending upon package, from $69.99/month) – via internet, **not satellite**
- **fuboTV** (119-173 channels from $69.99/month, primary focus is sports)
- **Sling TV** (32+ channels from $35/month, several plans)
- **Hulu with Live TV, Disney Plus and ESPN** (75+ channels, from $69.99/month; more for ad-free)
- **Philo TV** ($25/month for 60+ channels; no news or sports channels)
- **Paramount+** (movies & TV shows, includes Showtime, NFL, NCAA & PGA, from $9.99/moth; price varies with or without ads)
- **Acorn TV** (British TV programs, $6.99 per month or $69.99 per year)
- **BritBox TV** (BBC, Channel 4 programming, $6.99 per month or $69.99 per year)

Free Streaming Apps

In addition to the above pay apps, there are a number of free apps that offer great content.

PBS App

If you enjoy watching PBS news, documentaries, arts, science, history or lifestyle programs, there is an app for Android and Apple/iOS; download from the respective Play Store. You can install it on the Amazon Fire Stick and stream it to your smart television, or install it on any Android, Apple or iOS device. PBS content is licensed only for the U.S., so use a VPN set to a U.S. location.

Most programs are free to watch for several weeks to a month or two after the original air date; after that period of time, you can continue to view programs via **PBS Passport** if you are a member of a local public television station (usually for an annual donation of around $75).

PBS Passport gives donors and supporters access to an on-demand library of programming such as American Experience, Antiques

Roadshow, Nature, Nova, Frontline, Masterpiece Theater (including Downton Abbey), Independent Lens, Finding Your Roots, and other programs in addition to a rotating selection of Ken Burns documentaries.

Activate your Passport membership via your Facebook, Google, or PBS account. For each device, register it with the same account used to activate Passport; *there is no limit to the number of devices that you can sign in to at one time.*

Pluto TV

Pluto TV has content from ViacomCBS and includes TV and movies, local TV news and sports in over 200 channels, including British TV and the Game Show Network. It is just like watching a cable TV channel with commercials, but over the internet. The app is available for Android, Roku, Apple iOS, Mac and Windows desktops.

The Classic TV category has channels for *Dark Shadows,* the original *Hawaii Five-O, Gunsmoke, Star Trek, The Carol Burnett Show, Laverne & Shirley, Mission: Impossible, Johnny Carson* and many more. The Home + DIY category has an *Antiques Roadshow* channel. The Latino category has over 20 channels, all in Spanish.

Under Sports there are twenty channels, including CBS Sports HQ, PGA Tour channel, and Fox Sports. The Crime category has channels for *Forensic Files, Cops, Cold Case Files* and *Court TV*.

Pluto TV is completely free because it is ad-supported; you cannot disable the ads with a paid subscription option. It is available **only in the U.S., Canada, Australia and the UK**, so you will need a VPN to access the content if you are outside of these countries. Go to https://pluto.tv to get started.

Filmrise

Filmrise is a nifty app that has a selection of TV shows and movies in its library for free streaming (some with commercials). Its content leans towards investigative, true crime and detective shows. The app is in the Google Play, Amazon Play and Apple app stores.

TV shows have categories such as True Crime (*Forensic Files, Dr. G Medical Examiner, Unsolved Mysteries, Cops, Behind Bars*) and British Drama (*Brideshead Revisited, Midsomer Murders, Sherlock Holmes*). The Classics category has *Batman* (the 1960s series), *Lost in Space, The Rifleman, My Favorite Martian* and *3rd Rock from the Sun* among others.

Its movies tend towards action-adventure, courtroom dramas, crime, espionage, thrillers, documentaries, and mysteries.

Freevee (TV series, documentaries and movies
Formerly called IMDb TV, Freevee (owned by Amazon) is a free advertising-supported streaming app that includes series such as *The X Files, Doctor Who, Mad Men, Kitchen Nightmares, Forensic Files, Mayday Air Disasters, Columbo, The Waltons, Adam-12,* and *Dragnet.* Movies rotate but recently included *Fifty Shades of Grey, A Few Good Men, Gone Girl,* and *The African Queen.*

Peacock (NBC Universal app)
Peacock has a free tier with ads that has movies and TV shows; for $4.99 per month you get fewer ads, 50+ channels, and all NBC live sports; for $9.99 per month the service is ad-free and you can download programs.

BBC iPlayer
The BBC iPlayer (https://www.bbc.co.uk/iplayer) has content from BBC channels, including BBC One, Two, Three and Four, BBC Scotland, BBC Radio and BBC News. You have to create an account and register to sign in to view live programming.

"Unofficial" streaming apps
"Unofficial" Android and Apple streaming applications will let you stream TV shows, movies and sports events. These apps are not downloaded from a Play or App Store, but rather from the app's website. From time to time, they may be taken down or no longer function.

> **Note:** *If you choose to use an app that has not been vetted by the Apple store, Google Play store or Amazon store, be sure to download the app **only** from the app's official website and carefully scrutinize the permissions that the app asks for, and if it's something not necessary for normal use (like Contacts), deny permission. Exercise caution with "unofficial" apps as they may be malware.*

Installing and configuring these apps is beyond the scope of this book, but you can find this information online, or hire a "techie" to do it for you; usually it is not difficult.

Always use a good VPN when streaming, which will help you avoid geographic restrictions, prevent ISP throttling and data capping, and provide overall privacy and security.

I am not endorsing the use of any of these apps.

BeeTV

BeeTV is a free Android app that will run on any Android device. It goes out and searches for links to servers that have video content. It doesn't actually store any content itself, it simply goes out and looks for streaming links for content. Periodically it runs 30-60 seconds of ads between (not during) your choices.
https://beetvapk.app/

> *BeeTV lets you access some copyrighted material for free, so use it only for streaming publicly available content. Streaming copyrighted content may be illegal.*
>
> *If you don't find active links for what you're looking for, check back later because the links update constantly, or change your VPN location to a different country. While a title may be indexed, there may not be any active links to stream content.*

Subtitles are available in various languages. There is no sign up, no registration and no subscription. You can download content to an Android device if it has sufficient storage space.

The user interface, in my opinion, is not the greatest and is not very intuitive, but once you play around with it you will figure it out. There is a search engine if you are looking for something in particular.

Kodi

You may remember the app Kodi if you are "of a certain age;" it's a free open-source media player application that allows users to view or play most videos, music, podcasts and other digital media. Kodi, unlike BeeTV, is available as a native application for Android, Linux, Mac OS X, iOS and Windows operating systems.

Because there is a native Android version for the app, you can install it on your Amazon Fire Stick and stream video content (always with a VPN) – but again, do not download anything to the Fire Stick because there is no storage.

Kodi itself does not host any content, but plugins to the software will allow users to access content from other sources online. Using Kodi has a bit of a learning curve, but is easier to master than usenet (don't worry if you're unfamiliar with what that is).

> **Note:** *Kodi lets you access some copyrighted material for free, so use it only for streaming publicly available content. Streaming copyrighted content may be illegal.*

How to use or configure Kodi is beyond the scope of this book, but you can find more information online at many websites, including:

- https://kodi.tv/download
- https://www.firesticktricks.com/best-kodi-addons.html

Other "unofficial" video streaming apps

There are other free "unofficial" Android or Apple apps to watch TV or movies. Sites such as Best Droid Player (https://www.bestdroidplayer.com) or Digit Bin (https://www.digitbin.com) have reviews for streaming apps.

Other "unofficial" Android or Apple video streaming apps are listed below (subject to change at any time); you can do your own research. *I am not endorsing the use of any of these apps.*

- Live Net TV
- Swift Streamz
- Exodus Live TV
- Duckie TV
- OLA TV
- Tgun.tv
- UKTV Now (British TV)
- TV Catchup (British TV)
- Thop TV (Indian cricket league, India TV & movies)

DVDs

While they may seem old-fashioned, DVDs are still in extensive use in many parts of the world. Authentic, licensed DVDs are encoded with a region code that prevents a DVD sold in one region from playing on a DVD player made in a different region. For example, the U.S. and Canada are Region 1; Region 1 DVDs will not play on a DVD player from a different region.

As a solution to the region issue, you can buy multi-region DVD players that will play DVDs from different regions, use the DVD drive on your laptop or desktop computer to play videos, or use software that will remove the regional code.

Many parts of the world tolerate mom-and-pop shops that sell pirated DVDs. Since these are clones of genuine, authorized DVDs, often there will be multiple soundtracks, with the original English soundtrack one of the choices if it is a movie originally made in English.

I am not condoning the pirating of DVDs, but rather simply pointing out the reality. In much of Latin America, pirated DVDs are sold from 75 cents to $1.50. The recently signed U.S.-Canada-Mexico trade agreement specifically prohibits the copying and pirating of DVDs.

Pay & Free Options for Digital Books and Audio

There are a variety of different sources for digital books and other content, giving you access to a large choice of content as the availability

of printed English language books, CDs and videos may be limited at your overseas location.

Amazon Kindle – Pay Service

Amazon digital books are probably the best-known among U.S. consumers; they are designed to interface seamlessly with the Kindle book reader or Fire tablet sold by Amazon. The actual reader devices are usually not too expensive ($50 to $150), because Amazon is using the "razor-and-razor-blades" strategy in the hopes of getting you to make ongoing content purchases rather than the one-time purchase of the device.

> *You do not have to have a Kindle device to read Kindle e-books; by using the standalone app that can be downloaded for free for Apple, Windows or Android devices, you can read Kindle e-books without a Kindle reader. You can purchase Kindle books a la carte for download to your library, and you will "own" the digital copy of the book.*

Amazon's **Kindle Unlimited** service is sort of like Netflix for books; you pay a monthly subscription fee (currently $9.99 per month; thirty-day free trial) to access digital books that the rights holder has elected to enroll in Kindle Unlimited (it does not include all books in Kindle format). Kindle Unlimited is a separate product that is **not included** in Amazon Prime membership.

With Kindle Unlimited, you're not actually purchasing the book, you're just "borrowing" it. You can add up to ten books at a time to your account to read. Once you're done reading the book, you "return" it (remove it from your library). If you are an avid, high-volume reader, Kindle Unlimited can be a good option.

Amazon Prime - Book and Audio Perks
While you don't get Kindle Unlimited with an Amazon Prime membership, **Prime Reading** *is a separate service that is part of Amazon Prime. It includes over 1,000 rotating book and magazine titles as well as 50 rotating audiobooks, plus selected Audible.com audio content such as documentaries, serialized dramas, comedy shows and podcasts. Two million songs and music are also included in the Amazon Prime subscription that 150 million subscribers enjoy worldwide.*
Amazon First Reads *is another free perk for Prime members; each month, Amazon editors pick about a dozen soon-to-be-released books and allow Prime members to download a copy for free to their library.*

If you really want to go for it with music, **Amazon Music Unlimited** offers over 70 million songs for $7.99 a month after a free thirty-day trial period.

Internet Archive – https://www.archive.org
The Internet Archive is a U.S. 501(c)(3) non-profit founded in 1996 whose mission is to provide universal, worldwide access to a digital library of books, video, audio, software and images. It also has over twenty years of web page history via its "Wayback Machine" archive. It is one of the top 300 web sites in the world and is used by millions of patrons every day.

U.S. books published prior to 1923 (public domain) are available for download (to keep) from the Internet Archive.

Among the Internet Archive's free holdings are:

- 28 million books and texts;
- 14 million audio recordings (including 220,000 live concert recordings)
- 6 million videos (from 2 million TV news programs to Grateful Dead videos)
- 3.5 million images
- 580,000 software programs (games, educational software & more - no licensing)
- 475 billion web pages
- Over 15,000 Grateful Dead concert recordings

The Internet Archive began to digitize books in 2005 and today scans 1,000 books per day in 28 locations around the world, working in cooperation with libraries and publishers.

> *The Internet Archive's **Open Library** site has hundreds of thousands of more recent books that can be borrowed that have been contributed by **libraries around the world**.*
>
> *Books in the **Open Library** under "Books to Borrow" can be "checked out" digitally by logged-in patrons (all you need is a free user ID and password). You can read books in your web browser or in some cases download them into Adobe Download Editions (ADE), a free piece of software used for managing digital book loans.*
>
> *Some **Open Library** titles are available only as "print disabled" books, which have been specially formatted in the DAISY (Digital Accessible Information System) format for users who cannot read regular print books. These titles are only accessible on a specialized device to patrons having a key issued by the Library of Congress. See below for more options for the vision impaired.*

Under Books, in addition to searching for subject, title or author, you will find specialized libraries such as:

- FedLink (federal agencies' libraries and digitized resources; the National Agricultural Library alone contains over 177,000 digitized publications)
- Smithsonian Libraries (Smithsonian publications, art and design, history and culture)
- Genealogy (Federal Census records, family histories, county & local histories)
- Lincoln Collection (digitized historical documents relating to Abraham Lincoln from the Allen County Public Library of Ft. Wayne, Indiana)

Library of Congress Digital Collections - https://loc.gov/collections/

While the digitized collections represent only a fraction of what the **Library of Congress** has in its archives, the digital content is pretty cool.

Among the digital holdings of the **Library of Congress** are:

- Chronicling America: Historic American Newspapers (1777-1963; word searchable)
- Antique maps of the U.S. and other countries; county maps from 1800s
- Civil War photographs and maps
- Railroad maps throughout the U.S. (1828-1900)
- Abraham Lincoln Papers (40,550 documents)
- African-American perspectives from the rare book collection (digitized books)
- Travels in America (253 published narratives of travel from 1750-1920)
- Numerous audio recordings of music, singing, and interviews
- Many collections of historic photographs, 1840s-1900s
- Manuscripts from the Federal Writers Project (1936-1940)
- Sanborn Fire Maps (1800s city fire maps, for genealogy; identify families)

Google Books – https://books.google.com
Google undertook a project to digitize millions of books, most in the public domain but some with the permission of the publisher or author. As of October 2019, Google Books had over 40 million titles. A reader can search by author, title, or keyword for book subjects.

- Books in the public domain (pre-1923) can be downloaded in full for free in a choice of formats such as EPUB, PDF or plain text;
- For in-print books where the publisher has granted permission to Google Books, at least 20% of the pages will be available to preview;

- A "snippet view" is shown when Google does not have the permission of the copyright owner for the book; two to three lines of text surrounding the queried item will be displayed;
- Books that have not been digitized will not have a preview, but will still show up in a search.

Google Books is particularly helpful if you are interested in an antiquarian book that would be in a Reference department (non-circulating book) of a library.

As part of the **Library Project** of Google Books, various libraries have provided scans of their public domain books out of copyright, which are *fully downloadable*. The project began with Harvard University Library, the New York Public Library, the University of Michigan Library and Stanford University Library. It has expanded to include such institutions as:

- The Austrian National Library
- The Bavarian State Library
- Columbia University Library
- University of Virginia Library
- University of Texas at Austin (500,000 volume Latin American collection)

Google Books also has digitized magazines that publishers have given it permission to digitize.

National Library Service for the Blind and Print Disabled

The **National Library Service for the Blind and Print Disabled**, part of the Library of Congress, administers a free national library program that provides Braille and recorded materials to people who cannot see regular print or handle print materials.

Any American citizen living abroad who is unable to read or use regular print materials as a result of temporary or permanent visual or physical limitations may apply for service at https://www.loc.gov/nls/about/services/overseas-services/.

National Library Service patrons living abroad receive services directly from NLS headquarters in Washington DC. Overseas patrons are eligible for the *free download service* and iOS and Android apps.

The overseas service librarian works directly with overseas patrons to help them locate and receive library materials. The NLS will provide vision-impaired patrons who live overseas with **digital talking book players free of charge**.

BookBub – https://www.bookbub.com/welcome

BookBub is a free service for readers that provides publishers and authors with a way to find new readers who can discover their books. Its marketing tools allow publishers and authors to promote their books.

BookBub claims to have 15 million readers, and offers thousands of free and discounted e-books. You can download books to Kindle, iPad, Kobo, smartphones or any e-reader. It offers real-time updates from your favorite authors, book recommendations, and blog posts.

Online Access to U.S. Libraries

Many U.S. libraries and universities offer online access to digitized collections, provided that you have a library user card. If you already have a local library card, you may wish to retain it for use abroad; you may be able to check out digital books, music or videos online, usually for 14 days. If you have to sign up separately to access digital content online, do that before you leave the U.S.

Some libraries will allow you to download MP3 files (music, audio programs, interviews etc.) to a device for playing later offline.

Certain public libraries will allow non-resident users to purchase a digital library card for an annual fee; check into whether the library you're interested in has that option.

Broward County Public Library

The Broward County (Florida) Public Library offers a **free** electronic library card to *anyone online*; you do not need to be a resident of Broward County, nor do you need to get a physical library card. Among its online offerings are TV shows and movies that can be streamed once you've logged in using your library credentials.

Apply online for an immediate Library Instant eCard at *https://www.broward.org*

Two apps that work with the BCPL (and many other public library systems) are **Hoopla** and **Kanopy**. **Hoopla** offers audio and electronic books, music, TV shows such as *Call the Midwife* and films. **Kanopy** likewise offers e-books, movies and documentaries with an emphasis on educational offerings. Sign up for Hoopla and Kanopy from your library's website.

Lest you feel guilty about availing yourself of Broward County's generosity, the Ft. Lauderdale airport had a large exhibit encouraging air travelers transiting through the airport to sign up for a library account online.

> *If you already have a library card from your U.S. place of residence, check to see what is available online.*

University libraries may offer more extensive online digital resources. While usually access is limited to faculty, staff and students, some universities do allow members of the public to purchase a digital library card for an annual fee.

> *The free internet library card catalog **Worldcat** (https://www.worldcat.org) indexes the card catalogs of libraries all around the world, including thousands of U.S. libraries. If there's a book you want, see if it might be available in electronic form.*

Chapter 10
Healthcare, Medicare & End of Life Planning

The Cost of U.S. Health Care
Get Your U.S. Medical Records Digitized
Dental Care
What about Specialized Medical Devices?
Prescription Drugs
A Brief Overview of U.S. Medicare
Healthcare Outside the U.S.
Planning for When You Need Help at Home
Getting Assistance with Accessing Local Healthcare
911 Emergency Services (or the Lack Thereof)
End of Life Planning & Health Care Directives
Wills & Estate Planning

The Cost of U.S. Health Care

For many of us, the exorbitant price of health care in the U.S. is one of the reasons we are interested in moving abroad – the rest of the world pays **10%-20%** of what we pay in the U.S. for good health care.

A number of years ago when I was on vacation in England, I tripped, fell and fractured my wrist. It wasn't anything complicated, and the local National Health Service clinic fixed me up just fine, with an X-ray and temporary cast.

The next day I went to an NHS hospital orthopedic ward, where they took another X-ray, changed my cast and advised me about travel and further follow up care once I got home to the U.S. The total cost for all of this first-rate care to me as a tourist? Under £200! That was about USD $235 at the time – and my travel insurance reimbursed me for it.

Contrast that to when I fractured a rib in the U.S. A trip to the local Emergency Room, an X-ray, and 'oh, you have a fractured rib, and there's nothing more we can do for that' cost a total of $8,500, which fortunately my insurance paid.

If health care is an important factor to you (i.e., if you're over the age of 45 or have any chronic conditions or history of past conditions such as cancer), you'll need to choose a place to live that won't bankrupt you when you seek medical attention. The good news is that just about *anywhere* in the world will cost less than health care in the U.S.

Get Your U.S. Medical Records Digitized

Part of your preparation to move abroad should include gathering any relevant medical records, reports, diagnostic scans, etc. and if possible, digitizing them. This will make them available to future doctors in your new country of residence with a minimum of fuss.

It's generally a good idea to have a conversation with your U.S. health care providers before moving abroad if you have any ongoing care or health issues that need monitoring. Let them know of your plans to move abroad, and solicit advice regarding managing your condition(s).

Note that in many parts of the world, **you** keep your X-rays, scans and blood test results and must bring them to the doctor's office; the doctor does not store them for you.

Dental Care

There is excellent dental care available outside the U.S. for a fraction of the price. In fact, many U.S. residents who live near the southern border regularly visit Mexico for dental care because it is much more affordable.

Dental implants, root canals, crowns and other procedures that can cost thousands of dollars in the U.S. cost far less in other countries, and often there are English-speaking dentists in many places.

I visited a Colombian dentist in Medellin just for a routine cleaning and to get some bleaching done, and the cost was very reasonable, about $20 at the time.

In Ecuador, I go to a fantastic local dentist who is meticulous; he suits up like an astronaut against the coronavirus, all dental instruments are individually sealed in separate packaging after sterilization by an outside vendor, and he spends as much time as needed to get things right. But not many expats go to him – he doesn't speak English. I found him via the glowing recommendations from his existing patients, and I have to agree with their assessment.

What about Specialized Medical Devices?

In some countries insulin pumps are not available, nor the specialized insulin and supplies needed for them. Certain brands of implanted cardiac pacemakers or hearing aids may not be supported locally. Many countries routinely do knee or hip replacement operations, but more advanced devices may not be available locally. *Inquire first before moving*.

Prescription Drugs

If you are on any type of prescription medication that you need to take on a regular basis, check into its availability in a foreign location that you are considering.

Do your homework before deciding to move abroad as to whether needed medications were available in the foreign country. You want to know about possible prescription drug supply problems in your new home *before* you leave the U.S.

A Brief Overview of U.S. Medicare

Medicare is the U.S. government-funded health care system for those age 65 and older which also covers those who are permanently disabled as recognized by the Social Security Administration. Persons who are on dialysis, have ALS (Lou Gehrig's disease) or certain other serious conditions can also qualify for Medicare.

Medicare does not pay for health care incurred outside of the U.S., even in an emergency, so if you are living outside the U.S. you will want to decide whether to sign up when you turn 65 or continue paying for Medicare if you are already enrolled.

Over 64 million people are currently enrolled in Medicare as of 2022, and due to the Baby Boom generation, projections indicate that over *80 million* will be enrolled by 2030 (almost 23% of the projected population). Medicare spending is projected to increase from just over $740 billion in 2018 to just over $1.2 trillion by 2026, or from 3.7% of GDP to 4.7%. Low-income individuals who qualify for both Medicare and Medicaid (government-paid health care for very low-income people) are known as **dual eligibles**.

> *There is a 10% penalty added to the monthly premiums for every year or part of a year that a beneficiary does not enroll at age 65 - unless the individual is still working and is covered by qualifying (U.S.) employer health insurance. Living outside the U.S. does not exempt you from the penalty for late enrollment.*

If you are already covered by Medicare when you move out of the U.S., you will need to decide whether to continue paying for Medicare (see below) or whether to cancel coverage.

Canceling Your Medicare Coverage

If you decide to cancel your existing coverage (be **very sure** about this because of the steep permanent penalties to re-enroll), you will have to fill out **Form CMS 1763**. Medicare may require a telephone interview to make sure you understand all the implications.

Some expats have reported difficulties in getting the deduction from their Social Security monthly benefit stopped after canceling their Medicare coverage, so be sure to monitor the situation.

*If you also have health care coverage from another source, such as the Veterans Administration, Tricare or private retiree insurance, be sure to check on whether canceling your Medicare coverage will **affect that other coverage**.*

The health care benefits under Medicaid, the program for indigent persons, vary widely by state but nursing home care is a mandated benefit in all states. Like Medicare, Medicaid does not cover medical care outside of the U.S. The interplay of Medicare/Medicaid benefits is beyond the scope of this book, so if you want to know more, consult resources such as Medicaid.gov or AARP (American Association of Retired Persons).

Medicare actuarially only covers about 50% of expected expenses. For example, it does not cover dental work or dentures, eyeglasses, hearing aids, long-term care or nursing home care (unless you are being discharged from a hospital under certain circumstances).

Medicare Coverage and Benefits

Medicare consists of four parts:

- Part A (hospital and hospice benefits)
- Part B (physician and ancillary services)
- Part C (Medicare Advantage capitated plans)
- Part D (prescription drugs)

Most enrollees pay premiums for Part B and Part D, and because Medicare pays for about *only half* of expected medical expenses, most enrollees also purchase supplemental insurance (known as **Medigap** coverage). A detailed discussion of Medicare is beyond the scope of this book, but there are plenty of resources available that go into more detail – see https://www.cms.gov (Centers for Medicare and Medicaid Services) for more information.

Most people pay their monthly premiums through deductions from their Social Security benefits. Premiums vary depending upon the income (but not age) of the beneficiary. For 2022, Part B premiums varied from $170.10 to $578.30 based on 2020 income tax returns.

Part D premiums for prescription drugs in 2022 vary from zero to $90 or so depending upon your income and the benefit plan selected.

The cost of Medigap plans varies from around $95 to over $300 per month, although costs can vary widely depending upon the level of benefits selected, geographical location and the age of the beneficiary. Enrolling at age 65 will get you better rates as you age instead of waiting to enroll until you are older.

Add up all these additional Medicare costs, and you could be paying $300 to $550 a month (or more) for coverage that as an expat you cannot use. Only you can decide whether you want to continue being covered by Medicare.

If you think that at some point you might want to return permanently to the U.S., or if you want to have coverage during visits back to the U.S. for possible accidents or illnesses, *you may want to continue paying for Medicare Part B and other coverage.*

Nursing home/rehabilitation facilities are not covered under Medicare unless you were a hospitalized inpatient for at least three consecutive days and are discharged directly to the facility from the hospital.

> *The online publication "Medicare & You" is available at www.medicare.gov and is updated every year for changes to coverage. It explains in over 100 pages what Medicare covers and doesn't cover in greater detail.*

Health Care Outside the U.S.

For short trips outside the U.S., travel insurance is fine, but if you'll be living permanently in a foreign country as a resident, you may want (or be required) to have some sort of health care coverage.

Foreign Country Resident Health Insurance

In some countries and depending upon your age, there may be medical underwriting when you apply for health insurance as a resident. Having medical records, reports and scans digitized will make it much easier to furnish any needed information to the insurance company. There may be age restrictions; for example, Guatemala will not let you enroll in the government health care system after your late 50s.

Some countries as a condition of residency will require that you have some sort of health insurance coverage (public or private), such as Spain or Ecuador. Others will let you decide whether you want health insurance or not.

Can't I Just Pay Out-of-Pocket?

Often a viable option for Americans abroad is to simply pay out-of-pocket for health care as it is incurred, because the cost is so reasonable. You might still want to have some kind of coverage for catastrophic care – depending upon the country, major surgery such as heart bypass surgery could cost USD $40,000 or more. A chronic condition could end up being the most costly, something like dialysis. It's your call.

Before choosing to pay out-of-pocket, check to see if your residency visa requires you to maintain some sort of health insurance; some countries require this.

To give you an idea of how affordable paying out-of-pocket can be: friends of mine in Colombia told me about how one of them had a bout with kidney stones – excruciatingly painful. The American couple had recently arrived in Colombia and didn't yet have their health insurance in place.

An overnight stay in the hospital (after an Emergency Room visit) **with MRI**, consultations by two different urologists, and an IV with pain medication ended up costing a total of **USD $530**. Luckily, my friend (who was an RN) ended up passing the kidney stone before a lithotripsy session was needed. This was in a **private hospital** with top-notch care.

Quality of Nursing Staff

In some countries, hospital and ICU nurses in general may not be as highly educated or trained as in the U.S. (more like LVNs in the U.S.) and may be more reliant upon the physicians to tell them what to do, although this can vary.

In general, a hospital in a big city will have better-trained nurses and support staff than a hospital in a small town or rural area (just as in the U.S.). Depending upon the country, it may be advisable to hire your own private duty nurse while you are hospitalized.

Obtaining Blood Transfusions

In many parts of the world, volunteer donations to blood banks are not common (if there are blood banks), which results in hospitals having fewer pints of blood and blood products on hand. *If the hospital runs out of blood (which may happen frequently), you may have to recruit donors yourself. If you have an uncommon blood type, you may be out of luck.*

Usually, the patient's family would round up blood donations from friends and relatives, but if you as a foreigner don't have family nearby, or they don't speak the language, you could run into trouble. In areas where there are numbers of expats, the expat community often compiles a roster of expats by blood type who are willing to donate blood if needed.

How to Identify Better Hospitals Abroad

In the U.S., the Joint Commission on Accreditation of Health Care Organizations (JCAHO) is a Chicago-based organization that conducts inspections and issues certifications to different types of health care providers, including hospitals.

The **Joint Commission International** performs a similar function for providers and facilities outside of the U.S. One good sign (but no guarantee) is if a hospital or other health care provider has JCAHO International accreditation.

For example, Colombia has a highly regarded health care system with highly qualified physicians and excellent hospitals in the major cities.

Health care outside the major cities is more basic but still good. The cost of health care in Colombia is very reasonable compared to the U.S.
The World Health Organization ranks Colombia's healthcare system as #22 out of 190 countries that it ranked (the U.S. was #37); no other Latin American country ranked higher.

The Mechanics of Paying for Healthcare in Foreign Countries

Most hospitals, clinics and doctors' offices outside the U.S. are not set up to do insurance billing and *do not have any staff* who handle billing. **It's strictly a cash-and-carry business**, unless you're in a country with a national health system such as in most of Europe.

In fact, in some parts of the world, it can happen that a critically ill or injured patient arrives at a hospital and treatment is delayed until they determine who will be paying the bill, and in the meantime the patient dies.

In many countries, there is no law similar to the U.S.'s Emergency Medical Treatment and Labor Act (EMTLA) that requires hospitals to evaluate and stabilize patients without regard to ability to pay.

You will generally be required to pay in advance for elective procedures. In the case of a private hospital admission, unless you have insurance, if the exact amount of the bill isn't known in advance, typically you'll be asked for a sizable deposit up front, either in cash or on a credit card – usually at least USD $5,000 or $10,000.

> *Sometimes an inpatient will not be allowed to leave the hospital (even if medically ready to be discharged) until the bill is paid **in full**. The hospital may even post a security guard outside the patient's room to stop you from leaving!*

A public hospital may not ask for a deposit up front, but you could receive a bill later if you're not enrolled in the public health scheme or let your coverage lapse. If you own real estate, the hospital (public or private) may place a lien against your property.

Government Healthcare or Private Insurance?
Your choices come down to whether to enroll in the government health care system or go with a private insurer. Both have their pros and cons; the situation can vary greatly depending upon the country, the government's commitment to health care and its financial situation at any particular point in time, and the trustworthiness of private insurance companies.

The government-run health care system will often be substantially cheaper in monthly premiums than a private insurer, but you may be restricted in your choice of hospitals and doctors. Additionally, if the government hospital or health care system is experiencing financial problems, they may lack necessary supplies and equipment, or even be closed altogether.

Monthly premiums for the public health system in Colombia are 12.5% of your monthly income in 2022. In Ecuador it's about USD $75 a month per person in 2022 based on the monthly minimum wage of USD $425 for those with no Ecuadorian source income.

Public hospitals in some countries may not have a good reputation due to budget problems. Some lack even linens for the beds, which the patient or his family has to provide.

Hospitals may be short-staffed with insufficient nursing personnel, which often leads families to keep a family member with the patient at all times to help with meals and bathing or to summon help. You as an expat may want to pay out-of-pocket for a private duty nurse to be at your hospital bedside.

Dealing with Private Insurance Companies
A private insurer will give you more choices for hospitals and health care providers, but will cost more in monthly premiums and will have deductibles and co-pays (things very familiar to Americans).

You will usually first have to pay all costs out of pocket and then submit claims for reimbursement, with the possibility of having to appeal claims denials. For an elective, pre-authorized surgery at a hospital with which the insurance company has a contract, you might be required to pay upfront only your share of the expected costs. Be prepared for lots of paperwork and bureaucracy.

Choose a private insurer carefully, as government regulation of insurance companies outside the U.S. may not be as rigorous; in the case of a claim denial, you may be on your own in battling the insurance company.

> *Having private insurance does not guarantee that you'll receive care. During the coronavirus pandemic, there were instances where demand exceeded capacity and having private insurance didn't make much of a difference. In normal times, though, private insurance may get you faster or better care than in the public healthcare system.*

Depending upon the private health plan, procedures for hospitalization will vary. In some places, for example, you can buy a "membership" at several different levels for a private hospital that gives you *carte blanche* access to clinic, outpatient and inpatient medical services for a monthly fee. It's not really insurance, it's more like a discounted prepaid health care scheme.

In Colombia it is possible to obtain reasonably priced private health insurance that covers not only pre-existing conditions and doctor's house calls but also veterinarian house calls for your dog!

What I Do in Ecuador

In Ecuador, you as an expat are required to maintain some sort of health insurance, either through joining the public system (IESS) or private health insurance. I pay about $75 a month for IESS coverage and treat it more as catastrophic coverage. I am prepared to pay out-of-pocket for a hospitalization if necessary.

If all I need is to visit a primary care physician or specialist in an office visit, I pay out of pocket because it's faster and easier and not very expensive. An English-speaking primary care doctor charges around USD $20-$35 for an office visit *up to an hour long*, and a specialist USD $30-

$50. I had some benign skin lesions removed by a dermatologist in his office for USD $25.

Many private physicians are also IESS doctors; you can see a private surgeon in his office first and then schedule a surgical procedure through IESS (after the usual bureaucratic approvals) using the same doctor.

Many Latin American countries operate on this principle, where private doctors also participate in the public health system, including Mexico and Guatemala.

The Ecuadorian public health care system will refer patients to private hospitals and clinics for procedures and surgeries if their capacity is insufficient and the problem is urgent. For example, if you urgently need a hip replacement but the local system cannot schedule the procedure, they will send you to a private hospital.

This is really the best of both worlds: paying for public health care but enjoying the private health care system. Note that this practice may not be sustainable given the government's severe budget strains from the coronavirus pandemic, ensuing economic crisis and endemic corruption.

You might not be willing to wait ten months for a knee or hip replacement if you are in a lot of pain. Additionally, private health care providers may refuse to provide care if they are not being paid by the government.

Retired Military? Tricare is Available Overseas

You may be surprised to learn that Tricare, unlike Medicare, will cover you overseas. In some locations you may have to pay out-of-pocket first and submit claims for reimbursement; in other locations there may be participating local Tricare providers.

You must maintain your Medicare Part B coverage (although you can't use it outside the U.S.) and you will be responsible for all deductibles and cost share payments. The Tricare Overseas Program Contractor handles all non-U.S. medical claims and can assist you in finding a provider, obtaining authorization for care, etc.

You can find more information at
https://www.tricare.mil/Plans/HealthPlans/TFL/TFL_O

Planning for Needing Help at Home

At some point you may not be able to manage on your own. If you don't have a spouse or adult children with you in your new home, or if you/they don't speak the local language, you're going to need assistance with managing everyday tasks.

Many locations around the world have home health agencies who can provide staff 24/7, and you should be able to contract for housekeeping and cooking help, but someone will need to oversee all these caregivers and workers other than the ill or injured expat.

Ideally you can develop a network of trustworthy friends locally who will agree to act as care coordinators. These persons will need to be able to access your funds, so they really should be people you trust.

One system that can work well is to appoint a formal committee (three people works well). In order to take any significant action or spend money beyond a pre-approved limit, two of the three people must agree.

There should be provisions for when someone wants to resign their duties, and a mechanism for naming a new person to the committee. The committee can either serve as volunteers or if the job becomes more time-consuming, be compensated for their time.

It's probably best to have a second set of friends or family given a power of attorney over funds (if any) in the U.S., and a designated amount each month can be sent to the country where you're living to cover expected living and medical expenses.

Getting Assistance with Accessing Local Healthcare

At some point it is likely that you'll want some assistance in navigating the local healthcare system, whether public or private, especially if there are language issues. Under stress, your language abilities may vanish. In places where there are numbers of expats, English-speaking *medical facilitators* frequently help expats find the appropriate medical care, for an hourly fee.

Betty Alderete, a medical facilitator with medical training who formerly lived in Cuenca, Ecuador who assisted English-speaking expats with accessing health care in Cuenca, has the following tips in selecting a medical facilitator:

- Choose a facilitator who has some medical knowledge in the area of your condition(s) and is familiar with your condition(s); *do not use a facilitator who has no medical training* to function only as an interpreter;
- Choose a facilitator who knows who are the best specialists in your community for your condition, and more importantly, *whom to avoid*;
- Do not choose a doctor solely on the basis that he/she speaks English; many times, the best specialist *may not speak English*;
- Don't base your choice of doctor solely on a lower price; sometimes the best specialist may charge a little extra, but in any event will cost much less than in the U.S. It is not worth endangering your health to save a few dollars.

> *Just because a private hospital looks good, doesn't mean it's the best choice. Betty once had an American client who didn't speak Spanish who was likely having a heart attack. The client insisted on going to a certain private hospital, against Betty's advice. In the Emergency Room, they ran an EKG but the physician on duty said (in Spanish) "Gee, I wish I could make heads or tails out of this."*
>
> *Betty couldn't believe it because she could see for herself that the EKG clearly showed that her client was indeed having a heart attack. At that point she literally dragged the client to a different hospital several city blocks away, where they repeated the EKG and immediately went into emergency treatment mode, since they knew what they were doing.*

Betty has seen many clients who started out with a facilitator who acted only as an interpreter (with no medical training) and ended up in avoidable medical crises. By the time Betty got involved, the clients were in serious trouble, but due to her knowledge of local specialists, she was able to find them the correct care. She also assists clients in weighing the choices when several treatment options are presented.

Note that cultural customs regarding doctors may differ in foreign countries; doctors may not volunteer relevant information and it's up to the patient or his/her family to know what questions to ask.

911 Emergency Services (Or the Lack Thereof)

Keep in mind that some areas outside the U.S. do not have a 911-type emergency service that you can call, and that getting an ambulance may take much longer than what we are accustomed to in the U.S. Ambulances may lack basic lifesaving equipment such as IVs, defibrillators or oxygen. *A taxi may be faster than waiting for an ambulance.*

Even if there is a 911 system, streets may be unmarked or unnamed and houses may not have numbers; the ambulance may not be able to find your location right away.

In Cuenca, Ecuador there is a private company that provides 24-hour 911-type emergency services with a panic button the client can push, for a monthly fee of about USD $35. The client's home address is pre-programmed into their computer system.

End of Life Planning & Health Care Directives

You'll be doing a huge favor to your loved ones, friends and family if you address how to manage healthcare needs before you become seriously ill.

Who do you want to make medical decisions for you? Does this person have a medical power of attorney *valid under local law*? Does this person have access to your funds to pay the hospital? Do you want to receive all possible treatment or would you rather just receive palliative care with no heroic measures? Do you wish to be "unplugged" when it is clear that there is no prospect for recovery?

Investigate what the requirements are under local law for a health care power of attorney and advance health care directives. Wherever you end up living, it is important to draft legal documents valid under local law that spell out your wishes **before** a health emergency arises where you are unable to speak for yourself.

It's best to think about accessing local health care *before* the need arises. In areas where there are existing populations of expats, there may be groups that assist expats with addressing these matters, tailored to the particular country's legal requirements.

> *Well before it's needed, investigate local law regarding powers of attorney and create a durable power of attorney and health care directive valid under local law so that if or when the time comes, you will be able to receive the health care YOU want.*

Wills & Estate Planning

Nobody likes to talk about dying, but administering an estate of a U.S. citizen who dies overseas can be a long, drawn-out expensive affair if you don't have things ready to go ahead of time.

What do you want to have done with your mortal remains after death? Do you already have a cemetery plot purchased somewhere? Do you want to be cremated and have your ashes scattered at a particular place? Make your wishes known!

Get familiar with the local laws of the country where you will be living; choose *both* a local estate attorney and a U.S. estate attorney, and get wills drawn up in both countries. Your U.S. will should be drawn up in the state where you are claiming to be domiciled. **Keep both wills (U.S. and foreign) up-to-date.**

Depending upon the extent of your assets and where they are located, you may also need to consult with an estate tax attorney in the U.S. or in your foreign country of residence.

Go through all your bank and brokerage accounts, including retirement accounts. Review any life insurance policies.

- Do all accounts have beneficiaries named?
- Are the beneficiaries still alive?
- Do you need to make any changes?

For assets in the U.S., consider placing assets into a living trust, which will avoid the need for probate. Pick a dependable estate attorney in the U.S.

Most importantly, have an executor named and *give that person the pertinent information* that they will need, such as an inventory of assets and bank and brokerage accounts, online user names and passwords, etc.

Create an informal letter of Instructions for your executor, specifying where documents are kept and listing your assets and liabilities. You may want to create a list of steps that your executor should take after your death. This letter can be deposited in a sealed envelope with an attorney or trusted friend, to be opened in the event of your death.

> *To get a better understanding of how U.S. probate and estate administration works when a U.S. citizen dies, there are books for non-attorneys that explain the basics. Two good ones are: **Nolo Press's "The Executor's Guide: Settling a Loved One's Estate or Trust," by Mary Randolph, J.D.** (2021) and **"The Complete Book of Wills, Estates & Trusts 4th Edition"** by Alexander A. Bove (2021).*
>
> ***Give some thought to where you want your assets to go when you die.*** *Even if you're 35 years old, car accidents and coronavirus pandemics do happen. If you own significant property in your adopted country, you will need to consult a local lawyer about drafting a will that comports with local law and carries out your wishes.*

What Happens When a U.S. Citizen Dies Abroad?
Depending upon the foreign country concerned, when a U.S. citizen dies abroad, the next-of-kin in the country (or if none, in the U.S.) may have a right to decide what happens with the remains.

If there are no next-of-kin in the U.S., then an advance directive or will valid under local law will be essential.

After obtaining a local death certificate, your executor or administrator will want to obtain a *Consular Report of U.S. Citizen Death Abroad* which can be used in lieu of a U.S. death certificate if there will be a U.S. probate to distribute assets.

The first 20 copies of this U.S. government document from the consulate are included in the State Department's fee. Depending upon the extent of the deceased's assets in the U.S., you may want to request additional copies to have on hand for U.S. banks, insurance companies, or others who need legal proof of death. The consulate will notify Social Security of the death abroad.

*Note that the Department of State has **no funds** to assist in the return of remains or ashes of U.S. citizens who die abroad.*

> *In many countries, funeral homes have prepaid plans where, once they have the local death certificate, they will quickly and efficiently carry out your wishes. The notarized contract will specify whether you want to be cremated, have your remains or ashes repatriated to the U.S. (or other country) for burial, or buried elsewhere. Usually, it is much less expensive to have ashes repatriated to the U.S. than a coffin with an embalmed corpse. If the deceased was enrolled in a public healthcare system, check whether the plan has a funeral benefit (many do).*

Chapter 11
Computer Security for Expats

General Computing Best Practices to Follow
Data Backup
Creating & Managing Passwords
Managing Email/Text Messages & "Phishing"
Insecure SMS Text Messages
Virtual Private Networks
Wi-Fi Security
Defragging your hard drive(s)
Online Privacy

A s an expat, the internet is how you will conduct your financial affairs and banking, pay bills, access your funds in the U.S. for living expenses abroad, and keep in touch with family, loved ones and friends. Anything that threatens this access is an exceptional menace.

While I am not a computer guru by any means, in this area I believe you must be very careful. Too many scam artists and hackers are out there.

> *You may find this whole topic somewhat overwhelming if you are not technologically inclined. You might want to find a reputable IT guru to help you with technology issues; having someone available for tech support can be very helpful. Ask around for recommendations, whether in the U.S. or abroad.*

Most of the topics covered in this chapter apply equally to Apple/Mac products and to Windows computers, but because Windows inherently has greater security problems due to many different vendors supplying hardware and software, I will mention Windows-specific issues more often.

Watch Those "Helpers" Closely

Be careful whom you allow to modify your computer(s)'s settings, and try to watch and understand what they are doing to your system. You don't want someone to create NEW problems for you with how they have configured some essential function, and you certainly don't want to lose any files or data. For future reference, ask them to write down all changes that they make to your operating system or applications.

I had an expat friend who had an IT guy (another expat) install new software and change some settings on her computer. When she encountered problems with her laptop nine months later, he had left the country and she had no idea what he had done to her laptop.

General Computing Best Practices

IT security expert Brian Krebs, formerly a tech reporter with the *Washington Post*, lists three rules to avoid computer scams:

(1) **If you didn't go looking for it, don't install it** – meaning if you're at a site that says 'in order to view this content, you need to install this software' it's probably a bad idea to do so and it's likely to install some sort of malware, ransomware or virus on your computer. If you think you need to install something, go to the vendor of that software and install it from them.

(2) **If you've installed something, update it and keep it updated**. Malicious software will install itself on your computer if your software is not kept updated with the latest security patches and your computer will no longer belong to you.

(3) **If you don't need a software program any more, uninstall it.** Hackers actively look for unpatched programs that haven't been updated to fix security weaknesses.

Turn on automated software updates. ***Keeping your software up-to-date*** is the most important step you can take to boost security. This may be a hassle, but it's one that you cannot afford to ignore. Hackers are always exploiting more vulnerabilities, while security professionals play catchup.

Most modern software will update itself if you let it; turn on all auto updates. Needless to say, running expired or pirated software that can't be updated for security patches is a bad idea.

Back up your data. *If your system gets compromised, there's an excellent chance that all your data will be held for ransom. Your data will be encrypted and will only be unlocked if you pay a ransom to the bad guys – and said payment will just encourage them to keep doing it. Extortion has now gone mainstream.*

Hospitals around the world have found themselves locked out of their computer systems due to ransomware, affecting the delivery of health care to critically ill patients.

U.S. municipalities have likewise found themselves locked out of their computer systems, impeding the functioning of basic local government services, unless a ransom is paid.

Essentially the entire Costa Rican government was shut down by hackers in 2022 and held for ransom.

Malware and Virus Protection
You need to have good virus and malware protection. Your life is on your computer or laptop as an expat. I use MalwareBytes for malware; its user license also covers smart phones, so it's on my phone too.

In general, Apple products are less susceptible to viruses and malware, and usually have built-in safeguards that watch for dangerous apps. That said, you may wish to consider third-party software for additional security.

Windows Defender, the built-in Windows overall protection feature, is a good supplement to third party software protection but should not be your only protection. Testing has shown that using it alone still leaves too many vulnerabilities for the bad guys to exploit.

Malwarebytes in conjunction with Windows Defender is a reasonable compromise, but there are many possible combinations of products that will give you good protection (nothing will be perfect).

Free versions of antivirus programs, such as AVG, can be effective if used correctly, but remember that a free version of any software will have limited features. AVG's free version will not run scans automatically; you must remember to run scans yourself.

Firewall software products can protect you from malicious websites and generally have variable settings. I have used ZoneAlarm in the past, which identifies known dangerous websites and will stop you from unknowingly accessing them.

*Beware of scammers posting links on legitimate companies' support websites that appear to be affiliated with the company. I fell for this once and the bastards ended up putting malware on my laptop and demanded $89 to remove it. Lesson learned. Be paranoid. Be **very, very** paranoid.*

Data Backup

As an expat, this is not optional. You **MUST** back up your data. *Repeat after me: "I will back up my hard drive(s). Every time I use my computer."*

With ransoming of people's computers now being a "thing," having your data and applications backed up is essential. If a hacker does get access to your data and files and demands a ransom, you can simply exercise the nuclear option and reformat the hard drive and then re-install all your applications and data.

Additionally, what if your hard drive crashes? All your data and apps will go poof, just as if a hacker held your computer for ransom. ***Back up your data.***

There are several options for backups: a physical, external drive or a "cloud" backup. An external drive can run backup software that will run in the background and back up your files automatically, and is cheap. But what happens if the external drive itself crashes or fails? What if you have a fire, flood or other disaster and your external drive is damaged or destroyed?

A "cloud" backup service will automatically check for new or changed files and back them up online to a remote server – you must have internet, of course. There are any number of "cloud" backup services – do a Google search and you can find one. Read the reviews from reputable magazines such as CNET or PC Magazine, or Tom's Guide (www.tomsguide.com).

Free is not always the best idea. GoogleDocs and Drop Box will allow you to store documents in the cloud, but are not designed nor meant to be used for data backup. They have limited free storage and it would be an entirely manual process on your part.

> *The first time you do a cloud backup, it may take a **really** long time ... mine took a week the first time running 24X7 the first time for about 450 GB of data over a fiber optic high-speed internet connection. I was not expecting my first online backup to take so long, but luckily I had enough time to finish the backup before I had to move out of my apartment. **Allow plenty of time for your first cloud backup.** After the first-time back up, things go much more quickly as it is only the incremental changes that are backed up.*

Research the various online backup options and decide which plan fits your needs and budget. CrashPlan has a plan for small businesses and Carbonite has plans for individual (non-business) users.

Make sure you back up all your data before having major repair work done to your computer or before installing system updates.

Other online data backup companies for individual users include*:*

- *iDrive Personal*
- *Backblaze*
- *Acronis Cyber Protect*
- *SOS Online Backup*
- *Livedrive*
- *OpenDrive*

- *Sync.com*
- *pCloud*
- *Icedrive*
- *MEGA*

Creating & Managing Secure Passwords

This is an important subject. ***Never use*** the same password for more than one website. So many sites have been hacked that the bad guys will try using your password on other websites. Do not pick something that is easily guessed, such as your year of birth.

The best way to construct a password that will be almost impossible to crack is to create a sentence that you can remember, and use the first letter of each word. For example, "The last time I went fishing was in 1980" becomes **Tltlwfwi1980**. "We ate 20 Nestle Tollhouse chocolate chip cookies" becomes "**Wa20NTccc**." Pick a phrase that you will be able to remember, and **don't re-use the same phrase for different sites**.

The more characters a password has, the harder it is to "crack" by brute force (using a computer to guess all possible combinations until the correct password is found). An extremely high-end computer (that no average hacker would have) could possibly crack a nine-character password in 67 minutes, a ten-character password in 3.27 days, an eleven-character password in 229 days, and a twelve-character password in 44 years.

With current technology, an eleven- or twelve-character password is the "sweet" spot for now. The phrase above "The last time I went fishing was in 1980" has thirteen characters, so would be pretty crack-proof.

> ***Do not save passwords in Web browsers***; *a browser is much easier to hack than a proprietary app, despite regular security updates. While it is convenient to have your browser automatically log you into a website, it's a bad idea to save the password in the browser. You can also set your browser to automatically "forget" a password once you leave a website.*

PIN numbers

Personal ID numbers (PINs) are usually used in banking for ATM card withdrawals, debit card purchases or credit card cash advances. Create six-digit PINs if permitted, not four digits. Don't ever use any of the following PINS, because they are almost 20% of those currently in use: 0000, 1111, 1212, and 1234. You should also never use your birth date, the last four digits of your SSN, or similar numbers; these are much too easy to guess. Use different PINs for each account.

How Can I Manage All Those Passwords?

Some of us have so many user IDs and passwords, it's literally impossible to keep track of them without some sort of system.

Password Managers

Password manager programs work in the cloud; all you have to remember is the master password. If you already have a security program installed, there might be a password manager app included; check and see.

Among desktop/laptop standalone password manager apps, there are free apps as well as paid applications. Free standalone password manager applications generally limit you to a single device and may limit the number of accounts. The paid password manager apps usually charge fees starting at $35 a year.

The issue with a password manager app is obvious: if it ever gets hacked, the hackers have the keys to the kingdom. Researchers at the University of York in England in 2017 and 2018 were able to hack various password managers by using security flaws in the Google Chrome browser extension and in Android, and in 2019 security consultants were able to hack password apps as well using known vulnerabilities in browsers.

If you do choose to use a password manager app, avoid using a PIN to unlock the app from a smart phone; use your fingerprint or your face instead. And always download the mobile app from the official Google Play or Apple store, not from a third-party site.

Create a strong master password for the password manager, using a unique phrase or sentence that you'll be able to remember. Enable multi-factor authentication (such as a code sent to your cell phone or email address) for further security.

Check online computing publications such as CNET or PC Magazine for their latest recommendations for password manager apps, as this information changes frequently.

Most computer security experts believe that using a good password manager, in conjunction with good security practices, is not a bad idea. **However**, if you are not taking proper precautions to keep out malware, keystroke loggers, spyware, ransomware or unauthorized remote access software, then no password manager app will be safe from hackers and you have bigger problems to worry about than managing your passwords.

Alternative to Password Managers
You could use a lower-tech solution to manager your passwords, such as a password-protected Word or Excel document. You will want to keep an updated copy of this file somewhere else in addition to your computer and your cloud backup, such as a thumb drive or external hard drive – and don't name it something like "Password list."

In an emergency, you will need the cloud backup service login information in order to restore your files to a new computer or laptop, so be sure to keep the backup copy of your password file up to date.

Managing Email/Text Messages and "Phishing"

"Phishing" is the use of email or text messages to lure you into thinking that a message is from a trusted source (the bait) to get you to click on a link or open an attachment. Usually, the link or attachment will install some sort of malware onto your device which will then make it unusable unless you pay money (ransom) to the bad actor.

An attacker may send e-mail posing as a reputable credit card company or financial institution that requests account information, often suggesting that there is a problem and that you will be unable to access your account unless you provide requested information. When users respond with the information, attackers use it to gain access to the accounts.

Information about known phishing attacks is available online from groups such as the Anti-Phishing Working Group (**http://www.antiphishing.org**).

> *One way to check on a link received in an email: hover your mouse pointer over the URL hyperlink and look in the lower left-hand corner of your screen; the actual URL will display there. If the link says "Bank of America" but the actual URL is to an entirely different location, then you know it's a scam. The scammers may use a fake URL that has Bank of America in the name, though, so be careful.*

Malicious links and attachments are very common. Try to make it a rule not to click on links within emails. I know, your friends and family like to forward links to interesting articles, social media posts or videos, but exercise caution when you click on a link.

I let all my friends and family know, I am very reluctant to click on a link in a message from them unless there is enough information that I know it came from them and not from a hacker.

Social engineering attacks
In a social engineering attack, an attacker uses social skills to obtain or compromise information about an individual, organization or its computer systems.

For older expats, a fraudster might collect information from Facebook about a person's grandchildren or other family members and then pretend to be a grandchild, asking the grandparent to wire money for an emergency of some sort. Scammers will mention specific details such as names of the grandchild's actual friends, to make their story more believable.

Do not respond to a request for emergency funds until you have confirmed that the story is true. If your family member claims to be in jail, check with the jail to confirm that they are there. Some jails have the inmate population names and photos online in a searchable public database.

More recently, a new scam is phone calls from fraudsters claiming to be with the IRS or a state tax agency, telling the victim that unless funds are immediately wired to them, he/she will be immediately arrested.

These calls are always false – the IRS will never ask you to wire money to them, and if they were going to arrest you, they certainly wouldn't tell you in advance.

Be suspicious of unsolicited phone calls, visits, or e-mail messages from individuals asking about personal or financial information. Do not reveal any information, do not respond to solicitations, and do not click on links sent in e-mail.

"Disposable" E-Mail Addresses

Many times, you are asked for an e-mail address to access a website or sign up for a loyalty card, even if you will be using the service just once. If you don't want to receive endless amounts of marketing information, use a service such as 10minutemail.com, which will give you a functioning e-mail address for 10 or 20 minutes. When the time is up, the e-mail address self-destructs; 10minutemail claims to not retain any personal data.

> If you are registering for a website with your real email address, for a site where you will be logging in repeatedly, there is a way to track who is sharing your e-mail address.
>
> Type "+" before the @ symbol and add the website's name. For example, if you have a Yahoo account and your e-mail address is jsmith@yahoo.com, you would make it jsmith+amazon@yahoo.com. The mail server will ignore the part of the address after the plus sign and before the @domain name. You will then be able to see with whom Amazon is sharing your e-mail address.

Text Message Phishing

While many computer users are wary of phishing attempts via e-mail, they may not yet be as cautious about text message or WhatsApp phishing on a smart phone. Your phone is run on software just like any other computer and is also susceptible to being hijacked or encrypted and held for ransom. Be just as cautious when responding to text messages as you would with a suspicious e-mail. *If a bank is texting you, look up their customer support phone number independently and contact the bank to confirm the text message.*

The IRS will never text you, so you can **disregard any text message** claiming to be from the IRS and block the sender. Likewise, unless you are undergoing an audit and already dealing with a revenue agent or auditor, it is *very* unlikely that the IRS would call you.

Search Engine DuckDuckGo.com
*Canadian IT professional Tim Williams first told me about DuckDuckGo when I was living in Mexico several years ago. DuckDuckGo is a search engine that emphasizes protecting users' privacy and avoiding personalized search results; it does not profile its users and **shows all users the same search results** for a given search term. The search results are a combination of over 400 sources, including Yahoo! Search, Wolfram Alpha, Bing, Yandex and others. It does not store IP addresses or log user information, and uses cookies only when required.*

Insecure SMS Text Messages

As discussed in *Chapter 5, Keeping in Touch with the U.S.*, many banks, credit card companies, brokerage firms and online shopping sites use SMS text messages as part of two factor authentication (2FA) to prevent fraud. If you cannot receive SMS text messages, you may be denied access to your financial or shopping accounts.

However, SMS text messaging is not very secure. IT security expert Brian Krebs runs an IT security consulting business and online blog, www.krebsonsecurity.com.

In March 2021 Brian highlighted a fatal security flaw with SMS text messages. The flaw (known for years) involves transferring SMS services of a phone number (but not voice or data services) to a new carrier utilizing service providers that do not use the North American central registry for phone numbers.

This method does not involve more common fraud techniques such as sim swapping; unethical wholesale resellers only need sign a generic letter of authorization where they promise that any changes will be authorized by the user. *No notification to the user occurs, though – they just make the change.*

> *Brian's advice is (wherever possible) to remove phone numbers from your online accounts and avoid selecting SMS or phone calls for second factor or one-time codes. Some services **absolutely insist** on SMS text messaging, as insecure as that is. In that case, take advantage of a third-party app to generate one-time codes for multi-factor authentication (see below).*

Third Party Authenticator Apps (Two Factor Authentication)

For online financial institutions or shopping sites that *insist* on a U.S. phone number for SMS text messages as an identifier, you can use a third-party authenticator app such as **Authy, Google Authenticator** or **Microsoft Authenticator**.

The website must allow the optional use of an authenticator app, so not all websites will work with an authenticator app.

These apps generate a Time-based One Time Passcode (TOTP) within the app, which you then must enter. In effect, it's an app-based token generator.

You can use **Authy** with any account that uses **Google Authenticator**, such as Gmail, DropBox, Facebook and many more. Once **Authy** is installed on your device(s), even if an attacker executes a sim swap, he will not have access to the authentication code, which is generated on your device. Authy also has a desktop app.

The advantage to **Authy** over **Google Authenticator** is that is offers a secure cloud storage feature that permits you to back up all your encrypted 2FA tokens (from websites enrolled in the app). In the event that your phone is lost or stolen (or dies), you can reinstate your 2FA websites without having to manually and painfully restore 2FA authentication app-by-app as is required with **Google Authenticator**.

If you install **Authy** on more than one device (highly recommended), this will simplify the reinstatement process and make it more secure, because the second device will already be registered and available to use as identification verification.

If you want to know more about Authy, the company's website is www.authy.com. An explanation of the app is at their blog at https://authy.com/blog/understanding-2fa-the-authy-app-and-sms/. Authy's web site itself does not give a good explanation of the app.

Ironically, to install **Authy**, you must use SMS text messaging to receive the verification code, but this is a one-time event and once the app has been installed and configured, you will be more secure against SMS hijacking.

Microsoft Authenticator can be installed on multiple devices and synchronized across all of them, unlike Google Authenticator which only works with one device. Microsoft Authenticator has a backup feature similar to Authy's that makes moving to a new phone or device much easier.

If this entire subject has your head spinning, then let's move on to the next topic: Virtual Private Networks.

Virtual Private Networks (VPNs)

What the Heck is a VPN?
When you connect to the internet, there is a physical or wireless connection between your computer and the local network, which then has a (usually public) connection to the internet which terminates in another local network at the destination's computer.

A Virtual Private Network (VPN) bypasses these local, physical networks and the public internet "pipe" that carries the traffic and creates a private, secure virtual connection that goes end-to-end from the sending computer to the receiving computer. It uses existing internet connectivity but creates a virtual "pipe" of its own to carry traffic.

Why Should I Use a VPN?
Without going into too much detail, VPNs can change the apparent location of the users, sometimes multiple times. Websites such as Netflix or Amazon block known VPNs to prevent the circumvention of their geographic locations, as do some countries who wish to maintain a firewall for their citizens (i.e., China).

Additionally, a VPN can thwart online surveillance by internet service providers (ISPs), governments, hackers and cryptocurrency miners as well as help avoid internet speed throttling and potential legal hassles. Most VPNs are encrypted, but not all.

> *It's a good idea to use a VPN all the time on your **laptop, desktop, tablet and cell phone devices**. There are free VPNs but there is a trade-off: they sell your information to advertisers. In my opinion, it's worth paying money for a VPN. You needn't use something as expensive as ExpressVPN (about $100 a year) unless you're going to be streaming video content from Netflix or other video-on-demand providers such as Amazon Prime.*

Annual costs for a VPN range from $35 to $100 a year, depending upon what you need it to do. At the present time, the best VPN for streaming videos (Netflix, Amazon etc.) seems to be ExpressVPN, as many other VPNs are blocked by these content providers.

Look at online reviews of various VPNs from reputable websites such as cnet.com, pcmag.com, tomsguide.com or security.org and pick one that is recommended by them that fits your budget and expected use. See **Chapter 9, *Digital Entertainment, News & Sports Outside the U.S.***, for further discussion of VPNs relating to streaming video content.

Wi-Fi Security

Laptops, smart phones and other Wi-Fi enabled devices can connect automatically to familiar networks. While convenient, this can also be risky because hackers can set up a rogue Wi-Fi network with the same name as a legitimate one. This was demonstrated at the 2016 Democratic National Convention by reporters, who were able to access roughly *half* of the delegates' e-mails and text messages.

Periodically, make it a habit to remove networks that have been "saved" to your mobile device by going to the network or Wi-Fi settings and selecting 'delete.' This will require you to log in again to access the Wi-Fi network.

When using public Wi-Fi that does not require any authentication or log in (such as at a city park, coffee house, McDonald's or similar place), always use a VPN with your device. NEVER do any banking or financial transactions over a public Wi-Fi network.

If you decide to buy a household gadget connected to the internet (Ring doorbell, nanny monitor or security camera, etc.) be sure to change the default password to something unique that you have not used anywhere else. Mischievous hackers can wreak havoc on your household.

Defragging Your Hard Drive(s)

Over time your hard drive data can become fragmented, meaning that parts of files can be scattered across your hard drive. This slows down access to the file and can cause your computer to run more sluggishly over time. More importantly, in the case of a hard drive crash, fragmented data can be much harder or impossible to retrieve by a hard drive recovery service.

*If you have an SSD drive (solid state), you should **never** defrag it, because doing so will shorten the life of the drive. SSD drives have no moving parts and thus will not suffer much degradation in performance from fragmentation, but do have a finite number of "writes" of data to them.*

It is a good idea to defrag your old-fashioned "spinning" hard drive periodically to get fragmented file parts physically relocated adjacent to each other on your hard drive. Defragging does not change the *reference* to the location of the file (it will still be in the same folder or directory where you saved it) but only moves file fragments so that they are written adjacent to one another on the physical drive. Think of it as flossing your teeth for your hard drive.

All versions of Microsoft Windows come with a built-in defrag utility, but there are superior third-party products on the market, many of them free. Check online reviews for the latest reviews and recommendations.

Online Privacy

Why should we care about online privacy?
Privacy isn't about having something to hide, it's about protecting who *you* are and the right to the self, about letting *you* decide what to reveal to the world about who you are on your own terms.

As Edward Snowden the NSA leaker pointed out, Nazi propaganda minister Josef Goebbels was the originator of the "if you have nothing to hide, you have nothing to fear" argument. ***No system of mass surveillance throughout human history has ever existed without being abused; it's just human nature.***

Privacy is about *you* deciding whether some corporation can sell your personal information to make money. There was a famous incident a number of years ago about a national drugstore chain that harvested social media information to send targeted marketing to its customers.

It sent advertising to a teen-ager about pregnancy-related products as well as coupons for diapers and formula. The irate parents complained to the drugstore chain only to find out that their underage daughter was indeed pregnant and that this large corporation knew about it before they did.

*A **personal observation**: more and more websites seem to be encouraging you to log in to access their content using Google, Facebook, Twitter etc. user credentials rather than creating a unique user ID and password for that site. While this may be convenient for you, it also grants the third-party website access to information sharing with Google, Facebook et al. Not a good idea. Create a unique user ID and password*

> *for each site and **never use** Google or social media credentials to log into sites.*

There are plenty of online articles and videos about online privacy and security, from U.S. newspapers such as the New York Times to tech publications such as PC Magazine, CNET etc. Just do an online search; there's no shortage of information.

> *Most web browsers have an Incognito setting that can be used without cookies that makes it more difficult for web sites to track you. Some news websites limit the number of visits per month for non-subscribers; you may be able to read additional articles using the incognito setting (although some will not permit you to view content in incognito mode).*

What Can I Do to Protect my Online Privacy?

There are a number of online resources that can walk you through steps that you can take. The information presented here may seem a bit overwhelming, and nothing is obligatory, but you might want to take a look to see exactly what steps you can take. Several suggested online sites with pro-privacy advice are below.

Techlore Privacy Videos

One reputable source that focuses on online privacy is Techlore, a company that was founded by an IT expert who grew concerned about privacy abuses he saw in his Big Tech job.

Techlore offers a very good YouTube video, *The Ultimate Guide to Privacy, Security and Anonymity*, on YouTube (about half an hour) that walks you through three levels of security with the steps you as an individual can take to reduce your exposure to Big Tech, hackers and others: https://www.youtube.com/watch?v=a1i-3xwcSGA

The Techlore website offers further information and videos and is at: https://techlore.tech/index.html

Chapter 12
Identity Theft & Medical Billing Problems

General Tips to Protect Identity Information
Steps to Take before You Leave the U.S.
Online Data Breaches
Credit Bureau Breaches
Medical Identity Theft
Medical Billing Errors
Income Tax Return Fraud
What to do if You're a Victim of Identity Theft
Identity Theft Insurance

P reventing identity theft and credit problems is doubly important for expats, since it may be more difficult to resolve issues due to distance. Identity theft is now the fastest-growing financial crime in the U.S.

Identity theft occurs when someone steals your personal identifying information and takes out a mortgage or credit cards in your name, or runs up medical bills in your name.

You don't want to be cut off from your bank or brokerage accounts, credit cards, ATM cards or other sources of funds while living overseas.

General Tips to Protect Identity Information

- Permanently freeze your credit bureau files as soon as you have decided to move abroad, preferably at least 60 days in advance of your move. See the section below for more on this.

- Treat any e-mail received from a bank, IRS/state tax agency, brokerage firm, business or charity as potentially fraudulent. If they are asking you to take a particular action, contact the sender using independently verified contact information, ***not the contact information contained in the e-mail***.

- Never respond to requests for your personal information or account number by clicking on a link. Instead, contact the originator (***look up the contact information independently***) and inquire whether there is an issue.

- Develop the habit of reviewing your credit file from one of the three principal credit bureaus every four months; you are entitled by law to one free report each year. See more about this below under *What About Credit Monitoring Services?*

- Report possible online crime or fraud, such as fraudulent emails pretending to be from a bank or get-rich-quick schemes, to the Internet Crime Complaint Center, www.ic3.gov/complaint.

Steps to Take Before You Leave the U.S.

Opt Out of Unsolicited or Pre-Approved Credit Offers
At least 60 days before you leave the U.S. (as far as in advance if you can), sign up for permanent opt out of credit offers from the three main U.S. credit bureaus. Call 1-888-5-OPT OUT or visit https://www.optoutprescreen.com to stop receiving pre-approved credit card applications.

Cut Down on Junk Mail
Contact the Direct Marketing Association at www.dmachoice.org and request to be put on their "do not mail" list. While most reputable marketers will abide by this request, the sleazy or fraudulent ones will likely ignore it. However, it is still worthwhile to do.

If a company ignores your "do not mail" request, you can file a complaint online with the Better Business Bureau, which may have some effect if they care about their reputation.

Offers from Companies with Whom You Are a Customer

While you cannot compel companies with whom you are a customer to stop sending you pre-approved offers, you can formally request that they NOT send you marketing materials or pre-approved offers.

Tell them that continuing to send you unsolicited or pre-approved offers poses a risk to their business and your financial safety. They may or may not honor your request; there is not a lot you can legally do if they ignore your request, other than evaluate whether you want to continue to be their customer. Protest with a complaint letter in any event if they insist on sending you pre-approved offers.

Online Data Breaches

Almost every day there seems to be a new data breach reported in the news. Data breaches represent the threat that the information obtained could be sold on the "dark web" to bad actors to use in obtaining credit in your name.

There are two basic types of online data breaches nowadays:

(1) Breaches by foreign government actors that seem to be more focused on collecting information about U.S. government operations and U.S. corporations, that could be used to blackmail persons with top secret security clearances or gain a national economic advantage; or

(2) Breaches by organized criminal IT hackers, who extort money from victims or commit financial crimes by impersonating victims, always with the goal of earning money from such activities.

The first type of breach is quite serious, but for the average individual the second type of breach probably poses more of an immediate personal threat. If you keep all your computer files backed up, you won't have to pay a ransom. You can exercise the "nuclear option" and simply wipe everything off your computer and start over.

There is a free online resource for anyone to check if their email address or phone number is possibly being circulated by bad actors due to an online account having been compromised or "pwned" in a data breach: **www.haveibeenpwned.com**.

This site is entirely free to search so as to benefit as many people as possible. A Microsoft security professional, Troy Hunt, created the site in his spare time as a public service. Enter your e-mail address or user ID and see if anything pops up. You can also sign up for notifications if your e-mail address turns up later. I myself was just recently notified by this website that my email address was included in a site that was breached.

Credit Bureau Breaches

The U.S. is a society where pretty much your whole life history is contained in credit bureaus – your date of birth, your Social Security number, where you were born, everywhere you've ever lived, where you've worked, your salary or hourly pay, close relatives, which credit cards you have, available lines of credit, car loans, mortgages, the value of your house, the amount of rent you pay, evictions or foreclosures, any legal judgments against you, it goes on and on. The more the bad guys know about a victim, the easier it is for them to impersonate you.

The worst part of this is that you cannot opt out of credit bureaus; we consumers never agreed to share this information with them but have no voice in the matter. We are not the customers of the credit bureaus, we are the **product** that they sell – the information about us (just like Facebook). So when this information is breached, it puts your whole financial life at risk.

The U.S. has three principal credit bureaus (there are additional smaller ones):

- Equifax
- Experian
- TransUnion

Criminals can use the information contained in your credit file to obtain loans, credit cards and mortgages or to open bank accounts in your name without your knowledge, which will then be used to commit fraud.

In September 2017, Equifax announced that the information of over 147 million people in the U.S. had been compromised in a breach that occurred between May and July of 2017 via a website vulnerability. Among the information stolen was name, date of birth, Social Security number, home addresses, driver's license numbers with state and date of issuance, and tax ID numbers.

The company admitted that it was informed in **March 2017** that hackers could exploit a vulnerability in its system but failed to apply the necessary security patches.

Experian had its own smaller hack involving 15 million customers of T-Mobile in a breach that occurred between September 2013 and September 2015.

Freeze Your Credit Bureau Record

I recommend that you *freeze* your credit files with all three major credit bureaus (Experian, Equifax and TransUnion). Freezing your file stops most potential creditors from accessing your file, which is what happens when you (or a fraudster) apply for credit. Because this hinders the granting of credit, the credit bureaus don't want you to do a freeze. I say, *too damn bad*. They're the ones who let themselves get hacked.

> *If you haven't already done so, go to the Social Security Administration's website and create an online Social Security account before you freeze your credit bureau record. See **Chapter 7, Banking & Finances**, for further information.*

When a freeze is in effect, consumers can still access their own information using a special PIN code. Thieves and other companies who make pre-approved credit offers will not be able to access your file.

You will need to unfreeze your credit report when applying for a loan or a credit card, but you can replace the freeze after you have obtained the credit line. Unfreezing may incur a small fee.

> *Apply for any additional loans or credit cards that you'd like to have before you freeze your credit file and move abroad. You can still apply later, but it will be more of a hassle.*

There are **permanent** or **temporary** credit file freezes. Consider putting a **permanent** freeze on your credit file before you leave the U.S. You can do a five-year temporary freeze online (which of course the credit bureaus prefer), but a permanent freeze with a PIN to unlock the freeze has to be done by mail to your current address of record and takes some time to implement.

Once you request the permanent freeze online, the credit bureaus will send paperwork to your address for you to sign and return. When I requested a permanent freeze online **six months** before I left the U.S., I did not receive any paperwork in the mail to sign and return (even though the credit reporting agency must comply with a request within five business days). My suspicion is that they "forgot" to process my request because they dislike freezing credit files. I had to follow up to get them to do it!

> *Note: If you have both a P.O. Box and a street address, request a credit freeze for both addresses.*

Information on how to do this is available at each of the three companies' web sites. **Do this before you leave the U.S.** You will be given a PIN number, which you do not want to lose. In order to access or unfreeze your file, you will need the PIN number, **so keep it in a safe place**.

Change of Address for the Credit Bureaus
You would think that a company whose entire business consists of updating your credit file with information regularly received from creditors would automatically update your address when notified by creditors, wouldn't you? Well, guess again.

Not long ago I found out that Experian still had my address from *six years ago* on file and had failed to update it, although they could see the address that creditors were reporting to them. In order to update it, I am supposed to send them via fax a photocopy of my driver's license with the new address on it, a photocopy of my Social Security card, and photocopy a piece of mail with the new address on it, along with a letter requesting the change. ***Seriously?***

When I did my change of address notifications, it never dawned on me that credit bureaus would be too stupid to update my address.

What about Credit Monitoring Services?

Credit monitoring services are commercial services that you can sign up for that will alert you about activity posted to your credit file at the three credit bureaus.

The main drawback to credit monitoring is if something problematic turns up in your file, Elvis has already left the building and the event, whatever it is, has already occurred. It's better than not knowing at all, but preventing such things is better.

Note that due to various class action lawsuits, the larger credit bureaus under the terms of the settlements have agreed to offer free credit monitoring to class members (basically anyone with a credit file) for one or two years. You are likely eligible for free credit monitoring for some period of time. Check into it.

Credit monitoring services such as LifeLock, IdentityGuard, PrivacyGuard, myFICO and others generally cost from $100 to $150 a year. It's your choice. If you will sleep better having one of these services and aren't eligible for free, limited term monitoring, then do it.

A free alternative, if you will be disciplined about doing it, is to obtain a free credit report from each of the three big credit bureaus. ***Avoid*** *the website that charges you, www.freecreditreport.com, and go to the government website,* ***https://www.annualcreditreport.com,*** *instead. You can obtain one free report each 12 months, so by spacing your requests four months apart, you can cover all three bureaus in a year.*

Medical Identity Theft

This is a newer sort of identity theft, but it's becoming all too common. If someone is able to get ahold of your health insurance or Medicare ID card and can learn your date of birth, assuming that they're the same sex as you and near you in age, they can impersonate you to receive health care benefits. Low-paid medical billing clerks sell this information for $20 to criminal networks.

The problem with medical identity theft is that you can end up being dunned for bills run up by someone who used your identity to access health care. Additionally, medical information for someone else will now be in your medical record, which could endanger proper treatment for you. Unfortunately, there is no central "fraud alert" that can be placed on a medical file.

Scammers may also call you, spoofing the telephone number of a hospital, demanding payment or bank account information. Call the hospital back by looking up the number independently to confirm that the call is legitimate.

If you will continue to have U.S. public or private health insurance coverage while living abroad, definitely be on the alert for someone using your name to access health care. It's become a big business.

> *Look at all Explanation of Benefits reports you receive from your health insurance company; if you don't recognize a service or a provider's name, it could be a sign of medical identity theft.*

Your personal information held by medical practices is a prime target for identity theft thieves, who also target payroll departments. Once a thief has your Social Security number and date of birth, he or she can do a whole lot of damage to your credit rating, not to mention your stress level.

Medical Billing Errors

Medical billing may not occur to you as a topic to worry about as you're planning to move out of the country, but it can cause a lot of aggravation and stress. I'm including this as an issue because of personal experience.

Medical billing is notoriously error-ridden. It seems to me that more and more billing offices don't know what they are doing. If the service is billed correctly to begin with (not always a given), the insurance company may incorrectly process the claim, or the medical provider's billing office may incorrectly handle the insurance company payment and bill you for a balance that you do not owe. In any event, you need to follow up promptly and correct all errors.

The problem is that an incompetent billing clerk may cover up his/her incompetence by simply not billing something (it's called suppress billing) until someone higher up catches on, which can be one or more years later. It is a nightmare for anyone to deal with, but doubly so if you are living outside the U.S.

You need to be very vigilant about medical bills.

What I'm going to recommend may seem a little extreme to you, but given all the problems connected to medical billing and debt, prevention (or at least early detection) of medical billing problems is your goal when moving overseas.

Here is my recommendation:

Well before you leave the U.S., contact every single medical provider that you have visited in the past 18 months (two years if you really want to be thorough) and get confirmation in writing that you have no outstanding balances payable with them. Dentists, doctors, chiropractors, optometrists, labs, imaging centers, hospitals – make a list and contact them all.

Don't believe this is necessary? Among the **actual experiences** that I myself have had include the following:

- I had a doctor's office bill my insurance for an office visit *a year and a half* after the visit. Of course, the insurance company refused to pay it, as claims for service must be submitted within one year as required by the contract with the insurance company signed by the doctor. The insurance company's Explanation of Benefits (EOB) indicated that I was not responsible for the bill. I thought to myself, *"Oh well, that's their problem – they didn't bill my insurance within the required time frame."*

When the doctor's office billed me the entire amount (in violation of their contract with the insurance company), I refused to pay it, saying that if they had billed the insurance company in a timely manner, they would have been paid (I had already paid my cost share portion). The doctor's office actually sent my outstanding bill to a collections agency *two years* after the date of service!

I tried to get a copy of the Explanation of Benefits from the insurance company for this doctor's office visit, since I had foolishly not kept the EOB when I received it. I spent *weeks* trying to get a copy of the EOB from the insurance company without success – I could never get anyone at the insurance company to send me a copy because it was so old.

When the doctor's office sent my bill to collections, I was absolutely livid and threatened to take the medical practice to small claims court. Without the EOB from the insurance company, it would be difficult to prove that I did not owe the amount billed. Since I was working full time, I would have had to take an entire day off of work. I ultimately ended up paying the claim out of pocket, but not without a very angry letter to the doctor.

> **Keep all of your Explanation of Benefits from insurance companies.** *Digitize them, scan them into your computer and keep for future reference – you never know when you might need one. Shred the paper EOBs since they contain confidential information.*

- I received a bill from my podiatrist for services from **15 months earlier**, never having received anything in the interim, for custom-fitted orthotics that had to be sent back multiple times to be re-worked. The doctor told me that because of all the problems with the new supplier, he would only charge me half the usual price, which I paid at the time that the orthotics were given to me. But this never got communicated to the billing clerk. Result: a $250 bill 15 months later. Seriously?

- A clinical laboratory sent me a bill for $1,200 for allergy tests. They had billed my insurance, which had sent them payment and an EOB, which the billing clerk did not understand and ignored. I literally had to do this billing clerk's job and entered over 40 individual charges for services into a spreadsheet, showing the amount billed, the amount the insurance paid, the contractual adjustment, and the patient's remaining balance. The correct patient balance due was under $100, which I paid along with a letter to the laboratory and the spreadsheet. I never went to that clinical laboratory again.

- Avoid paying with cash for an insurance co-pay and always get a receipt from the medical office for a co-pay. Cash payments in doctor's offices have a way of "disappearing" into the pockets of staff; you will then be billed a second time for the co-pay that you've already paid. It's always an innocent billing "mistake" when the co-pay doesn't get credited to your account. Pay by credit card if possible, so there will be a record of the payment.

- Over **two years** after I left the U.S., a primary care practice in the U.S. sent me a check for $60 to refund co-payments that apparently were collected in error. I couldn't remember exactly what the issue was about, and wasn't going to expend a lot of effort in figuring it out. But here I was abroad with a damn paper check.

This sort of crap happens all the time. And this is just *my own personal experience* dealing with medical bills – I have never had any serious medical conditions. It can be a nightmare.

The danger to you as an expat is that sometimes these problems do not surface until one, two, three years afterwards, when you will be living overseas. You ask, *"What do I care? I'll be overseas."* Wrong. As long as you have bank accounts or other assets in the U.S., the creditor (the medical provider) could take you to collections or sue you.

Many debtors don't receive proper notice of legal action, and when they don't appear for the court hearing, the creditor gets a default judgment and can garnish a bank account or income stream. Most courts just rubber stamp whatever the creditor tells them. The horror stories are legion.

Even if they aren't successful in collecting the debt, there will be a black mark on your credit report. This may affect your future ability to rent a house or apartment or obtain employment in the U.S.

Don't let that happen to you!

Income Tax Return Fraud

One of the most popular uses for stolen identification data from credit bureaus is to file false income tax returns with the Internal Revenue

Service before you file your own return and claim inflated refunds. You then are left to deal with the aftermath of the identity theft plus the massive headache of dealing with the IRS. *If possible, file your income tax return as early as possible each filing season*.

The IRS now allows any taxpayer to request a sig-digit PIN that will be required in order to file a tax return with the IRS, using the online "Get IP PIN" tool. Once the IRS has issued a PIN for that year, its use will be required to file a return.

Previously this option was only available to those who had been victims of identity theft. **Each PIN is good only for the tax year for which it was issued.** The IRS will mail you a new IP PIN via snail mail each January once you are enrolled in the program.

The signup process requires you to validate your identity with a series of questions and will send a text code to a mobile phone in your name; *it will reject any VOIP-based numbers such as those tied to Skype or Google Voice*. If you are unable to receive the text code, the site will offer to send an activation code via postal mail to your address of record.

If you are unable to complete the identity validation process online, your income is $73,000 or less (married filing jointly $146,000 or less), and you have a valid Social Security number and access to a telephone, you can fill out Form 15227, Application for an Identity Protection Personal Identification Number (IP PIN) and mail it to the IRS.

Go to www.irs.gov and search for "Get IP PIN" for further details.

What to do if You're a Victim of Identity Theft

Dealing with the aftermath of identity theft is bad enough for someone in the U.S. For an expat living abroad, it's even more difficult. Not only will it cost more money to clean up the theft, you may be required to return to the U.S. for things that must be done in person. It's best to try to prevent identity theft in the first place.

For all of the below steps, keep careful records of whom you spoke with (names, dates and phone numbers) and copies of correspondence and documentation that you send to each person or organization. From the U.S., it's advisable to send correspondence certified mail, return receipt requested in order to prove that you mailed correspondence and documents. From abroad, using a registered delivery service such as DHL or FedEx is best.

- Start with notifying the companies where fraud has occurred, ask them to close or freeze the account, and change all logins, passwords and PINs. Place a fraud alert with all three credit bureaus and obtain copies of your credit reports; look for unauthorized accounts or abnormal activity.

- File an online complaint with the Federal Trade Commission at their identity theft website (https://www.identitytheft.gov). Create an online account with the FTC's identity theft website, which will enable you to create and update a **recovery plan**. The personalized plan will walk you through the steps of notifying all involved parties. You will be able to create pre-filled form letters to send to creditors and track your progress in resolving the identity theft.

- Close new accounts fraudulently opened in your name, remove bogus charges from your accounts, correct your credit report, institute a credit freeze or extended fraud alert, and review your credit reports frequently.

- Review your online Social Security earnings history to see if someone has used your SSN for wage reporting. Report a misused Social Security number with the Social Security Administration (in rare cases, you may be able to get a new SSN assigned to you).

- Stop debt collectors from trying to collect debts that you do not owe; contact the debt collector promptly and give them a copy of your identity theft report obtained from the FTC.

- Contact businesses with fraudulent accounts and explain that this is not your debt, ask them to stop reporting it to the credit bureaus, and ask for information about the debt and how it happened. You can use a sample letter from the FTC's website.

- Replace any stolen identification such as driver's licenses, passports or Social Security cards. Replacing a driver's license may involve a trip to the U.S.

- If you think that the identity thief might have opened accounts with cell phone, land line or utility companies (cable, electricity, water etc.), contact the National Consumer Telecom and Utilities Exchange (www.nctue.com). Request your NCTUE Data Report, which is a record of all telecommunication, pay TV and utility accounts in your name reported by member companies. It contains information about your account history, unpaid accounts, and customer service applications. Review it for any accounts you don't recognize.

- For fraudulent apartment or house rentals, contact the landlord who rented the property to the identity thief and ask them what tenant history services they use. Contact those companies, ask for a copy of your tenant history report, and ask what steps you need to take to correct fraudulent information in the report.

- For government benefits, contact the agency that issued the benefit and explain that someone stole your identity. Ask what you need to do to fix the problem and get benefits reinstated.

  You may need to appear in person or send written correspondence.

- If someone has opened a checking account in your name, obtain a free copy of your ChexSystems report, which compiles information about your checking account(s) nationwide (https://www.chexsystems.com and select 'Identity Theft'). Contact every financial institution where a fraudulent checking account was opened, report the fraud, and ask them to close the account. Place a security alert on your ChexSystems consumer file.

- For investment accounts, contact the broker or account manager and inform them of the identity theft and have a fraud alert placed on the accounts. You may need to close the accounts and open new ones. Change all login IDs, passwords and PINs.

- For fraudulent income tax returns, contact the IRS and complete Form 14039, IRS Identity Theft Affidavit. File and complete income tax returns. Request an identity theft PIN that will be used with all future income tax return filings. If you are unable to resolve your situation satisfactorily, contact the IRS's Taxpayer Ombudsman, which is an independent office within the IRS that assists taxpayers who have been unable to resolve problems through regular channels.

- For medical identity theft, get copies of your medical records from doctors, clinics, hospitals, pharmacies, laboratories and health plans where the thief may have used your identity. Review your medical records and report any errors to the provider with a copy of your FTC Identity Theft Report. Review insurance Explanation of Benefits (EOB) reports for any unfamiliar services and contact the insurance company.

There may be additional steps needed for child identity theft, student loan theft or a bankruptcy fraudulently filed in your name. Go to the FTC's identity theft website listed above for further information.

All of the above is definitely a lot of work and will take time to pursue. There are identity theft insurance products on the market to help with this situation.

Identity Theft Insurance

Companies selling Identity theft insurance usually offer three services: monitoring of credit bureau activity, alerts when there is such activity, and help in recovery due to identity theft. Depending upon the product, identity theft insurance may or may not reimburse you for funds stolen from a bank account or investment account, however.

> *Note that the most important thing a consumer can do is **permanently** freeze his/her consumer credit file at the three principal credit bureaus. You can do monitoring yourself if you are disciplined enough to remember to request a free annual report every four months between the three bureaus. Knowing your legal rights is more important than having identity theft insurance. Prevention is better than dealing with the aftermath.*

What's the Difference Between Identity Theft Insurance and Credit Monitoring?

Identity theft insurance differs from plain credit bureau file monitoring in that it may offer additional benefits such as reimbursing you for time off from your job, costs of certified mailing, court appearances, legal assistance, consultations with identity theft experts, scans of social media posts for reputational risk, health insurance fraud alerts, notary fees, public record searches, and monitoring of black-market chat rooms and "dark web" sites.

Options for Purchasing Identity Theft Insurance

You can obtain identity theft insurance from companies that sell standalone products or from the credit bureaus themselves for this service. The standalone products tend to be more expensive than simple credit file monitoring, and depending upon the extent of coverage can cost from $18 to $35 **per month** and may cover up to $1 million in losses.

If you have a U.S. property or renter's insurance policy, you can usually add on an identity theft rider for $35-$75 a year; this coverage will not reimburse you for actual losses from fraudulent activity in loans, bank, investment or credit card accounts but may pay for other expenses.

Websites such as Consumer Reports (www.consumerreports.org), Nerd Wallet (www.nerdwallet.com) or Credit Karma (www.creditkarma.com) have articles that go into further detail about the pros and cons of identity theft insurance.

Chapter 13
U.S. Federal Income Taxes

Mechanisms to Alleviate Double Taxation
Foreign Earned Income Exclusion
Foreign Tax Credit
Self-Employment Tax – Social Security & Medicare
Preparing & Filing Your U.S. Federal Income Tax Return from Abroad
Reporting of Foreign Bank Accounts & Financial Assets
Other IRS Reporting – U.S. Owners of Foreign Companies

This isn't most people's favorite topic, but it is an important one. Many expats don't realize that the U.S. taxes its citizens and residents on their *worldwide* income, not just the income earned in the U.S. Our Internal Revenue Code can trip up anyone, it is so arcane and complicated.

While we all sometimes feel like making the IRS our whipping boy, understand that it's the *U.S. Congress* that drafts all income taxation laws; the IRS just administers the laws that Congress passes. Direct your ire at Congress.

For U.S. citizens or permanent residents, just because we're living overseas doesn't mean that Uncle Sammy doesn't still want to hear from us every year by June 15th (overseas residents get an extra 60 days to file).

> *When doing your change of address notifications, be sure to include the IRS; send them **Form 8822, Change of Address**, when you know your new (preferably U.S.) mailing address.*

If you've kept your legal domicile in a state with an income tax, it's probably a good idea to file a resident tax return with **that state** every year, too. See **Chapter 14, State Income Taxation, Driver's Licenses & Registering to Vote**, for an explanation of the difference between *residency* and *domicile* and other important information.

> *If this whole topic gives you the heebie-jeebies and overwhelms you, then let a professional income tax return preparer who specializes in expat returns deal with preparing and filing your return. You should however have a basic understanding of how the process works. See **Chapter 18, Further Resources**, for a list of potential tax return preparers who specialize in expat returns.*

Another reason not to ignore your federal income taxes: the **Fixing America's Surface Transportation (FAST) Act of 2015** authorizes the IRS to request the U.S. State Department to revoke or deny renewal of U.S. passports if there is outstanding unresolved, legally enforceable federal tax debt (including penalties and interest) of at least $53,000. *Your U.S. passport could be at risk if you accumulate a substantial tax debt.*

Note: even if you acquire citizenship in another country, as long as you are a U.S. citizen or resident, you are subject to U.S. taxation until you renounce your citizenship.

Mechanisms to Alleviate Double Taxation of U.S. Citizens and Residents

Because of the U.S.'s *worldwide* income tax scheme, foreign source income may be taxed twice – once by the country where it is earned and again by the U.S. There are several long-standing provisions to lessen or eliminate being taxed twice on the same income. The two principal mechanisms are the **foreign earned income exclusion** (FEIE) and the **foreign tax credit** (FTC).

> The **foreign earned income exclusion** *allows you to exclude in 2022 up to $112,000 of earned income (**the amount changes each year**). Earned income means income from services rendered – salaries, wages, self-employment income, etc.*
>
> The **foreign tax credit** *reduces your federal income tax dollar-for-dollar, but only up to your U.S. federal income tax liability on the same income. If the foreign taxes are greater than the U.S. federal income tax imposed on the same income, the credit is limited to the U.S. income tax.*

Foreign Earned Income Exclusion (FEIE)

The foreign earned income exclusion (Internal Revenue Code Section 911) lets you exclude certain income earned from the performance of services while physically outside the U.S. from your U.S. gross income. Examples are salaries and wages, commissions, bonuses, professional fees, self-employment income, active business profits (from services performed outside the U.S.) and tips.

Earned income *does not include* things such as interest, dividends, capital gains, most types of rental income, passive business income where you did not furnish any services, alimony, Social Security benefits, pensions or annuities.

Note that not all U.S. states recognize the foreign earned income exclusion, California and New York being among the most prominent examples.

The foreign earned income exclusion is claimed on **IRS Form 2555, Foreign Earned Income** (part of the Form 1040 tax return) and is elective - you are not required to claim it. You are entitled to elect either the foreign earned income exclusion or the foreign tax credit; you cannot take both *on the same income.*

You can, however, take a foreign tax credit on income *exceeding* the maximum foreign earned income exclusion (i.e., income not excluded from U.S. income tax) that was subject to foreign income tax.

> Note that you **must file a tax return to claim the foreign earned income exclusion**. Many expats mistakenly believe that because their foreign earned income can be excluded, that they don't need to file a tax return because they won't owe any tax after applying the exclusion. This is a serious error, because you really won't know whether you owe tax or not until you go through all the (convoluted) calculations.

To qualify for the foreign earned income exclusion, you must meet one of two tests: the **bona fide resident test** or the **physical presence test**. Even if you meet *both* of these tests, it's important that you **use only one** on your tax return.

If you fill out Form 2555 incorrectly with *both* of these parts filled out, the form will be rejected and you will get a notice from the IRS disallowing your foreign earned income exclusion *in its entirety* and assessing interest and penalties. ***Claim only one of the two tests***.

Option 1: the Bona Fide Resident Test (FEIE)

If you can meet its requirements, the bona fide resident test is better to use, because it gives you more flexibility to spend time in the U.S.

To quote from the IRS:

> "To qualify for bona fide residence, you must reside in a foreign country for an uninterrupted period that includes an entire tax year. An entire tax year is from January 1 through December 31 for taxpayers who file their income tax returns on a calendar year basis. During the period of bona fide residence in a foreign country, you can leave the country for brief or temporary trips back to the United States or elsewhere for vacation or business.
>
> Once you establish bona fide residency in a foreign country for an uninterrupted period that includes an entire tax year, you will qualify as a bona fide resident starting with the date you began the residency and ending with the date you abandon your foreign residence. This means you could qualify as a bona fide resident for parts of one or two other tax years in addition to the full tax year(s) of bona fide residency."

The **bona fide resident test** is a facts-and-circumstances test. *You do not automatically acquire bona fide resident status merely by living in a foreign country or countries for one year.*

Can I Qualify if I'm Working Abroad Under a Contract for a Specified Time Period?
No. If you go to a foreign country to work on a contract for a specified period of time (even if it ends up being extended repeatedly) *you will not qualify* as a bona fide resident because the specified term of the contract is regarded as proof that you have no intention of remaining in the country indefinitely as a bona fide resident.

What if I Purchase a House Abroad? If I Rent? If I Live in a Hotel?
If you purchase a house in the foreign country, that is a strong indicator of bona fide residency. Renting your housing is better than residing in a hotel or employer compound. If your spouse and children reside with you in the foreign country, that too is a factor in your favor.

> *Note: You will not be regarded as a bona fide resident of a foreign country if you make a statement to the foreign authorities that you are not a resident of that country and the authorities have determined that you are not subject to their income tax laws as a resident.*

Can I use the bona fide resident test with a tourist visa?
No. *Form 2555, Foreign Earned Income* in Part II, the Bona Fide Residence questions ask what type of visa under which you entered the country and whether the visa limits the length of stay or employment in the country. Tourist visas do not allow you to do any kind of work for remuneration and almost always limit your length of stay; **you are not a resident**.

Mexico, for example, lets Americans or Canadians enter on a tourist visa for 180 days; many Americans or Canadians reside indefinitely in Mexico on a tourist visa, never getting temporary or permanent residency. Every 180 days or so they leave the country and then re-enter to start the clock running again.

Option 2: the Physical Presence Test (FEIE)

The other test that will qualify you for the foreign earned income exclusion is the physical presence test. You need to be *physically present* in a foreign country *or countries* **330 full days** during any period of 12 consecutive months including some part of the year at issue.

The 330 qualifying days do not have to be consecutive. This test does not depend on the kind of residence you establish, the type of visa (tourist visa is OK), your intentions about returning to the United States, or the nature and purpose of your stay abroad.

There are complicated rules on how to count travel days to and from the U.S. or over international waters; being outside the U.S. does not necessarily equal being present in a foreign country. **IRS Publication 54 - Tax Guide for U.S. Citizens and Resident Aliens Abroad** has more information on how to calculate travel days.

You will not meet the physical presence test if you are not present in a foreign country or countries for at least 330 days during a twelve-month period *regardless of the reason*, including illness, family problems, your flight out of the U.S. being cancelled, or your employer's orders.

In some special circumstances such as wars or natural disasters (or a coronavirus pandemic), the IRS may announce exceptions to the 330-day rule for specified locations.

Can I use the physical presence test with a tourist visa?

Yes – with a caveat. Let's say that you are a free-roaming remote worker or digital nomad who works from different countries using tourist visas throughout the year. You could meet the requirements for the physical presence test, as long as you were careful to limit travel to the U.S. or over international waters. And for the physical presence test, **Form 2555, Foreign Earned Income**, doesn't ask about the type of visa.

This treatment could still *possibly* result in complications because of tax information-sharing between the U.S. and other countries. Close to 60 countries have an information-sharing agreement with the U.S.

What if one of them (say Germany) requested a list of every U.S. taxpayer who claimed the foreign earned income exclusion for income earned in that foreign country -- you then might face some unpleasantness for having worked in the country on a tourist visa.

It is true that many countries won't get too excited about you working remotely via internet for an employer located outside of their country, even on a tourist visa, as long as you're not taking a job away from a local. It's your call.

Foreign Housing Exclusion/Deduction - FEIE

If you qualify for the foreign earned income exclusion under either the bona fide residence test or the physical presence test, there are additional benefits relating to foreign housing.

There are separate calculations for employees versus self-employed persons. The foreign housing allowance for employees is an additional exclusion from income, whereas for self employed persons it is an additional deduction from self-employment income.

The calculations can get complicated and there are special calculations for high-cost locations. IRS Worksheets for Form 2555 will walk you through these calculations, or you can utilize tax preparation software.

Foreign Tax Credit (FTC)

Uncle Sam allows you to elect a foreign tax credit instead of the foreign earned income exclusion, if it is more beneficial. The foreign tax credit is a dollar-for-dollar reduction of your U.S. federal income tax liability.

The foreign taxes paid must be *income taxes*; other types of foreign taxes, such as Social Security taxes, net wealth taxes, sales taxes, value-added taxes, or gross receipts taxes are not creditable because they are not *taxes on net income*. A country's withholding tax on capital exiting the country, for example, would not qualify for the foreign tax credit because it is not a tax measured by income.

Foreign tax credits are claimed on **IRS Form 1116, Foreign Tax Credit (Individual, Estate or Trust).** You cannot take a credit for foreign taxes that are:

- deducted on your U.S. income tax return (if you itemize deductions) or

- paid on foreign earned income that was *excluded from your U.S. gross income*

The only time you can claim both the FEIE and the FTC (for earned income) on the same return is if your foreign earned income is higher than the exclusion limit (for 2022 $112,000).

For example, let's say you have $250,000 of foreign earned income (I wish!). You can exclude the first $112,000, and then for the remainder you can claim the foreign tax credit after some calculations on Form 1116. *You won't be able to claim any foreign tax credit or deduction for the* **excluded** *foreign earned income.*

If you have local (foreign) bank accounts, check to see if there is local income tax withholding at source on the interest income. You may be able to claim a foreign tax credit on your U.S. income tax return for the foreign income tax withheld. This is a separate calculation from claiming a foreign tax credit for foreign taxes paid on earned income.

Which method is better – Foreign Tax Credit or FEIE?
As a rule of thumb (there are always exceptions), it's more beneficial to claim the foreign earned income exclusion if the local income tax rate is **lower** than what you are subject to in the U.S. (or zero); if the local income tax rate is **higher** than your U.S. tax rate, then the foreign tax credit may be more beneficial. Do the calculations both ways.

Restrictions on Switching Between Methods
If you elect to exclude your foreign earned income (FEIE), the election remains in effect for all subsequent years until revoked. If one year you take a credit for foreign taxes paid on earned income instead of excluding foreign earned income, the election to exclude foreign earned income will be considered revoked and unavailable for the next five years.

You attach a statement to your return stating that you wish to revoke the election to exclude foreign earned income. *If within the next five years, you wish to re-elect the foreign earned income exclusion, you must apply to the IRS for approval via a private letter ruling, which involves significant expense and time.*

Check to see if there is an income tax treaty between your foreign country of residence and the U.S., as there may be additional benefits that you could be entitled to as a U.S. citizen residing in the foreign country. See **IRS Publication 901, U.S. Tax Treaties**, *for further information, or do a Google search.*

Self-Employment Tax - Social Security & Medicare

Note: *Unfortunately, self-employment income earned abroad is subject to Social Security/Medicare taxation,* **even if the self-employment income itself is excludable** *from gross income for income tax purposes. Doesn't seem quite fair, does it?*

Self-employment tax is **separate** from income tax and consists of two components: Social Security tax (old age and disability benefits) and Medicare (retiree health care benefits). It is assessed at the rate of 12.4% for Social Security and 2.9% for Medicare, for a total combined rate of 15.3% on self-employment income.

These rates are double what W-2 employees of U.S. companies pay, because the employer pays the other half, but *self-employed individuals must pay both portions*.

The self-employed individual does get a deduction for one-half of these taxes in calculating net taxable income, however, so the tax treatment is equalized somewhat.

The Social Security portion of the tax has an earnings ceiling of $147,000 in 2022, beyond which Social Security taxes are not assessed. As a result, the maximum Social Security tax for a self-employed individual in 2022 will be $18,228 ($147,000 x 12.4%), but there is **no earnings ceiling** for the 2.9% Medicare tax – it is assessed on *all earnings*.

Are My Earnings Self-Employment Income?

Generally, if your foreign business is operated as a sole proprietorship, the profits will be considered self-employment income. If there is a legal entity separate from the owner under local law, and the owner is receiving a salary, **sometimes** that will not be self-employment income. Consult a U.S. income tax professional.

If you are working remotely (online) as an *independent contractor* (not a W-2 employee) for a *U.S. company*, it is likely that the U.S. company will issue you a Form 1099-MISC reporting the income, which will be subject to U.S. self-employment tax (even if you can exclude it as foreign earned income).

The IRS is quite efficient at matching up these Forms 1099 to your income tax return. If the income isn't there, you will get a "love letter" from Uncle Sam noting the discrepancy and assessing the additional self-employment taxes.

Consult a local in-country tax advisor about whether your self-employment activity is subject to tax in the local, foreign country. If you have a business with employees, you will be paying at a minimum applicable local income and employment taxes.

If you are a remote worker, many foreign countries are not exactly set up to know about what you are doing from your laptop, and if your compensation is not deposited to a local country bank account (i.e., your pay goes to a U.S. bank account), they are unlikely to know about it. If your work is not displacing any local jobs, they may or may not care. In any event, probably it would be best to keep things low profile if you're working online for a U.S. employer.

Why pay self-employment tax on self-employment income earned abroad that is not from a U.S. company? There are two reasons that this can be beneficial:

- You will be accruing quarters of coverage that will count towards your eventual Social Security retirement benefit; **and**

- By paying into the Social Security system, you will also accrue quarters towards disability insurance coverage should you become permanently and fully disabled and be unable to continue working.

Exception to paying self-employment Social Security/Medicare taxes

The one exception to paying **self-employment** Social Security and Medicare taxes for U.S. citizens and residents living outside the U.S. is if the U.S. has a Social Security agreement with the foreign country where you are residing to eliminate dual taxation of Social Security taxes.

Currently there are 30 countries with such agreements, principally European countries but several in Latin America and Asia plus Canada. To claim exemption, you must obtain a statement from the appropriate agency of the foreign country verifying that your self-employment income is subject to Social Security tax in that country.

Visit the Social Security Administration's web site about agreements with other countries to determine if one might apply to your situation: https://www.ssa.gov/international/

What if I'm Treated as a W-2 Employee by my U.S. Employer?

If you're an online remote employee (not an independent contractor) of a U.S. company, they will treat you as any other W-2 employee and withhold your portion of Social Security and Medicare payroll taxes as well as paying the employer's share of these taxes. You may be able to ask your employer to reduce or eliminate your federal income tax withholding if you will qualify for the earned income exclusion.

There may be state income tax complications in this scenario – see **Chapter 14, State Income Taxation, Driver's Licenses & Registering to Vote** for further information. A number of U.S. states don't recognize the foreign earned income exclusion for state income tax purposes.

Preparing and Filing Your U.S. Federal Income Tax Return from Abroad

If you're up for the challenge, you may be able to use TurboTax, H&R Block or another consumer tax return software product to prepare and e-file your income tax return yourself without too much difficulty. Most of these products have versions that can handle foreign earned income, foreign tax credits, depreciation (if you have business property or rental real estate), foreign bank account reporting to the IRS, etc.

Interestingly, H&R Block Software in 2021 announced the rollout of a new consumer tax preparation product designed especially for expats (*gee, do you think there may be a trend here?*). Its expat software product starts at $99 for simpler federal returns and costs more for those with self-employment income or rental properties. The product is available only for calendar year 2020 and future years' tax returns.

In order to download one of these tax return preparation software products, you may need to use a VPN set to a U.S. location. Many of them have licenses that limit their use to only within the U.S. When you e-file, you definitely want to use a VPN for security reasons.

Note that for the foreseeable future, you **really, really** don't want to paper file. The IRS is still digging itself out from under unprocessed income tax returns. E-file.

---

*If your income is under $73,000, you may qualify for a free filing product. Go to the IRS's web site (**www.irs.gov**) and select "Do Your Taxes for Free" to view the commercial products available. Some Free File commercial products will also do state tax returns. Check to make sure that the free version offers all the forms needed for your return.*

Do not use Google *to search for a free e-file product, as some companies have been found to intentionally misdirect Google searches to products where you pay to prepare your income tax return, even if you qualified for a free product. The links at the IRS's Web site to free file products include some state income tax returns (varies with the vendor).*

The IRS has an online publication, **Publication 54 - Tax Guide for U.S. Citizens and Resident Aliens Abroad**, which may be of interest.

Be aware that while the IRS provides publications about various tax topics and instructions on how to fill out its tax return forms, these instructions are not considered "***substantial authority***" that can be relied upon in the event of a dispute with the IRS. As ridiculous as this sounds, if you rely on an erroneous IRS publication to prepare a tax return, this does not get you off the hook in an audit or in tax litigation.

*If you plan on operating some sort of local, foreign-based business, in my opinion it is **essential** to work with a local in-country accountant and tax advisor to keep out of trouble with the tax authorities of the foreign jurisdiction. The local tax authorities generally have no problem making an example of foreigners who are not following the law.*

Many local jurisdictions around the world are enacting restrictions on Airbnb or similar short-term rentals; check into local ordinances **before** starting such a business activity.

If you have a multi-member LLC or S corporation, are the owner or beneficiary of a domestic or foreign trust, have other complications (or if you just don't want to deal with this stuff), you might want to consult a U.S. income tax professional who specializes in expats.

*If the idea of doing your own U.S. income tax return is just too much to bear, see **Chapter 18, Further Resources**, for possible tax return preparers who specialize in doing U.S. expat tax returns.*

Reporting of Foreign Bank Accounts & Financial Assets

If you have a foreign bank account or have certain foreign financial assets, there may be additional U.S. filing requirements. The penalties for failure to file these forms can be steep, so you'll want to make sure to prepare and file these forms if required.

Why is Uncle Sam requiring this information? The government discovered that wealthy people were stashing significant assets abroad and were not reporting the income to the IRS. Regrettably, many non-wealthy people have been caught up in this search for non-reported foreign financial income and must report this information as well.

*The reporting burden on foreign financial institutions is such that many offshore banks, brokerage firms and mutual funds no longer want U.S. citizens or residents as customers and will refuse to have you as a customer. See **Chapter 7, Banking and Finances**.*

Form 8938, Statement of Specified Foreign Financial Assets

Form 8938 is required to be included in your U.S. income tax return if the total value of those assets exceeds a specified threshold, from USD $50,000 to USD $300,000. The reporting threshold varies depending upon whether you live in the U.S. or not, and on the filing status of the tax return (single, head of household, married filing jointly, married filing separately and so on).

Specified foreign financial assets include any financial account maintained by a foreign financial institution and (if held for investment) any stock, securities, other interest in a foreign entity, and any financial instrument or contract with an issuer or counterparty who is not a U.S. person.

This is a **broad definition** and includes, for example, loans made to foreign persons, foreign investment annuities, life insurance contracts with an investment component, interests in foreign estates, foreign pension plans or foreign deferred compensation plans, and ownership interests in foreign businesses.

*Note that Form 8938 has different, higher thresholds than does the other foreign bank reporting form, **FinCEN Form 114** (see below). **You may be required to file both of these forms.***

There are special rules for specified closely held domestic entities, including corporations, partnerships or trusts, which hold specified foreign financial assets that generate passive income. See the instructions for Form 8938 for further information.

Form 8938 is filed with your individual Form 1040 income tax return, or if the foreign financial assets are held by entities, with Form 1041 (trusts), Form 1065 (partnerships) or Form 1120 (corporations).

Penalties for not filing Form 8938

If you are required to file Form 8938 but do not file a complete and correct Form 8938 by the due date (including extensions) for your return, you may be subject to a penalty of $10,000. It's a big deal.

If the IRS mails you a notice of the failure to file and you do not file within 90 days, you may be subject to an additional penalty of $10,000 *for each 30-day period* during which you continue to fail to file Form 8938 after the 90-day period has expired. The maximum additional penalty for a continuing failure to file Form 8938 is $50,000.

If you underpay your taxes as the result of a transaction involving an undisclosed specified foreign financial asset, you may have to pay a penalty equal to 40% of that underpayment. If you underpay your tax due to fraud, you may be subject to a penalty equal to 75% of the underpayment.

As if all of this weren't enough, if you fail to file Form 8938 or fail to report a specified foreign financial asset that you are required to report, the statute of limitations for the tax year may remain open for all or part of your income tax return until three years after the date that you file Form 8938.

FinCEN Form 114, Report of Foreign Bank and Financial Accounts (FBAR)

This is a *separate, different* reporting form used to report any financial interest in, or signature authority over, a bank, securities, or other financial account in a foreign country. *It is not part of your federal income tax return filed with the IRS.*

You do not need to file the report if the assets are with a U.S. military banking facility OR if the combined total of all assets in foreign account(s) is $10,000 or less during the entire year.

> *Any foreign bank, securities or financial account balance over USD $10,000 triggers a requirement for the **FinCEN Form 114** FBAR report, regardless of country of residence.*

The FBAR report is filed electronically with the Financial Crimes Enforcement Network, **NOT** with the IRS or with your federal income tax return.

Penalties for Not Filing FinCEN Form 114 (FBAR)
A person who is required to file an FBAR and fails to properly file may be subject to a penalty not to exceed $10,000 per violation.

A person who willfully fails to report an account or account identifying information may be subject to a civil monetary penalty equal to the greater of $100,000 or 50% of the balance in the account at the time of the violation.

You can file your Form 114 **for free** by going to the FinCEN website (https://www.fincen.gov/report-foreign-bank-and-financial-accounts) and entering your information online.

> **Note**: *Just go directly to the FinCEN website yourself and fill out your report online; the reporting is very simple. There is no need to use third party vendors who are happy to charge you $100. Be sure to save or print out a copy of your Form 114 before you submit it online. When you receive the FinCEN acknowledgment of receipt, save or print out a copy of that, too.*

The due date for filing the FBAR is April 15th, with an automatic extension to October 15th if you need more time.

Other IRS Reporting – U.S. Owners of Foreign Companies (Corporations/Partnerships/Disregarded Entities)

This topic may not apply to some readers of this book, but if you're thinking of establishing or investing in a business abroad (maybe as part of acquiring a residency visa), *you need to know about these requirements.*

If you as a U.S. person acquire a 10% or greater interest in a foreign company, corporation, partnership, or other locally recognized separate legal entity, you are required to file an information return (included with your own tax return) in the year you acquire the 10% interest.

If your ownership interest is 50% or greater, you will have an annual information return filing requirement that reports the book earnings and expenses as well as a U.S. tax concept known as earnings and profits.

Think this would never apply to you? Some friends of mine living abroad were considering investing in a local business owned by a U.S. expat. They wanted me to look over the accounting records and give them my opinion. I ended up giving them a memo with eight or nine pages of issues about the business.

Among those issues was the fact that since they were going to become over-50% owners in the business, they would also have this annual filing requirement for an information return, with a $10,000 penalty for not filing it each year. They had **no idea** of the existence of these reporting requirements.

The Forms **5471 (Corporations), 8865 (Foreign Partnerships)** and **8858 (Disregarded Entities)** are used to report information for *each foreign entity* in which you have a qualifying ownership interest to the IRS and are usually included with your own tax return.

These are not do-it-yourself forms unless you are a U.S. tax accountant familiar with calculating tax basis and E&P adjustments to book income to calculate the earnings and profits reporting amounts.

Failure to file one of these reports, or filing a substantially incomplete form, carries a $10,000 penalty for **each form, each year**. Substantial, repeated noncompliance can trigger a $100,000 penalty per occurrence. Enough said.

Chapter 14
State Income Taxation, Drivers Licenses & Registering to Vote

State Income Tax Concepts for Expats
Should I File a State Income Tax Return?
Working Online and State Income Tax Complications
U.S. Driver's Licenses
The Real ID Act (Welcome to Bureaucratic Hell)
International Driver's Licenses
Voting from Abroad

I t's best to make an informed decision about state residency, and many people are unfamiliar with state income tax law or concepts. Often, by the time that an expat gets a tax bill and realizes that there is a problem, it may be too late to do anything about it.

This chapter will help you to better understand the intricacies of state residency as they relate to expats.

State Income Tax Concepts for Expats

As a general rule, U.S. states use a concept known as **domicile** to determine whether you are taxable in their state **as a resident**. Domicile does not necessarily mean that you live in the state or own or rent property there, and in a tax audit, a state can assert that you are domiciled there even if you do not physically reside there. Are you confused yet?

Domicile refers to the place to which you will return, even if you are not living there currently. *It is your home base in the U.S.*

For expats, this can get a little tricky. You may consider yourself domiciled permanently abroad, with no U.S. domicile. The state may think differently.

Domicile is a facts-and-circumstances sort of animal. Examples that can indicate domicile include:

- In which state is your driver's license?
- Where are you registered to vote?
- Where are your bank and brokerage accounts?
- Of which churches are you a member?
- To which country clubs do you belong?
- In which state is your will drafted?
- Where is the crux of your social and family ties?

All of these indicia of domicile comprise **nexus**, a legal term that means ties or links to the state.

With the severe budget shortfalls that states are facing these days, they are getting aggressive in asserting that you have *domicile* in their state if you have money or assets. This will result in you being taxed as a resident.

It can even happen that two states *both* assert that you are domiciled in their respective states, resulting in a special tax hell that will likely require professional help to untangle (although this usually only happens to higher-income individuals).

If you have a driver's license in a particular state or are registered to vote there, those facts weigh very heavily in the state's favor when it argues that you are *domiciled* there and should be taxed as a resident.

> **Note**: *just by itself, a mailing address is not proof of domicile. If you use a friend or family member's address to file federal tax returns, but do not file a state return, you may receive a notice from the state asking why you did not file a state tax return. A simple response that the address used is a mailing address only and is not your residence or domicile will usually be sufficient to satisfy the state, <u>provided that you do not have any other nexus to the state.</u> Being able to point to another state where you are domiciled will also be helpful.*

California is notorious for sending prior year tax bills to people who had overseas job transfers (i.e., outside the U.S.) for several (even ten) years and then return to California. California's position is that your job overseas was "temporary" since you returned to California, and that you remained domiciled in California the whole time you were overseas.

New York State and New York City tax litigation case law has more cases than you can count of people who moved to Florida (a state with no income tax) but kept a house and country club membership in New York, spending part of each year in each state. New York may view you as still being a New York resident -- so when you sell an appreciated asset such as stocks or bonds, New York State will tax you as a resident.

Your Mission: Establish Domicile in a State with no Income Tax
If you currently live in a state with an income tax, you may want to think about state domicile to minimize state income tax hassles down the road. If you plan to be abroad for only part of each year and maintain residency in your current state, then this consideration may not apply to you.

The idea is to sever all possible ties to your former state of residence. ***Your goal is to establish domicile in a state that has no state income tax*** to minimize state income tax hassles and expense once you're living abroad**.**

Note that this does not mean that you have to live there or have a home there (although that helps), but getting a driver's license there, registering to vote there, and having a will drawn up there all point to being domiciled there for income tax purposes.

> *To research state residency options, one idea is to visit a big, multi-day RV show. Why an RV show? Because full-time RVers have the same issue that expats living overseas do – in which state do they keep their U.S. domicile, how do they get their mail, receive packages, register to vote, get a driver's license, etc.*

Driver's Licenses and Domicile

I know an American couple permanently living abroad who have Oregon driver's licenses. They were confident that they would have no issues with state income tax because they somehow had gotten an Oregon DMV clerk to put their *foreign address* on the Oregon driver's license (!!). I suspect that this was a low-level DMV employee not understanding what he/she was doing.

In any event, this would have *no effect whatsoever* on whether Oregon would consider them residents for income tax purposes, because having an Oregon driver's license **in and of itself** is a strong indicator that you consider Oregon to be your *domicile*.

Which State Should I Choose for Domicile?

This depends in part upon whether you want to have a U.S. driver's license as an expat; this will affect your choice of state for domicile.

> *Since the 9/11 terrorist attacks, it's now much more complicated to get a driver's license. To get a driver's license in most states, they will want to see proof that you have an address within the state (utility bill, property tax bill etc.). **South Dakota** will let you get a driver's license without a local residential address (see the section on **Driver's Licenses** below).*

As far as state-level income taxation goes, the following U.S. states do not have an income tax:

Alaska   Texas
Florida   Washington
Nevada   Wyoming
South Dakota

New Hampshire and Tennessee have a limited income tax that taxes only investment income (interest and dividends).

South Dakota Residency
Because of its desire to attract full-time RVers, South Dakota makes it especially easy to establish residency there for tax purposes. It wants you to purchase your RV in the state so that it can collect the sales tax and annual registration fees. There are even people who establish companies in South Dakota solely to put their $500,000 RV in it and pay lower annual fees to South Dakota.

Consider that in California, for a $500,000 RV, one-time sales taxes on the purchase could run north of $43,000 and the annual, recurring registration cost (based on value) could be around $32,500. That's what South Dakota is after: those sales tax and annual registration fees, albeit at lower rates than California's.

We expats usually aren't going to own an RV, but we don't need to tell South Dakota that; it can be our little secret. In my case, I have grandparents and an aunt buried in South Dakota, so I actually *do* have some connection to the state.

Don't Forget about State Inheritance or Estate Taxes
When deciding on a domicile state, if you have significant assets, keep in mind state-level inheritance or estate taxes. While I'm sure that you are not planning to die anytime soon, your heirs will thank you if you choose your state wisely.

Should I File a State Income Tax Return?

If you do decide to maintain domicile in a state with an income tax, it may be a good idea to file a state income tax return every year, even if you are not required to file. Why?

- If you never file a return, there is *no statute of limitations* and the state could come back years later and assess you for income tax. Once a return is filed, in most states, after three years from the date the return was due or filed, you cannot be audited (with some exceptions for fraud or large misstatement of tax liability).

- If in a subsequent year you have a state tax liability, your underpayment penalty (assuming that you do not make any estimated tax payments or have withholding) is based upon the prior year's tax liability. If you don't file a return, there is no prior year data.

- What if you have a large capital gain down the road? The capital gain exclusion of $250,000/$500,000 from the sale of a principal residence only applies if it's been your principal residence for two out of the past five years – after that, the gain is taxable.

- What if you win the lottery … or decide to go back to work at some point to earn some money … or start a business, teach online or write a book?

- What if you inherit property that generates income or capital gains when you sell it? You'll be looking at owing state income tax, without being to rely on the penalty safe harbor of the prior year's tax liability.

That said, many expats have maintained residency in a state with an income tax and do not bother to file a state tax return because they have no tax liability, and have not encountered any problems. It's your call.

Working Online and State Income Tax Complications

With the coronavirus pandemic, more people are working from home via the internet, sometimes in a different state from where their employer is located. This can introduce complexity into your state income tax situation.

Companies may be more willing to consider remote workers due to the pandemic, and some expats may want to earn additional income from online or internet-based work by working outside the U.S.

The American Institute of Certified Public Accountants (AICPA) in October 2020 conducted a survey and found that seven out of ten persons polled were unaware that working remotely could affect their state tax bill, and that 46% were unaware that each state has its own rules relating to telecommuting.

Many U.S. remote workers are going will face unpleasant surprises when they go to file their state income tax returns. It's best to understand ahead of time what might happen.

Assuming that the hiring entity is based in the U.S., your U.S. tax treatment will vary depending upon whether you are hired as an independent contractor or as an employee.

What Happens if I'm an Independent Contractor?
Independent contractors in the U.S. are treated for tax purposes as if they were operating a business and will be subject to self-employment taxes (see **Chapter 13, U.S. *Federal Income Taxes*, for further information).

There is no federal or state income tax withholding, no unemployment insurance benefits, no worker's compensation coverage, and no state disability insurance coverage. You will likely need to make quarterly federal and possibly state estimated tax payments.

State income tax treatment of *independent contractors* based outside of the U.S. will vary by state; some states will not consider you to be earning state-sourced income as long as you are not physically present in the state rendering services.

Other states may have different rules for sourcing your revenue as an independent contractor, so you must **investigate each situation carefully**. You may need to file one or more state income tax returns and pay state income tax.

What Happens if I'm an Employee?
Let the (possible) headaches begin. Your state tax treatment will vary (sometimes greatly) depending upon which state your employer is hiring

you from. ***This question bears careful research before starting an online job as an employee.***

If you're lucky, your employer will be based in a state that allocates your wages based on the physical location where you are working – so if you work online from abroad 100% of the time, your wages might not be considered to be state-sourced wages.

If you make occasional work-related trips back to the U.S., the travel could trigger state income tax for the period you are physically present working in that state.

The "Convenience of the Employer" Trap

Five states (Arkansas, Delaware, Nebraska, New York and Pennsylvania) have a rule called "for the convenience of the employer" – which is in practice horribly *inconvenient* for remote workers. Connecticut has enacted some transition rules and is in a somewhat murky position for 2022 and beyond. Massachusetts and New Jersey have a version of the rule.

Essentially, what this rule does is not recognize or allocate wages based upon where the employee physically was when working remotely and instead allocates 100% of the wages to the employer's physical office location. The fact that the employee works remotely (even from outside the U.S.) is deemed to be for the convenience of the employer and is ***disregarded*** for purposes of sourcing the wages.

Say you're working remotely 100% from the Caribbean; you could end up paying state payroll and income taxes if your employer is based in one of the above five states. But wait; it gets worse.

If you're a resident of one state and work remotely for an employer located in one of the "convenience of the employer" states listed above, you *can end up having wages being double taxed at the state level*, even after applying credits for state income taxes paid to another state (because of the different wage sourcing rules). If your head is about to explode from reading this, you're not alone.

Let's say you live in Virginia and are domiciled there and work 100% remotely for a company based in New York. New York defines all wages earned by remote employees, no matter where located, to be New York source wages, while Virginia uses the worker's physical location where the services were provided.

So you have a situation where New York State is taxing 100% of wages (as New York source), and Virginia is also taxing 100% of wages (because you are physically working in Virginia and are a Virginia resident). Because each state is applying different rules, no credit for taxes paid to another state would be available in this situation.

If you were domiciled in Virginia but working remotely for a New York company from outside the U.S., New York's rules would still subject you to taxation and payroll withholding. Under Virginia's rules, the wages would not be Virginia source and would not be subject to Virginia taxation.

Congress could pass legislation that addresses these problems, and with the large increase in remote workers due to the coronavirus pandemic, might even get around to doing something, but until it does, exercise caution regarding state taxation when working remotely as an employee.

For further information, sites such as the Mobile Workforce Coalition (https://www.mobileworkforcecoalition.org/) have more information about state-level income and payroll tax issues.

U.S. Driver's Licenses

I suggest keeping a U.S. driver's license; financial institutions, credit card companies and credit reporting bureaus will sometimes want to see a state-issued ID that matches your U.S. address.

If you want to remain low profile about living abroad, it's better (but not obligatory) to have a U.S. driver's license or state-issued ID rather than a foreign driver's license. You might run the risk of having bank or brokerage/mutual fund accounts closed on you involuntarily if they learn that you are living abroad full-time. See **Chapter 7, *Banking and Finances***, for further information.

If you're no longer driving – say you have vision problems, or are 85 years old – I recommend that you get a state-issued ID card, which is usually issued by a state Department of Motor Vehicles (DMV). Just get **something** that is state government-issued ID from the same state as your mailing address, with your in-state address on it.

> As discussed above, the state where you have a driver's license or state-issued ID card can lead to state income tax issues – the state will likely consider you to be **domiciled** in that state and subject to resident income tax.

Having a U.S. driver's license may make renting a car easier when you visit the U.S. It is usually possible to rent a car in the U.S. with a foreign driver's license, but you may run into issues with some rental agencies. Check beforehand if you will be renting a car with a foreign country driver's license.

> If you will be driving in your foreign country of residence, definitely get a local driver's license. It is likely required by local law to possess a local driver's license, unless you are a short-term visitor on a tourist visa.

Changing the State of your U.S. Driver's License
Changing the U.S. state of your driver's license can be easy or it can be a real horror.

I've had driver's licenses in six different states. New Jersey was by far the most difficult experience, although Hawaii would come in second. South Dakota had by far the easiest process.

South Dakota is the only state I'm aware of that will let you get a driver's license without having proof of an in-state physical residential address (copy of a utility bill, property tax bill, etc.) – a private mail box from a mail service will suffice to get a driver's license. You must show one piece of mail addressed to you at the mail service (or the mail service contract) plus a receipt for one night's stay at a campground, hotel or motel in South Dakota.

With careful advance planning and a contract with a mail forwarding service in South Dakota, it is possible to fly into the state, stay overnight and leave the next morning with a nice new South Dakota driver's license.

To see the specific documents that you will need to get a South Dakota driver's license or state-issued ID card, you can visit South Dakota's driver's license Web site here: http://dps.sd.gov/licensing/driver_licensing/.

South Dakota's driver's licenses and state-issued ID cards are valid for five years. The state allows one renewal by mail in each ten-year period, but you must present a receipt for an overnight stay in the state at a hotel, motel, campground or RV park in the year of renewal; in effect, that means an overnight trip to South Dakota every five years.

> *If you've changed the state of issue or name on your driver's license, update your ID with all banks and brokerage accounts so that they have your current ID on file. You may be asked to produce it later for a withdrawal or to close the account, and if it doesn't match you will need a second form of ID.*

A number of states are starting to implement **digital driver's licenses**, which allow you to register your state's driver's license in a government-approved, encrypted app that will display the license on your smart phone. As of mid-2022 it is available only on Apple devices, but it is likely that Android devices will follow. **You still need to carry your physical driver's license** with you, even if you have a digital driver's license.

The Real ID Act (Welcome to Bureaucratic Hell)

Because the U.S. has no national identity card, the driver's license or state-issued ID card (usually issued by the DMV) serves as *de facto* identification.

Congress passed the Real ID Act in 2005 in the wake of the 9/11 terrorist attacks, because the hijackers had used state driver's licenses to board aircraft in 2001. The act establishes minimum security standards for the issuance of driver's licenses (among other IDs). This law requires that states validate your **full name, right to reside legally in the U.S., proof of address, date of birth, and Social Security number**.

States have had difficulty complying with the Real ID requirements, and the federal government has granted multiple extensions to states. The latest deadline (after which non-compliant IDs will not be accepted by federal agencies) has been extended (again) to **May 3, 2023** due to the coronavirus pandemic – for a law that was passed *in 2005*.

Driver's licenses or state-issued IDs (usually by the DMV) that are not Real ID compliant after the deadline of May 3, 2023 cannot be used to access federal buildings, nuclear power plants, or **board commercial aircraft.**

It's that last item that is of primary importance for us expats. Yes, you can use a U.S. passport as ID to board a plane, but you'll have to be careful not to misplace your passport.

How can I tell if my Driver's License is Real-ID Compliant?
Most states' Real ID-compliant driver's licenses and ID cards have a black or gold star in the upper right-hand corner of the license or ID card (designs vary). More recently issued non-compliant cards will often say "Federal Limits Apply" meaning it is *not valid* for use by any federal agency, including for boarding aircraft.

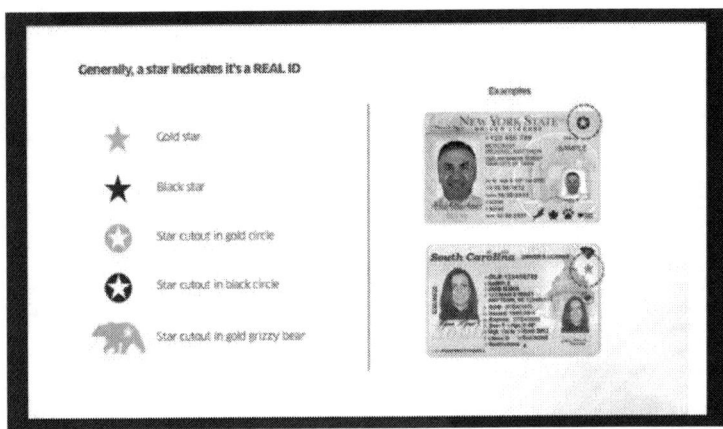

Illustration of Real ID stars

While all states have now implemented Real ID, estimates are that as of mid-2022 only about 50% of driver's licenses and IDs nationwide were Real ID-compliant, meaning that **half** of people still have non-Real ID driver's licenses or IDs not yet upgraded to comply with the new requirements (the license is still valid to use for driving a car).

If your driver's license is not Real ID-compliant, **prepare yourself for major hassles** when you renew your driver's license or state ID.

Residents with current, valid driver's licenses up for renewal have had to return in person to their state DMV office with original documents, resulting in long waits and crashed computer systems. States with large populations such as California or New Jersey have had major problems with Real ID, with people camping out overnight just to get a place in line.

*To prove your full legal name, date of birth, Social Security number, address, and proof of legal presence in the U.S., this means **original documents** (no photocopies allowed): a birth certificate, Social Security card, two documents with your principal address such as utility bills, property tax bills, rental agreements, etc., and a U.S. passport or green card if not born in the U.S.*

Sample California Real ID informational graphic.

South Dakota is Real ID-compliant, so you will need to comply with the requirements discussed above. If your current state's driver's license is already Real ID-compliant, it should be pretty straightforward for you to get a South Dakota driver's license.

My Personal Experience
*When I switched my U.S. driver's license to South Dakota, my old state was **NOT** Real ID-compliant whereas South Dakota **WAS** Real ID-compliant (states with smaller populations have found it easier to implement the Real ID Act).*

So yes, I really had to bring an original birth certificate (no photocopy), my original Social Security card, and documents that complied with South Dakota's requirements about principal residence. I even brought along my U.S. passport, just to be on the safe side. That said, South Dakota was a breeze and I was in and out of the DMV in under 15 minutes with a minimal of hassle.

Regardless of where you decide to have your U.S. driver's license, ***get it updated to be Real ID compliant before you leave the U.S.*** Yes, it's a headache and I feel your pain, but believe me, if you don't get it updated before leaving, you will have bigger headaches in the future.

Isn't There an Alternative to this Real ID Hell?
One option would be to get a non-Real ID-compliant driver's license; while you won't be able to use it to board aircraft, enter federal buildings, or visit a nuclear power plant, it will still be valid for renting a car or driving in the U.S. You could use your U.S. passport for boarding aircraft. It's your call.

Renewing Your Driver's License or State-Issued Identification
Once you are living abroad, keep an eye on the expiration date of your driver's license or state-issued ID card. You may need to plan a trip to the U.S. if you must renew it in person. Well before it expires, check into the renewal requirements:

- Can it be renewed by mail?
- Do you have to comply with the Real ID Act?
- Are there special requirements for seniors to renew?
- How far in advance of the expiration date can it be renewed?

> *In some states, the combination of the Real ID Act and the coronavirus pandemic is resulting in long lines at DMVs. Plan accordingly; check on what the situation is on the ground at the local DMV office before planning a visit in person. You may need to make an appointment online before showing up in person.*

The U.S. Department of Homeland Security has a Q&A document online at https://www.dhs.gov/real-id-frequently-asked-questions if you want further details about the Real ID Act.

International Driver's Licenses

An international driver's license **translates** your valid government-issued driver's license into nine languages (English, Spanish, Russian, Chinese, Italian, German, Arabic, Swedish and French) and allows properly licensed drivers from over 150 United Nations member countries (including the U.S.) to drive the roads of another member state.

Who Can Get an International Driver's License?
You must be at least age 18, have been driving for at least six months, and have a valid government-issued driver's license from a signatory country.

For how long is an International Driver's License Valid?
An international driver's license is valid for one year from the date of issue. It **does not replace** a valid government-issued driver's license, which must be carried with the international driver's license *at all times*.

Can I Drive (*as a Visitor*) with a U.S. Driver's License in a Foreign Country?
Check with the laws of the country or countries to be visited, as the requirements will vary. To rent a car, you may need to present both a valid government-issued driver's license **and** an international driver's license, even if it is not legally required; check with the car rental agency.

Can I Drive with a Foreign Driver's License in the U.S.?

Some U.S. states require both a valid government-issued driver's license **and** an international driver's license; check with the state DMV office in the state(s) where you'll be driving for requirements.

Most major U.S. car rental companies require an international driver's license **along with** a valid government-issued driver's license; check with the car rental agency when you reserve your car for their policies.

*If you plan on driving a car in a foreign country as a **visitor** using your **U.S. driver's license** (or would like to have an internationally recognized identification translated into multiple languages), be sure to get your international driver's license **before** leaving the U.S.*

How do I Obtain an International Driver's License in the U.S.?

The American Automobile Club (AAA) is the **only authorized U.S. issuer** of international driver's licenses. Avoid fraudulent or unauthorized issuers of international driver's licenses.

The online application to print out can be obtained at the following website:

AAA: https://www.aaa.com/vacation/idpapplc.html

You'll need to furnish two 2"x 2" photos (many AAA offices can assist with that for an additional fee), a signed copy of your valid U.S. driver's license and payment of the appropriate fees. The cost for the license itself is usually about $20 plus applicable mailing fees if you're not going in person to an AAA office.

How do I Obtain an International Driver's License from Abroad?

You must apply for and obtain the international driver's license in the **same country** that issued your valid government-issued driver's license. For example, if you live as a resident in France, you'll need to obtain the international driver's license in France. You **cannot use** the international driver's license within the country where it was issued.

Contact the foreign agency that issued the foreign driver's license for more information on how to obtain an international driver's license.

Voting From Abroad

As a U.S. citizen residing outside of the U.S., you are entitled to vote in federal elections, but the hassle factor is significant. If you maintain a domicile in a U.S. state, you are entitled by federal law to vote absentee in those state and local elections as well.

"Entitled" doesn't always mean "able to," however, and the process can be very confusing.

> *Keep in mind that as explained above, where you register to vote is an indicia of **domicile**, which can affect state taxation. Where you are registered to vote may give that state ammunition to argue that you are domiciled in that state, whether you live there or not. **Carefully choose where you register to vote.***

The Federal Voting Assistance Program (FVAP) (https://www.fvap.gov) is a voter assistance and education program established by the U.S. Department of Defense to ensure that U.S. citizens residing outside of the U.S. and active-duty members of the uniformed services are informed of their right to vote and have the tools to do so.

FVAP creates and disseminates educational materials to inform voters, election officials and other stakeholders about the absentee voting process, election dates and deadlines, and has election offices' contact information for every U.S. state and local jurisdiction.

According to the FVAP, there are almost three million Americans abroad who are eligible to vote in U.S. elections. 2020 was an exceptional year for its high rate of voter participation by Americans living abroad in the presidential elections.

> *When you obtain your ballet via the FVAP, additional federal voting safeguards apply to ensure your ability to vote from abroad. Let's say you never receive your ballot; you have more options with a FVAP ballot than if it is sent directly to you by the local jurisdiction.*

Every state is *required* by federal law to make ballots available electronically to overseas voters upon request, and election officials are *required* to send out requested ballots to overseas voters no later than 45 days before the election. While some states will allow you to return your ballot by email or fax, **more than 20 states** still require you to print it out, sign it and mail it back, which is a significant inconvenience for us expats.

In addition to the non-partisan, governmental Federal Voting Assistant Program, there are non-profit partisan organizations that specialize in assisting expats with voting from outside the U.S.

Democrats Abroad (https://www.democratsabroad.org) and **Republicans Overseas** (https://www.republicansoverseas.com) are happy to help U.S. voters with registering, figuring out how to request a ballot, and in getting the ballot to the proper place back in the U.S.

> *State and local jurisdictions do not always do a good job in explaining exactly what you need to do as an overseas resident, and the ballot instructions are not always clear, either.*

The Steps Involved in Voting from Abroad
As an expat voter living outside the U.S., you take the following steps to participate in a local, state or federal:

(1) Register to vote,
(2) Request a ballot *as an overseas voter*,
(3) Receive the ballot, and
(4) Return the ballot to the correct state jurisdiction.

Each step along the way should be carefully monitored to ensure that all is well with the process. Things can and do go astray occasionally.

Registering to Vote

FVAP's Web site has an overseas voting assistant guide (https://www.fvap.gov/citizen-voter) that will let you select the state from a drop-down menu that will show each state or territory's rules.

Registering through FVAP's Web site involves using the Federal Post Card Application (FPCA), which must be re-submitted each year to renew your voter registration.

It's a good practice to fill out this document at the beginning of each year to ensure that you're registered for all primary, general and special elections in your state. The FPCA serves as both your ballot request and voter registration.

If you go to **VoteFromAbroad.org**, you can also fill out the FPCA and if your state permits, you can sign it electronically and submit it via email. Some states will allow you to print out the FPCA, sign it, and then scan it in electronically and submit it via email; others will require you to mail in the paper FPCA form, which may entail using a private service such as FedEx or DHL at additional cost. VoteFromAbroad.org's website can help you determine your state's rules regarding submitting the FPCA.

A third alternative is to go directly to your state's voter registration site online and register to vote as an overseas voter, although this procedure may vary and have *fewer protections* than if you use the FCPA.

How to Receive Your Ballot

You must be sure that you are recorded as having requested a ballot as an *overseas voter*, which will entitle you to receive the ballot electronically no more than 45 days before the election (as required by federal law).

Using the Federal Post Card Application will give you the most rights under law in case of problems. You can also go directly to your state's voter registration site online and request an absentee ballot as an overseas voter.

How to Submit Your Ballot

Depending upon where you are registered to vote in the U.S. and where you are living outside of the U.S., you may have several options to return your ballot to your state.

You can consult FVAP's Web site for information about each state's rules for receiving ballots at https://www.fvap.gov/overseas, which includes a map that you can click on.

If You Must Return a Paper (Physical) Ballot

In the event that your state is one that insists on receiving a paper ballot, sometimes you can deliver the ballot to the nearest consulate or embassy and they will send it to the U.S. in the diplomatic pouch; *this service may be temporarily suspended due to the coronavirus pandemic.*

Using the diplomatic pouch can take your ballot up to six weeks to arrive, and **involves using the U.S. Postal Service** once the ballots are back in the U.S., so your ballot may not arrive before election day. Check to see if your nearest U.S. Embassy or Consulate has a ballot collection service.

FVAP's Free Ballot Fax Service (if allowed by your state)

Some states will accept faxed ballots even if they won't accept emailed ballots. Consult the FAVP's web site to see if your state falls into this category.

If it will accept faxed ballots, the Federal Assistance Voting Program web site offers a free email-to-fax service (https://www.fvap.gov/uploads/FVAP/Forms/TransmissionCoversheet.p df), or you can use online free web-based faxing services once your ballot has been digitized.

> *Use the fax service **only** if your state does **NOT** accept emailed ballots, but **will** accept faxed ballots (can these rules possibly get any more confusing?).*

What Do I Do if I Do Not Receive My State Absentee Ballot?

In the event that you are unable to obtain a ballot from the jurisdiction where you are registered, you can obtain a Federal Write-In Absentee Ballot, which serves as a backup for overseas U.S. voters. The FWAB must be **mailed** to the election official at the applicable local election office address, *it cannot be emailed or faxed.* You can download the FWAB at https://www.fvap.gov/fwab-privacy-notice which will walk you through the needed steps.

You must already be registered to vote and have already requested a state absentee mail-in ballot in order to request a Federal Write-In Absentee Ballot (used only for federal elections).

If you don't receive your state absentee ballot in time to vote, you're out of luck as far as voting for state or local election offices if there are no federal offices on the ballot.

If you receive your state absentee ballot after mailing your voted FWAB, you may also vote and return the state absentee ballot. If both are received by the deadline, only the state absentee ballot will be counted.

My Experience Voting in the 2020 Presidential Election
When I voted in the 2020 presidential election from Ecuador, during the coronavirus pandemic, I checked earlier in the year to confirm that that I was still actively registered to vote in South Dakota as an overseas voter and that they had my request for an electronic ballot by consulting the state's voting website.

*South Dakota emailed me the ballot, but I still had to print it out, mark my choices, sign it, and return the physical paper ballot to the county auditor's office. Since Ecuador currently has no functioning postal system, I had to pay DHL $25 (a discounted price from the usual $65-$75) to express air mail my ballot to South Dakota. **Each U.S. state does things differently.***

If you really want to be conscientious about removing any nexus that your former state of residence could use to allege domicile, it's not a bad idea to notify the voting authorities in the state with whom you wish to sever all ties by writing a letter asking to be removed from the voting rolls. Mention the state to which you're moving and your new mailing address (if you know it), just to make things official. See a sample letter at my website, https://sites.google.com/view/northoak-books.

Other Voting Resources for Overseas Voters

The U.S. State Department has a web page devoted to voting from abroad, at

https://travel.state.gov/content/travel/en/international-travel/while-abroad/voting.html.

This web page also has a link to a state-by-state voting assistance guide with more detailed information. You can also look up state rules at https://www.votefromabroad.org/states/.

Vote From Abroad.org (https://votefromabroad.org) is a nonpartisan site that will assist all voters regardless of political party affiliation.

Ballotpedia (https://www.ballotpedia.org/Sample_Ballot_Lookup) can give you locale-specific information about candidates and ballot measures for the jurisdiction where you are registered to vote.

Chapter 15
Miscellaneous Topics

Buying Real Estate Abroad
What About Working Locally?
Should I Buy a Car?
Getting Around Locally
Notarizing Documents
Renewing Your Passport

Buying Real Estate Abroad

It's usually good advice not to buy real estate in a hurry. Would you buy a house in the U.S. in a new city where you do not know the neighborhoods or much of anything about the city? Probably not.

In a foreign country the unknowns are much larger – cultural differences, legal differences and many others. _Don't be in a rush!_ At a minimum, spend at least six months renting before thinking about buying. A year or two would be better. If you don't speak the language, be very careful.

> _Exercise caution if you'll be buying real estate **to qualify for residency**. You will be unfamiliar with the country, the real estate market, the legal system, and possibly the language. You're likely to pay an above-market price. Are there any alternatives to purchasing real estate (or investing in a business) to get a visa? Find out what happens to your residency visa if you want to sell your property and buy a different property._

You do not want to purchase property only to find out that you don't like living in the neighborhood, you can't easily sell the property, or the costs for a caretaker to watch it for you and keep out squatters are burdensome. In some countries, squatters can gain legal title to a property after as little as two years of continuous occupancy.

In some countries it may be possible to rent before buying a property; this is generally a good idea if the owner who wants to sell is amenable to it.

Keep in mind that while you may be able to **buy** real estate or a business fairly quickly, **selling** can take far longer than in the U.S. You may be stuck with your purchase for a very long time. In many countries, there is no such thing as a Multiple Listing Service and you may incur advertising costs for months on end.

Don't assume that if you're buying property or a business in a resort location or in an area popular with expats that you will be able to easily sell your property (although that may be the case). It all depends upon market conditions and the law of supply and demand.

Foreigners in Vietnam are sometimes tempted to purchase a restaurant or bar in a tourist area after seeing the business running full bore, jammed with customers spending money. What they don't realize is that it's only like that for three months out of the year, and that during the rainy season, with torrential downpours every day, there's virtually no business.

Once they've sunk their money into such a business, their only option is to try to unload the business onto the next expat sucker before they go broke. Buyer beware.

It would be very interesting for a university business student to write a thesis analyzing failed businesses opened by expats to see why the business did not work. I have seen cafes with good food in a central location that targeted the expat market not succeed, whereas others in the same city thrived.

What was the difference? Were their prices too high? Location? Poor or inconsistent service or staff problems? You do not want to be the expat who poured $50,000 or more into a business only to see it fail.

With the coronavirus pandemic, it's hard to know how long the negative economic conditions will last. At the time of this writing (2022), there are signs that there may be real estate buying opportunities at reduced prices due to decreased demand, distressed sellers, or an appreciation of the U.S. dollar (or all three factors), although there is evidence of price recoveries underway in many markets.

Unexpected Events & Real Estate
What if you purchased a house or condo and then the military deposes the elected government or rioting occurs? Wouldn't it be nice to be able to bug out quickly and not have real estate to worry about?

In October 2019, the Ecuadorian government suddenly abolished all subsidies on gasoline, diesel, and propane (used for cooking and heating water), resulting in large fuel price increases overnight. All hell broke loose.

Here in Cuenca, we had fewer disturbances than elsewhere; still, streets were cordoned off by the military and the Ecuadorian Air Force flew in large cargo planes to deliver food and medical supplies because the city was cut off by roadblocks with armed protesters. Armed soldiers stood in front of supermarkets to guard against looters.

The government was left significantly weaker after the violent protests, which only ended when the president gave in to the protesters' demands and reinstituted the fuel subsidies.

Given that these kinds of events can and do happen, sometimes seemingly out of the blue, take your time before deciding to buy real estate.

What About Working Locally?

Let's get real. You will be a foreigner, perhaps with limited language skills, with few social connections or a social network to help you find a job. You may be able to find a job with a local business that needs English speakers to interact with expat customers, but you will be competing against the locals who also speak English.

In many countries the pay is significantly lower than in the U.S. for a comparable job; this is why people want to come to the U.S. to work. It's been that way for centuries.

You can definitely teach English, but you likely won't make much money doing that. It will be necessary to have a teaching certificate for teaching

English as a foreign language (this can be obtained online in about a month for native speakers of English with a university degree).

In much of the world, whom you know is as or more important than your actual abilities or competence. Depending upon where you are in the world, having first-class credentials may not get you a job.

Don't underestimate the insecurity or resentment that locals with limited opportunities sometimes feel (depending upon the location) when going up against a privileged, educated foreigner. How would you feel in their shoes?

It's best to plan for a worst-case scenario and assume you won't be able to find work locally; have enough money to support yourself without working locally.

Working online for a U.S. Employer

Working via the internet for a U.S. company may net you more money than working for a local company. If you have any contacts from prior employers who might be interested in your working online for them as an independent contractor, **that's your best bet** because they already are familiar with you and the caliber of your work.

There are special federal income tax benefits for U.S. taxpayers working from abroad; see **Chapter 13, U.S. Federal Income Taxes**, for more information. Note that state income taxation can be tricky for online workers; see **Chapter 14, State Income Taxes**, for further on this.

Self-Employment

Being self-employed is probably a better bet. If you have some skill that you can do working for yourself, whether online or in the local economy, that could enable you to earn some scratch. If you plan on hiring locals, you will get a much warmer reception.

> *If you're going to hire employees, be sure to comply with local labor laws. In some countries, it is difficult to fire employees, and sizable severance payments may be obligatory. There may not be much flexibility in scheduling employees' hours, and the employer may be required to pay for health insurance and Social Security taxes. There may be obligatory profit-sharing distributions to employees. In Latin America, an "aguinaldo" is common whereby the employer pays an additional month's salary in December; sometimes a second aguinaldo is payable in the summer – that's fourteen months' salary each year.*

Figure out what opportunities exist in the local economy. As the saying goes, find a need and fill it. Can you take advantage of lower local wages?

While there may be an obvious need for a particular product or service locally, you are likely *not* the first person to have noticed, and there may be very good reasons why this product or service is not available. Find out what the obstacles are: is the government the problem? Is it just not feasible economically to provide this service? Or is it simply a lack of experience and knowledge – that you happen to have and can deploy?

> *Be sure to work with a local accountant familiar with the country's tax laws, especially if you will have employees. It's also a good idea to have a working knowledge of basic accounting, so that you can run your business efficiently on a daily basis. Can you calculate profit margins, return on capital or break-even points?*

Here's a sample of online resources about working or blogging from abroad:

The Professional Hobo (Nora Dunn) – www.theprofessionalhobo.com
GoAbroad.com - https://www.goabroad.com/
Go Overseas.com - https://www.gooverseas.com/
Nomadic Matt - https://www.nomadicmatt.com/
Upwork (remote online work, various types) - https://www.upwork.com/

Hobo with a Laptop – https://hobowithalaptop.com/
Location Indie - https://locationindie.com/

Should I Buy a Car?

This will depend upon where you are living. There are places where a car will be essential, if there is no good public transportation. In the city a car could be more of a pain than it's worth. Some expats rent a car when they want to take a road trip, and take taxis or use public transportation the rest of the time.

How is the Parking Situation?
In some urban areas, parking for cars is difficult to find or expensive, and traffic can mean that it's faster to get around without a car. Hourly on-street parking may not involve parking meters; instead, you purchase a ticket at a nearby store and put it on the dashboard. If you go over the parking time purchased, your car may be towed.

Do you have a secure place to garage the car overnight? In many places it's not a good idea to park a car out on the street, as thieves will steal the wheels, the battery, the instrument panel, the power window mechanisms (anything not nailed down), including the car itself.

You'll Need a Local Country Driver's License
If you as a resident are going to be driving in your new country, you will want to get a local driver's license. Many countries will let you keep your home country driver's license when you get a local driver's license.

Tourists visiting a foreign country for a short time can generally get by with using their home country's driver's license with an international driver's license, but typically you'd be able to do this only for a short while (consistent with being a tourist). *As a resident you will absolutely need a local driver's license*.

For further information about international driver's licenses (which do not substitute for a local country driver's license), see *Chapter 14, State Income Taxes, Driver's Licenses and Registering to Vote*.

Local Driving Customs

Driving habits vary widely around the world. In some places, a stop sign or a red light is just a suggestion. Are you ready for that? Before you decide to get a car, get a feel for how crazy is the local driving situation.

In some countries, very few motorcyclists have a driver's license, which might explain why some drive like maniacs and have a high fatality rate.

- Are drivers on the road texting while driving?
- Are half of the cars on the road after dark driven by drunk drivers?
- Do the traffic police pull you, a foreigner, over for an imaginary traffic violation just to solicit a bribe from you?
- Are there traffic cameras gone crazy that issue computerized $100 traffic citations even when you're driving under the speed limit?
- How prevalent are uninsured drivers?

In some places, expats make it a practice that if pulled over by traffic police, they record the traffic stop with a cell phone camera for security reasons.

Some countries drive on the left side of the road, with the steering wheel being on the right. It's probably not a good idea to jump right in driving on the left side of the road if you're jet-lagged; give yourself a minimum of a day or two to rest up first.

---

*If you're going to own a car, **insurance is essential**. In some countries, as a foreigner you may be targeted for "staged" accidents or subject to shakedowns. While having auto insurance might be mandatory, you'll find that in some places this requirement is widely ignored and basically **everyone is driving uninsured**. If a serious accident happens, the driver flees. The police arrest people first and do the accident investigation later. Having insurance may help avoid being jailed during the investigation, as the insurance company will post a guaranty bond and can help arrange for a lawyer.*

How Easily Can the Car Be Serviced or Repaired?
Should you decide to buy a car, make sure to buy a model and brand that is easily serviced locally, with good availability of spare parts. Do local mechanics know how to work on this make and model of car? Driving a common make and model will also make you slightly less conspicuous as a foreigner.

If the dealer is the only place that can service the car, just as in the U.S. you're likely to pay more for routine servicing than if you have a car that nearly all mechanics know. Some dealers overcharge foreigners for repairs, or recommend unnecessary repairs.

Are Car Prices Reasonable?
The prices for cars can vary widely, and in some countries can be double or triple of what they are in the U.S. or Canada due to import tariffs. In Mexico, cars cost about the same as in the U.S. because there is a large manufacturing and assembly base there. In more and more of the world, Chinese automobile brands are making inroads against the traditional auto manufacturers.

In many countries, motorcycles or scooters are a popular option for getting around, and of course are much less expensive than a car. Often a low-powered scooter does not require a driver's license—check local laws.

Should you decide to buy a car, it may be worthwhile to enlist the help of a trustworthy local or facilitator who specializes in automobile purchases; you will want to have an honest mechanic check over the car first, and may need help in negotiating the price, handling the transfer of title, and registering the car.

Getting Around Locally

Public Transportation
Taking local urban public transportation can be a great way to learn your way around your city. A sense of adventure and flexible attitude are helpful; even if you get on a bus going the wrong direction, you may

discover that the bus goes somewhere that you'll want to go in the future.

The driver may have the wrong destination sign in the window of the bus, the bus stops may not be marked by signs, or you may have to signal at the bus stop that you want the driver to stop to pick you up. It's all part of the adventure of learning the local bus system.

---

*MOOVIT is a nifty smart phone app for Apple and Android phones that has detailed **urban public transit route and timetable information** for over 105 countries for medium- or larger size cities. In the U.S. alone it has information for over 170 cities; for Germany it has 13 cities, for Argentina 44 cities. The app has maps that show you the route of each line with each bus or transit stop for the city in question, with timetables.*

You tell the app where you want to go, from what departure point (or where you are now), and the app will tell you which bus or light rail lines to take, where to transfer, where to walk to the nearest stop or station, and when the next bus arrives. You can follow your location while on the bus in motion in the map within app, so you know where to get off. The app depends upon crowd-sourced user feedback to alert it to changes in local transit operations.

It's enjoyable to chat with local citizens while waiting for a bus or while on the bus, who may not be accustomed to seeing foreigners taking public transportation. Make googly eyes at the cute baby and chat about the weather with the mother.

Be sure to familiarize yourself with the local crime situation first; there may be certain bus lines or times of the day or night that it is not advisable to use public transportation. Being a foreigner can make you more conspicuous and a target for robbery or theft. Observe what the locals are doing and follow their lead. Try to blend in if possible.

Being a Pedestrian or Bicyclist
It can be a real eye-opening experience to be a pedestrian or bicyclist outside the U.S. Attitudes towards pedestrians and bicycles will vary widely depending upon where you decide to live.

In many countries, pedestrians do not have the right-of-way and drivers expect pedestrians to take full responsibility for not getting run over. Holland or Denmark are probably as close to bicycle nirvana as you'll get, but other places (both in the U.S. and abroad) can be downright dangerous for bicyclists.

Roads, streets and highways may be designed with no thought given whatsoever to the needs of pedestrians or bicyclists, resulting in dangerous situations.

Drivers of cars, buses or trucks may be accustomed to ignoring traffic signals and stop signs, or may be looking at their cell phones instead of paying attention to their driving. Drunk driving, especially at night, is a real problem in many places.

In some places, even if there are crosswalks and pedestrian traffic signals, the signals may conflict with traffic signals for cars. I have seen intersections where the pedestrian green crosswalk signal conflicts with the oncoming cars' green left turn signal, directing traffic into the pedestrian's path as he/she uses the crosswalk.

Cities around the world are encouraging their residents more and more to use bicycles. Some cities have bike lanes to separate car traffic from bicycles, but more often the rule of the day is defensive bicycling. Imagine that you are invisible to cars, trucks and buses, because often they are just not paying attention to their driving, or are drunk. It may not be a good idea to bicycle at night.

That said, bicycling is a great form of exercise that also gets you from Point A to Point B, and saves money on bus or taxi fares. Are there other bicyclists you can join for a Sunday ride? Look into it.

Notarizing Documents

This is one of those topics that you don't think about until you need to have it done. It may not be a big deal when you're in the U.S., but when you're abroad it's a little more complicated.

Getting a *legal* U.S. notary seal or stamp on a document outside the U.S. generally involves a visit to U.S. Consular Services, either at the U.S. embassy in the capital city of your country or at a consulate.

> **NOTE**: *The only **legally valid** in-person notarizations executed outside the U.S. must be done by U.S. State Department officers. For a document whose validity you wouldn't want tossed out in court in the U.S., it's best to do it right and go to a U.S. embassy or consulate.*

> *In places where many U.S. expats live, there may be an expat U.S. notary public with a current commission in some U.S. state; this person may even be willing to notarize documents with their seal or stamp.* ***Be warned, though, that this notarization would not be considered legally valid in a U.S. court of law.***

As of 2022, Uncle Sam charges $50 ***per notarization seal*** to notarize documents, so it's not exactly cheap. You usually have to make an appointment in advance.

If a U.S. consular official visits your city every so often, you may be able to make an appointment during his/her visit to get your documents notarized without travel, but often when you need a document notarized, you have a deadline or time constraint.

A family member once sent me a document and asked me to get my signature notarized. When I explained that this would entail a five-hours-each-way overnight trip (the consulate only did notary appointments first thing in the morning) plus $50, he decided that it didn't really have to be notarized after all.

> *Note that in a foreign country, there may be the local equivalent of notaries public. They will first need the document translated into the local language (sometimes by a certified translator); they will then be notarizing the **foreign language document**, not the English document. Usually this will not be acceptable for U.S. purposes, where you need the document to be notarized by a U.S. notary with a valid state commission.*

Online notaries

A new wrinkle in notarizing documents is *online notaries*. Firms such as Notarize.com, Onlinenotary.net, NotaryCam, SafeDocs etc. will perform an online notarization of a single document for around $35. There are two types of online notary services:

A **remote online notary** is a legally commissioned notary authorized to perform notarizations remotely via the internet. During a recorded video call, the notary confirms the signers' identities and witnesses the person(s) signing the document.

The online notary must possess a traditional notary commission and be physically present in the state where his/her notary powers are granted, and under whose laws the document is being notarized. The signers may not need to be in the state (this varies by state). The state must have passed an authorizing law regarding remote online notarizations. Some states may impose additional requirements on the online notary such as training or certifications.

E-signing is the act of each person signing the document electronically, which is considered an e-signature. All U.S. states now allow e-signatures, or electronic signing of documents.

As of 2022, 29 states allow fully online notary services while all states recognize e-signatures.

For something relating to real estate that will need to be recorded by a county recorder, it would be prudent to first confirm with the county recorder that a remote online notarization will be accepted.

> *For purposes of notarizing documents* that will need to be apostilled (see *Chapter 3, How to Decide Where to Go,* for an explanation of apostilles), I would not recommend using an online notary. The U.S. Department of State or state agency apostilling the document may not accept an online notarization.

The American Association of Notaries

(https://www.notarypublicstamps.com/) is a non-profit professional association for notaries that through its free notary location search tool can help you find a notary public.

American Notary USA (https://americannotaryusa.com/) is a for-profit company that connects notaries with individuals and has a directory. You can search by city, state or zip code for a notary.

Renewing Your U.S. Passport

I thought I'd include this here because the U.S. State Department's website is not very clear about this. The majority of U.S. passports are issued for a ten-year period, after which you'll need to renew it for another ten years. You may, however, renew your passport *at any time* – it does not have to be within a certain period of time of expiration to be renewed.

Generally, you want to renew your passport *more than six months* before it expires because most countries will not let you enter if you have fewer than six months left on the passport.

---

*If you are planning on traveling and your passport is within a year of expiration, go ahead and renew it. **Don't wait.** You want to have it ready to go should you decide to take a last-minute trip or in case of an emergency.*

In 2022, some U.S. consulates or embassies abroad are renewing passports faster than in the U.S. (two to three weeks), but this may vary by country.

*In the U.S., the State Department has a backlog of renewals. Standard processing of passport applications is currently taking up to **10-12 weeks**; a small percentage of applications is taking longer than 12 weeks. "Expedited" processing ($60 fee) is still taking **six to eight weeks**. Because of U.S. Postal Service delivery problems, the State Department recommends using Priority Mail **Express**.*

You have been warned.

The procedure to renew your passport outside the U.S. varies depending upon the embassy or consulate in the country where you're living. If you live in an area with lots of expats, a U.S. official from Consular Services may come to visit every four to six months or so and you can make an appointment.

You may be able to renew it by mail if the embassy or consulate in your country offers that service. This will mean surrendering your passport to the tender mercies of DHL, FedEx or other local delivery service and crossing your fingers that nothing gets lost.

To renew in person while abroad, generally you need to bring the physical passport to be renewed, correct payment, and updated photos. **Check online with the local consulate or embassy nearest you for their exact procedures and payment preferences**.

See **Chapter 13, U.S. Federal Income Taxes**, to read about difficulties with your passport if you owe more than USD $53,000 in back taxes, interest and penalties to the federal government.

Chapter 16
Settling into Your New Home

Cell Phone Plans in Your New Country
Using a Facilitator
Common Sense Safety Precautions for Expats
Tips for Learning a New Language
Perception of Local Prices & Shopping
Noise & Noisy Neighbors
Sharing Contact Information

Cell Phone Plans in Your New Country

Probably one of the first things you will want to do after arrival in your new country is sign up for local cell phone service with a local phone number.

Why have a local country phone number?

- To be able to call emergency numbers for police, fire or ambulance
- To allow local tradespeople to contact you
- To allow delivery people to find your location and to call you (often using Google Maps and WhatsApp)
- To allow other expats or locals to call or text you
- To be able to make and receive calls from doctors and dentists
- To have a (possibly obligatory) phone number for banks & government offices

Before you jump into paying $35 for a monthly cell phone plan, explore all the alternatives. In much of the world, you can get a pay-as-you-go plan with very economical prices. In my years as an expat living abroad,

I have always used a prepaid cell plan because it meets my needs and is very economical.

> *If you are age 65 or older, check to see if there is a discount; some carriers offer discounts for senior citizens for phone or internet service.*

In Mexico I paid the equivalent of about USD $5 a month for *unlimited calling* to, from and *within* Mexico, the U.S. or Canada *plus* 3 gigabytes of data. By using Wi-Fi wherever possible, I rarely used the data and kept it in reserve for when the internet went out. It really did work from the U.S., too.

In Ecuador, for USD $10 a month you can get 10 GB of data and 200 minutes of calling to any (Ecuadorian) number. Additionally, you can designate up to five other numbers that use the same carrier for unlimited calling.

When making calls, I try to use Wi-Fi whenever possible, since that doesn't use any plan minutes, so 200 minutes a month is plenty for me.

> *Many parts of the world use WhatsApp for messaging, video and voice calls. Since streets may have no names and houses no numbers, it's especially useful for sending delivery people your exact location for deliveries.*

In most countries, to sign up for a prepaid plan you go to a cell phone store that sells sim cards and they will install it for you and set up the service. There may be a small charge for the sim card depending upon the carrier, but it's usually not more than a couple of dollars. They can also put a balance onto your account and you're all set with a local phone number and data in case Wi-Fi is not available.

You may be able to set up recurring payments online through your local bank (this is different from giving the cell phone company your bank account number); otherwise, you can pay for a reload in person at a store. I try not to give businesses a bank account number or a debit or credit card to pay recurring bills (like for internet service) if I can avoid it, because sometimes they continue charging you even after you've closed your account.

In Guatemala the wireless carriers are notorious for mysteriously draining your prepaid plan balance of unused minutes before the expiration of the term; it's clearly an abusive situation that the government apparently has no interest in addressing.

> *If you go in person to a store to reload your phone balance, be sure to stay in the store until you receive a text message confirmation from the carrier. I once had a store clerk try to rip me off for USD $10 by telling me that the network was "congested" and that it would be ten minutes before the balance would be registered. Because I knew better (the confirmation is always instantaneous), I refused to leave the store until she gave me my money back.*

See **Chapter 5, *Keeping in Touch with the U.S.*,** for more details about cell phones and how to keep a U.S. phone number at low or no cost without a sim card.

Using a Facilitator

As a recent arrival, you may wish to use a *facilitator* until you get more accustomed to your new home. Common in locations popular with expats, a *facilitator* is a local whose business is to assist expats with various tasks such as shopping for furniture and appliances (and arranging for delivery), accompanying you to a doctor's appointment, doing grocery shopping, assisting with setting up internet or utilities, or helping with banking.

Specialized facilitators can help with buying and registering a car or getting a local driver's license. Usually, a facilitator charges by the hour; rates will vary by country and locality.

Look for an online expat bulletin board or local English language newspaper, as often facilitators will advertise their services there. Check with other expats for recommendations. Choose carefully as there have been cases where facilitators have stolen funds from expats.

Common Sense Safety Precautions for Expats

Think like a New Yorker
New York City residents are quintessentially street-savvy people; try to think like a New Yorker back in the "bad old days" of the 1990s when the crime rate was much higher. Women wore a purse diagonally across their front, not on the shoulder.

I lived in Mexico for almost two years, visiting Mexico City multiple times and taking the subway and city buses around Mexico City. I spent three months in Medellin, Colombia and visited other parts of the country by myself. A friend and I took an overnight bus to Quito and then public transportation to our final destination in downtown Quito. Does that mean that Mexico, Colombia or Ecuador is safe for Americans to wander around and do dumb things? No, it does not.

It means having common sense and taking precautions. Research ahead of time if there are places you should not go. As a foreigner, you already stick out and may appear to be a tempting target for thieves or pickpockets. *No Dar Papaya* as the Colombians say (don't make yourself an easy target).

The U.S. State Department lists travel warnings for countries, regions or parts of cities, but this may not be a complete list or be very detailed. Often it will emphasize areas where U.S. government employees are forbidden to travel.

Plan Your Route Ahead of Time
Most important here is to *look like you know where you're going* and what you're doing (even if you don't). You don't want to look like a hopelessly lost and confused foreigner vulnerable to robbery or assault.

If you are walking to your destination, consult a map *before* you step out the door and plan your route. When I was new to Cuenca and unfamiliar with the city, I carried a piece of paper with a hand-drawn map with street names that didn't obviously look like a map, until I learned my way around. I avoided pulling out my phone or using a paper map while on the street.

If you will be taking the subway, streetcar or a city bus, figure out ***ahead of time*** which lines go to your destination, where to transfer trains or buses, and how to get to your final destination without having to check system maps.

Before leaving your house or hotel, check what the fare is, how the ticket machines work, and have the exact fares needed. You should be able to find this information online from the transit system, tourism or local government's websites. Make notes on a piece of paper that you will have with you to avoid looking uncertain, confused or lost.

If you're arriving in an unfamiliar city for the first time (or have much luggage), it may be worthwhile to pay for an official taxi and not take public transportation. It's still a good idea to know something about your route, in case your taxi driver decides to take the scenic route to run up the fare. Exercise extra caution if you will be jet-lagged from a time difference.

In Mexico City, unless I was with a male friend, I always rode in the "women only" subway car that every train has as the first car (enforced by uniformed transit system employees). I'm sure there are female pickpockets, but there are probably fewer of them in the "women only" car. You also avoid the perverts who masturbate or try to grope women on the train.

Follow the Local News if Possible
Are overnight intercity buses now being hijacked or robbed? Is there a new spike in crime in a certain location? Is there a form of crime unique to a particular city or country? Are the police or cab drivers trustworthy or not?

Don't Look at Your Cell Phone on the Street
Never look at your cell phone while you're walking down the street; keep it out of sight at all times while out in public. If I need to look at my phone (to consult Google Maps, for example), I try to step into a shop or a café before looking at my phone.

Why is looking at my phone while walking down the street a bad idea?

- First, by looking at it on the street, you are displaying it to everyone; the bad guys may assume that you as a foreigner will have a nice, expensive smart phone.
- Second, even in a "good" neighborhood, a thief can snatch your cell phone out of your hands and run or escape by motorcycle before you can do anything about it.
- Third, by looking at the phone you are not paying attention to your surroundings or being alert to who is around you (potential bad guys). *You're not being a New Yorker.*
- Fourth, you won't be interacting with locals or noticing interesting things if you're looking at your phone.
- Fifth, you might trip and fall due to uneven surfaces, which are quite common in many places. I've tripped and fallen a number of times. *Watch where you're walking.*

Don't Look Like a Rich Foreigner
I remember in Medellin, Colombia an American woman was wearing a rather big and flashy piece of jewelry on a chain around her neck, one of those solid gold bars. The thief isn't going to know whether it's gold-plated over silver, whether it's 14K or 18K or 24K gold. It was not a tiny, discreet little bar of gold worn under clothing. This wasn't the best thing to be wearing out on the street.

Wear Pickpocket-Resistant Pants
There are travel pants designed to foil pickpockets; one such brand is Clothing Arts, based in Brooklyn, New York. They make a line of men's and women's travel pants and shirts that are extremely difficult to pickpocket, with multiple layers of zippered pockets. A friend of mine likes to say that the pickpockets in Italy have advanced degrees, and it's true.

Cash, ATM & Credit Cards – Carry Only What You Need

- Carry only what you'll be using that day – cash, ATM card, credit cards. If you won't be using your ATM cards or credit cards, *leave them at home* in a safe place. There's no reason to carry around your U.S. driver's license in your wallet ***ever***. ***Don't***

carry everything in one wallet; if you should accidentally leave your wallet in a taxi, you may be facing a real crisis.

- Keep a supply of coins and small bills on hand for taxi drivers, so that they can't pull the "I don't have change" routine on you and overcharge you. In many places a taxi ride is only a dollar or two, so plan accordingly.

- Whenever you have the opportunity to break a larger bill into smaller ones, do it. Good places to do this are at supermarkets and larger department or chain stores, or a more expensive restaurant. Even if you have a smaller bill on hand and your total purchase is only $8, give them a larger bill and get change back.

- Like New Yorkers, you may want to keep some expired, useless credit cards and ATM cards in your wallet so that if you do get robbed or held up, you have something to give the robbers. They won't know until later that the cards are worthless.

Pick Your ATMs Carefully
Use ATMs located *inside* banks, supermarkets or shopping malls. Try to avoid ATMs out on the street. If there's a uniformed bank guard standing near the ATM (but not too close), that's good.

Many ATMS will only dispense larger denominations of bills, so plan accordingly.

How to Hide Cash at Home
You may want to use a portable disguised valuables container. You can either make one yourself (here's a video on YouTube on how to do it – "How to Make 6 Secret Hiding Spots" https://www.youtube.com/watch?v=H640jO_n1AQ). There are other similar videos on YouTube, so take a look. If you make your own, you can buy local brands of products that a thief in your country of residence wouldn't look twice at.

You can also buy professionally made disguised valuables containers at places like Bed, Bath & Beyond or online. These containers start out as actual containers – a can of soup, a Pringles potato chip can, a can of soda, whatever – and are then modified to hold cash.

Other expats stash smaller valuables or cash in a non-functioning electrical outlet in a room of the house.

Exercise Caution about Who Enters Your Home
As a foreigner, you may be viewed as "rich" by local standards and able to bear losses more easily than locals. Maids and cleaning people sometimes scope out your possessions and sell that information to burglars. I don't mean to suggest that all maids, gardeners and handymen are potential thieves (most are very honest and hard-working), but desperation can make anyone do bad things. *Be careful about whom you let inside your house.*

A safety tip: if a tradesperson, handyman or cleaning person is coming to your house and you will need to pay them, **before** they arrive in your house, have on hand the appropriate amount of cash when you need to pay them. Never let them see where you keep your cash in your house. You may want to hide your cash in more than one place at home.

How to Handle Panhandlers and Street Beggars
As a foreigner you may find people asking you for money more frequently than locals, because foreigners may hand out small sums more willingly than the locals.

Be aware that the person asking you for money on the street may be testing you to see if you pull out your wallet; you don't want to fall victim to a snatching or mugging. If you do decide to give money to people on the street, keep a supply of coins in a pocket that you can access *without bringing out your wallet.*

Groups that work with impoverished people do not recommend that you give money to people on the street, for the simple reason that you have no way of knowing their true situation. The pitiful man with no legs may actually have a good home with his family, who have stopped giving him cash because he will go on an alcoholic binge.

I am not saying that truly needy and desperate people are not out there asking for help, because they definitely are; the problem is differentiating between them and those who have substance abuse addictions or are pickpockets. Many locals won't give street beggars the time of day for this reason, as unfeeling as that seems.

A while ago, I was asked for money by a woman who looked to be about fifty years old, who held up an asthma inhaler and said that it cost $30 at the pharmacy, and that she desperately needed a refill. I wasn't going to give her $30, but I did give her a dollar. To my surprise, a few days later in another part of town she again asked me for money with the same story, apparently not recognizing me.

This time I told her about a nearby local non-profit that could, guaranteed, help her obtain the asthma inhaler refill for free – I knew the director personally. They could also assist her with rent, food and other necessities. She shook her head and said 'no, no.' She obviously wanted money and not the asthma inhaler. I imagine that if I had called her bluff and offered to go with her to a pharmacy to buy an inhaler, she would have turned down that offer, too.

I have printed out business cards with the contact information for food banks and groups that help indigent people, to hand out when people on the street ask me for money. I now give my money to the non-profits that work with the needy, who can properly assess their needs and help them get the assistance needed.

Don't Lock Yourself in or out of the House
In many parts of the world, it is entirely possible to lock yourself in or out of the house and be trapped. Many deadbolts require a key to open them from the inside; in the U.S. or Canada this is not allowed by the fire code, but it is very common elsewhere.

This also enables abusive family members to lock up other family members against their will. If you step outside for a moment and the door happens to slam shut, you can easily be locked out of the house.

This actually happened to me in Medellin, Colombia. I had just rented a furnished apartment and went out onto a balcony to check out the view.

A gust of wind slammed the door shut and there I was, stuck out on the balcony with no way back into the apartment.

I did not have my cell phone with me. Luckily there was a porter at the building's entrance and I was able to get his attention, and he called the owner of the apartment.

I later realized that the same thing easily also could have happened to me *inside* the apartment. If a gust of wind had blown the bedroom door shut, it could have locked the door with my keys and cell phone in the bedroom. I would have unable to get out of the apartment because I needed keys to open the front door. I was never warned about either of these hazards.

Safeguard Your Local ID card
I recommend, if it's legal, scanning and printing in color both sides of your resident ID card and getting the copies laminated into a card, and carry *that* around in your wallet. *Keep the original in a safe place at home.*

This laminated copy probably won't be sufficient for a bank, but for a store that just wants your ID number, it should be fine. This way, if your wallet gets stolen or lost, you still have the original ID card.

Get to Know Your Neighbors
When I lived in Guanajuato, Mexico there was an increase in residential burglaries. As is often the case in Mexico, the police were not very helpful or interested. So the neighbors of our *callejon* organized a Neighborhood Watch sort of thing, and held periodic meetings to discuss ways to improve security.

I attended those meetings to meet and get to know my neighbors, and it was very informative. I was the only foreigner who lived on our *callejon* and it was fascinating to observe my neighbors, including my landlord who lived next door, organizing against the burglars. They ordered laminated plastic banners to hang on exterior walls with messages warning off the thieves.

Exercise Caution about Business Partners
If you're planning on investing money in a business venture with partners, be careful with whom you go into business. It can be hard to know someone's true stripes until a disagreement arises, but local partners can become *very* upset at a disagreement and resort to violence.

I had a co-worker in New York whose dream was to own a scuba diving business. He obtained his diving instructor's license and left his job and invested in a dive business in Belize. He got into a disagreement with his business partners, who were defrauding him to the tune of about USD $150,000. He took them to court but before the case was decided in his favor, he was brutally murdered. His partners didn't appreciate the lawsuit.

Tips for Learning a New Language

Learning the Local Language
If you will be living somewhere where English is not the principal language, it's a good idea to learn at least a little of the local language. You will get so much more out of living in a foreign country if you are able to converse with people.

There are many different language learning programs and we all learn things in different ways. Try to find a program that matches your preferred learning style; if you are a visual learner, you probably won't be happy with an aural program that emphasizes listen-and-repeat only.

Tips to Make Learning a Foreign Language More Enjoyable
Since I have learned both German and Spanish as an adult, I have a few observations about the process. There is just no getting around it: learning a foreign language involves hard work and memorization.

- One technique that can help you to keep going when the going gets tough is to use a topic about which you are passionate, and practice the language using this topic (or topics).

  For example, if you are an avid soccer fan, you will likely enjoy foreign language lessons reading about and discussing soccer. If you are passionate about human rights abuses, then content about that topic will keep you interested when memorizing verb conjugations. If you live and breathe playing bridge, chess or poker, find local groups and play those games in the local language.

- Try reading the books of your favorite author(s) in the foreign language. Harry Potter or Stephen King books have been translated into almost every language. Forty years ago, when I was attending the University of Heidelberg in Germany, I bought paperback German translations of my favorite authors' books and read them, already knowing that I would enjoy the book. **Reading is the best way to improve your vocabulary**.

- If you're a fan of a particular U.S. TV show, watch it dubbed into the foreign language (U.S. TV shows and movies are popular worldwide). I watched *"Star Trek"* episodes in German, already knowing the English dialog by heart, so I could just focus on **how** to say something instead of on the meaning, which I already knew. I do the same now for TV shows dubbed into Spanish.

- Explore TV programming produced in the foreign language; if you can find a program that you really enjoy, you'll learn the language while having fun. I discovered a mini-series from Spain called *"The Time In Between"* (*"El Tiempo Entre Costuras"*) that was very well done; I have now read the novel upon which the series was based, as well as the sequel novel. There is a Spanish language version of the series *"Breaking Bad"* produced in Colombia (available on YouTube) that I found interesting.

- A book that I found very useful is *"**The Telenovela Method**"* by Andrew Tracey. While his book is about learning Spanish, the methodology works equally well for any language. In a nutshell, it involves watching TV and movies in the foreign language you are learning, using subtitles and closed captioning, and looking up every word you do not understand.

You learn to speak the way real people speak every day, and not the formal, "correct" textbook language. You watch programming that **you** are interested in and will enjoy. Andrew also points you to online language learning resources (some of them free) such as electronic flash cards that you customize for yourself.

I found a movie in Spanish that I just loved, "*La Dictadura Perfecta*," which is about political corruption in Mexico. It's very much black humor, and having watched it probably 25 times to improve my listening comprehension and vocabulary, I'm still not tired of it.

- If you like standup comedy, try viewing Netflix or YouTube videos. Depending upon your language level, you can begin with English subtitles, then switch to closed captioning (in the foreign language) as your comprehension progresses. Use a notebook to write down everything you don't understand. This is a great way to learn slang and colloquial expressions as well as cultural references. Very entertaining as well as educational.

> *The sooner you are able to converse in the local language, the more you will begin enjoying your new home and get to know local people. It will also save you money and possibly prevent you from being victimized.* **Consider time spent learning at least a little of the local language to be well spent.**

Go Exploring & Check Things Out

Make it your mission to explore your new home, its neighborhoods, customs and culture. Visit local stores, markets, secondhand stores, flea markets, fruit and vegetable vendors – ask the merchants what things cost.

Your new neighbors are a valuable resource of information – ask them questions. How often is garbage pickup? (Is there one?) How do you get bottled water or propane delivered? Do you even need bottled water? Is there a good tailor or seamstress nearby who can repair garments, whip up a new suit, or alter clothes if you've gained or lost weight? Do things go totally crazy around a particular holiday? Is there a problem with home burglaries in the neighborhood?

Perception of Local Prices & Shopping

Think about local prices in terms of local wages or purchasing power
While you are getting familiar with local prices, it helps to understand
what local prices are like. How much does a sales clerk in a store earn?
How about an electrician, plumber or auto mechanic? A university
professor? A physician? A surgeon or specialist? This will help you to
put into perspective the "local" cost of an item in relation to local wages.

This can be a real eye-opener. Things may start looking a LOT more
expensive. If a store clerk only earns the equivalent of USD $75 a week,
then spending USD $20 on a doctor's visit is a boatload of money.

Another useful exercise is to look up the U.S.'s per capita GNP (gross
national product), median per capita income or per capita household
income, and that of your new country of residence.

Let's say it's a 4:1 ratio. The next time you convert the price of something
into USD, multiply that price by four. So that "bargain" rental house or
apartment for USD $500 a month is actually the equivalent of USD
$2,000. If a skilled worker only earns USD $500 a month, then a USD
$500 rental would be **very** pricey.

Don't overpay for goods or services
The first year you are in a new place, you are very likely to overpay for
things until you learn the best places to shop. Some expats never do learn
the correct (not overpriced) price for things, and the locals are more than
happy to cater to these folks.

An expat in Mexico told me that she had been paying her cleaning lady
just slightly above the going rate ($2 to $3 an hour) for house cleaning.
Another expat paid this same cleaning lady $40 a week for two hours of
work (that's TEN TIMES as much), because *that's what she had paid her
house cleaner back home in the U.S.* The cleaning lady soon refused to
work for anyone else and my friend had to find a new cleaning lady.

By overpaying for things, you may unknowingly be making yourself a
target; the locals may think that you have a lot of money. By knowing
what customary, "normal" prices are and refusing to pay inflated prices,

you make yourself less vulnerable, and you will not be perceived to be a clueless "rich expat."

If you politely protest an incorrect price, the vendor may even be embarrassed enough to admit it and charge you the correct amount. If they don't, move on to the next seller and make your purchases from someone who charges honest prices.

Shopping when you're a new arrival

If you need to equip and furnish an apartment or house or make other significant purchases shortly after arrival, it would probably be best to enlist the help of a trustworthy local person.

A local will know where to go to get the best deals on certain types of merchandise. Is it better to buy furniture in a particular neighborhood, at the mall (doubtful), the flea market or at the local mom-and-pop furniture store where they make everything by hand in the back?

A local will also know about the small village 15 minutes away where you can buy your item for 40% less ... and can negotiate the price on your behalf if your language skills aren't yet up to par. Plus, it'll be fun to visit that small village and see what it's like.

Usually, the best prices will be found where the locals shop, and the highest prices in areas frequented by tourists or foreigners. The local produce or municipal market will almost always be cheaper than the supermarket, and will likely have better quality, fresher produce too.

On the other hand, most imported products will probably be found only in western-style supermarkets, so if you have a hankering for specialty items, you will most likely need to go to a supermarket.

Tipping for Services

Along with learning the correct, customary prices, you'll want to know in what circumstances tipping is expected, and if yes, what an appropriate tip should be. In most of Latin America, for example, a standard restaurant tip is 10% of the bill including taxes. In most of Europe, the tip is already included in the bill, so you don't want to add a tip a second time.

In many countries, taxi drivers do not expect to be tipped at all, although if the driver assists you with your luggage or packages, a small tip is always appreciated. It's a good idea to have a general idea of what the fare should be, so that you can detect excessive fares. Personally, I like to reward an honest taxi driver who is not overcharging me with a little extra something.

I also enjoy chatting with taxi drivers about whatever's been in the local news, and if I get a driver who is interested in discussing these things (not all are), he gets an extra-large tip. I once had a taxi driver here in Cuenca who read *The New York Times* in Spanish every day and was a very interesting conversationalist. He got a *really* big tip.

Noise and Noisy Neighbors

In many parts of the world, noisy neighbors and noise in general can be problematic by North American standards. There may be no local ordinances against barking dogs as public nuisances, and the police may be uninterested in noise complaints.

I am friends with a Colombian couple in Medellin who have had to move *five times* because of noisy neighbors. They always rent.

Imagine moving into a new place and then finding out there's a disco a block away about to open that will be blasting music until 3 a.m. on Friday and Saturday nights. Or that the neighbor across the street has *four* dogs that bark constantly at all hours.

I moved into a lovely, huge apartment in Cuenca in a desirable residential area near a university. I moved out less than six months later because of the noise. There was a pizzeria/bar on the corner that on Friday and Saturday nights had a live outdoors rock band (with loudspeakers) on their patio that would play past midnight. After having to sleep on the floor of my walk-in closet a few times due to noise, I had had enough.

Despite the neighbors circulating a petition against this business (which I enthusiastically signed), and countless complaints to the police and to City Hall from politically well-connected families, nothing changed. The last straw was when the university had a live heavy metal rock concert that went from 4 p.m. to midnight, with five-foot-tall loudspeakers aimed directly at our building. A new disco that was about to open down the street put the final nail in the coffin. It was time to move.

It can be hard to know about a particular neighborhood or block until you actually live there. Maybe it was quiet on the Saturday afternoon that you visited, but during the week the traffic and noise are unbearable. Is it underneath the flight path of the airport? Will that military barracks a block away have helicopters flying in and out all the time? You won't know until you live there.

Other Nuisances

I once rented an apartment that (unbeknownst to me when I rented it) backed onto a steel fabricating plant one block over *in the middle of a residential neighborhood.* The smells at times were very disagreeable, and there was the occasional metallic clanging as well.

Sharing Your Contact Information

You will undoubtedly be meeting new people (both expats and locals) as you travel to different places or settle into your new home, and will want to share your e-mail address and phone number with them. While you may be able to share information via smart phone, problems can arise if the person with whom you want to share contact information has an Android phone and you have an iPhone, or vice-versa.

If you carry a supply of business cards with you that have your contact information on them, you will always be prepared to hand out this information.

You can create business cards using MS Word (or other software program)'s free built-in templates. Decide on the information you want to put on the card: your name, e-mail address, a local phone number, a U.S. phone number or a small photo of yourself. There will generally be 16-20 cards on a sheet.

Save the file to a thumb drive and take it to a local copy or print shop that can print on lightweight card stock.

Chapter 17
Departure Travel Tips

Complications of One-Way Airline Tickets
Time of Day to Arrive at Your Destination
Luggage Tips
Traveling to/from Latin America?

Let's say you're all set to leave the U.S., all packed and have your one-way airline ticket purchased.   Everything's good to go, right? Well, not so fast ...

Complications of One-Way Airline Tickets

If You Will be Entering on a Residency Visa
If you already have your residency visa in hand before departing for your new foreign country destination using a one-way airline ticket, you may have fewer problems boarding your flight or entering the country. You'll be able to show your residency visa to the airline and immigration authorities.

If You Will be Entering on a Tourist Visa
However, if you will be visiting a country on a tourist visa (i.e., you'll be applying for residency after arrival), **many countries and airlines do not want you arriving on a one-way ticket**.

Why is it a Big Deal to Fly Using a One-Way Airline Ticket?

- The country may not want arrivals with one-way tickets because it may suspect that you are planning to overstay your visa or have other nefarious plans (like working illegally), or your financial resources may be in question.

- The airline may not want you flying on a one-way ticket because if you arrive at your destination and are denied entry by the immigration authorities (for any reason), the airline that brought you in to the country will be responsible for flying you back.

  Since airlines naturally enough do not want to have this expense, they may *deny you boarding* if you show up at the airport with a one-way ticket to board your flight. Often, having just a bus ticket to a destination in another country will do. Sometimes it's a matter of them just not liking your looks.

It can be hard to know which countries practice this policy, and it can be difficult know in advance. Colombia, Costa Rica and Ecuador for sure have this issue. I myself have flown into Mexico several times from various countries, without a return ticket, with only a tourist visa without any problems, but this is the kind of thing that **can change at any time.**

My general impression regarding Mexico is that if you are from the U.S., Canada or Europe and appear to have adequate resources (i.e., you're not a shaggy-looking backpacker, are an older respectable-looking person, or have a business class ticket), they won't bother you too much about a one-way ticket.

> *Keep in mind that whether you can board an international flight with a one-way ticket is totally at the discretion of the airline; they can deny you boarding at the airport if they feel like it.*

When I was returning to Mexico City from Quito in 2018, I was in the queue to check in for my flight and the airline was pulling people out of the line and denying them boarding. After I got home to Guanajuato, I found out what had been going on.

Mexico was worried that Ecuadorians were flying into Mexico for the purpose of crossing illegally into the U.S. and was denying entry to people who had visas, round-trip tickets, good jobs, houses and cars in Ecuador. As a result, the airline was denying boarding to people in Quito. This resulted in some very unhappy Ecuadorians who just wanted to go on vacation in Cancun.

Apparently, a few Americans and Canadians have also been denied boarding on flights to Mexico, but this seems to be people who for one reason or another have embarrassed the Mexican government (journalists, aid workers, and human rights activists).

At many international airports, immigration officials use closed circuit cameras to examine people in the arrivals immigration queue, and if they don't like your looks, they will ask you to come with them for an "interview" that can end with you being sent back to your point of origin. It can feel arbitrary and capricious.

There is some anecdotal evidence to suggest that passengers with a one-way business class ticket may receive less scrutiny by immigration authorities upon arrival at your destination. In any event, try not to look like a penniless backpacker.

> *Sometimes a round-trip airline ticket can cost the same as a one-way ticket, in which case it's simpler to just buy the round-trip ticket and avoid these issues.*

What Are the Options for Flights Departing from the U.S.?
If you'll be arriving in your foreign country using a tourist visa, a round-trip ticket is significantly more expensive than a one-way ticket, *and* you don't want to risk trying to fly "naked" on a one-way ticket, you basically have *four options*:

- You can buy a fully refundable roundtrip ticket from the U.S. (whose cost will likely be exorbitant) and then cancel the return ticket once you're inside your destination country and claim your refund;

- You can buy a cheap, non-refundable one-way onward passage to a third country and view it as insurance, and never use it. This is what I did when arriving in Ecuador; I bought a cheap one-way ticket from Quito to Bogota ($65) and never used it;

- You can try to purchase online a bus ticket leaving the foreign country in question for a third country. The problem is that often there are difficulties in making the online payment, as the bus company may not accept U.S. credit cards, and there may not be a way to buy a bus ticket unless you know someone locally who can go buy it for you; or

- You can use something like Onward Ticket (https://onwardticket.com/). For USD $14, you can book a legitimate and confirmed flight reservation in your name that is valid for a minimum of 48 hours. You receive your printable PDF ticket with a valid PNR (passenger name record, that letters-and-numbers reservation code) instantly, 24/7 in case an airline or immigration desk asks to see an onward ticket. Popular with digital nomads.

Time of Day to Arrive at Your Destination

As a general rule, if you are unfamiliar with a place or have never been there before, try to avoid arriving at night. There may be destinations where virtually all international arrivals only arrive at night, in which case you may not have a choice. See if you can spend the night at an intermediate stop so that you arrive at your final destination during the day. You will also arrive more alert and rested.

Late night arrivals mean you will likely be exhausted and groggy from jet lag and more likely to get overcharged by taxis, or leave behind belongings accidentally in a taxi.

If you are familiar with your destination or have someone meeting you at the airport, then arriving at night is a little less of a concern. It's still better overall to arrive during daylight hours, though; the bad guys tend to be out at night.

Personally, I like to arrive at an international destination by mid-morning or midday; that gives you enough time to go through customs and immigration, get to your hotel, relax and unwind, get something to eat, and then sleep for twelve hours (assuming you're able to fall sleep).

When you wake up it will be morning and you'll be on local time.

Luggage Tips

You may have a lot of luggage if you are moving out of the U.S. If this is the case, check into the price of a business class ticket. Not only is the weight limit per suitcase higher in business class (often seventy pounds vs. fifty pounds in coach), but you may be allowed to check more suitcases for free, and the charge for exceeding the number of free suitcases or weight allowances may be less.

> *Buy a luggage scale before you pack your suitcases and check the weight of your suitcases carefully. With a coach ticket, the additional charge for extra suitcases or overweight luggage can be $100 or more per suitcase, whereas with a business class ticket, the additional charge per suitcase might be only $25.*
>
> *With the extra luggage charges, the total overall cost may be the same or less for a business class ticket than for a coach ticket, plus you'll enjoy better food and more leg room during the flight.*
>
> *If you have a long layover between connecting flights, the business class lounge can be a nice place to hang out and nosh on the free food and beverages. Depending upon the airport there may even be free shower facilities and cubicles available for taking a nap.*

Keep an Eye on TSA Changes in Carry-on Luggage
The Transportation Security Agency (TSA) can change carry-on luggage requirements at any time for security reasons, so pay attention to the most current rules. Several years ago, there were rumors that the TSA was going to ban laptops in carry-on luggage, requiring you to check it instead. Depending upon the country of destination, that could mean that your laptop wouldn't ever arrive in checked luggage due to theft.

Shrink-Wrapping of Luggage
In some airports it is possible to get your luggage wrapped in a large-size *Saran Wrap* sort of plastic, which offers some protection from thieves

while in transit. Typically, the kiosks where this is offered are located in the departure terminal before you check your luggage with the airline.

Having suffered items stolen from my own suitcases, I find that it can be worthwhile to have this done if you are traveling to a part of the world where luggage thefts are common. It usually involves a fee of USD $10-$15 per suitcase.

Traveling to/from Latin America?

If you are heading to or from Latin America, you may wish to check into ticket prices for departures or arrivals from the Tijuana (Mexico) Airport on the border with San Diego. For non-Mexico destinations you may need to transfer to onward flights in Mexico City, but the savings can be substantial.

Cross Border Xpress Facility in San Diego, California
San Diego has a wonderful facility called the Cross Border Xpress which opened in December of 2015. It allows you to enter the Tijuana Airport Terminal from the U.S. (San Diego) side of the border, since the Tijuana airport is right on the border with San Diego.

At least four million passengers are expected to use the Cross Border Xpress facility in 2022 (30% of total passengers using the Tijuana Airport, which just completed a large expansion in May 2022).

You check in with your airline on the U.S. side of the border, get your luggage tagged for your flight, walk over a sky bridge (where you are crossing the international border), go through Mexican Customs and Immigration and you are then in the Tijuana airport. You must purchase a SkyWalk ticket in order to cross the border using CBX.

As of 2022, the price of SkyWalk tickets varies by time of year and direction, and is $18-$22 one-way, round trip $32 to $35; 20% discount if purchased through the website or CBX app. There are also commuter plans for frequent travelers, discount plans for family groups, and military discounts. Additional charges apply for unaccompanied minors ages 12-17 or for porter assistance including a wheelchair.

Tickets can be purchased online and printed out before you leave home via the CBX website https://www.crossborderxpress.com/en/.

> *If you will be remaining in Mexico more than 48 hours, there is also a tourist tax of around USD $28 that is collected upon entry at the Mexican Customs and Immigration checkpoint (this is for land entry, different from air entry). If you are just transiting through Mexico (24 hours or less) on your way to another country, this tourist tax should **not** apply (but they may try to collect it).*

When you fly into Mexico as a tourist on an international flight, this tax is automatically added to your ticket price, so you don't see it (there is also a departure tax on international flights). If crossing by the Cross Border Xpress, be sure to have enough cash on hand to pay this tax if needed.

> *If you will be staying in Mexico for more than 48 hours, when the Mexican Immigration official stamps your tourist visa (called an FMM) that documents that you've paid the tourist tax, make sure that the stamp is legible. I paid the tax when I entered Mexico, but had to pay it a second time when I was leaving because the stamp was so faint that it was hard to read and the immigration officials at the Mexico City airport refused to accept it as proof of payment. **Make them stamp it a second time if it's hard to read.***

If you pick a rental car company with locations at both the San Diego airport and at the CBX terminal, you can rent a car at the San Diego airport (which is near downtown San Diego) and return the car at the CBX terminal, which will save you from having to travel from downtown San Diego to Otay Mesa (about half an hour away).

Overall, I was impressed with how easy it was to use the CBX terminal. If you are returning to the U.S. from Mexico (or are willing to route your trip through Tijuana), it is quite a bit faster to go through U.S. Customs and Immigration at the CBX facility rather than at the San Diego or Los Angeles airports.

Wikipedia has a nice article about Cross Border Xpress at https://en.wikipedia.org/wiki/Cross_Border_Xpress in case you want to read more about it.

Chapter 18
Further Resources

Information Sources for Would-be Expats
Income Tax Return Preparers – Expat Tax Returns

You can find much information online about the expat life, including blogs (which may be undated and contain out-of-date information), videos and free newsletters. Below are additional sources of information that you may find useful.

I have included several resources for locations in Mexico because many readers of this book may be interested in Mexico due to its geographical proximity to the U.S. and relative ease of obtaining residency.

As you do research into the prospect of moving abroad, keep in mind that the below resources are *just a sampling* of what's available.

Don't forget to take a look at the checklists, timelines and sample letter that are at my website, https://sites.google.com/view/northoak-books.

Information Sources for Would-be Expats

Live & Invest Overseas
Based in Panama with U.S. owners, Live & Invest Overseas offers podcasts, newsletters, conferences and publications about every aspect of moving abroad. The company assists would-be expats in deciding whether it makes sense to move abroad for work or retirement.

Countries covered are in Europe, Asia and Latin America. The company offers many freebies such as location-specific publications and newsletters to entice you to make purchases. https://www.liveandinvestoverseas.com/

International Living
The grand dame of the move-overseas movement, International Living started out as a newsletter around forty years ago, and is now a successful magazine and online business advising those interested in living abroad about all aspects of the expat life.

International Living holds conferences about various places around the world that are popular with expats. You can sign up for daily postcards or receive various reports for free via email.
https://internationalliving.com/

Retire Early Lifestyle – Akaisha & Billy Kaderli
Pioneers of the expat move-abroad movement, Akaisha and Billy Kaderli got tired of the work rat race and chucked the career hamster wheel in 1991 at age 38. Akaisha and Billy's website has a free newsletter and much valuable information about the financial aspects of quitting your job and moving abroad.

Their blog documents their travels and experiences, has interviews with other expats and articles about how to create financial sustainability. They sell a number of books about how to retire abroad at any age from their website as well.
https://www.retireearlylifestyle.com/

Escape Artist
Escape Artist bills itself as "the most comprehensive source for information, resources, analysis and insights for the internationally minded." With offices in the U.S., Belize, Panama and Portugal, Escape Artist has six different free newsletters and many articles on topics relating to being an expat. Has an emphasis on investments and reducing U.S. taxation. Free weekly newsletter. https://www.escapeartist.com/

Nora Dunn's Blog *"The Professional Hobo"*
The blog of a woman who has been traveling full-time for twelve years, *"The Professional Hobo"* has a mix of articles about Nora's own travel experiences, the business of blogging, and interviews with others who live abroad full-time.

Nora has been a digital nomad since 2016 and addresses topics such as how to travel with minimal luggage, what's the best travel insurance to have, best money transfer services, how to change careers mid-stream, how to start your own blog, how to earn enough money to live on and handle finances while abroad, and much more. https://www.theprofessionalhobo.com/

InterNations

An expat networking non-profit, it has chapters in 420 cities around the world. Members tend to be younger and still working professionally, but the organization welcomes all ages.

InterNations holds over 6,000 events and activities worldwide each month. Sample activities include an Armenian Oriental dinner party in Brussels, a tour of Soweto in South Africa, beach volleyball in Singapore, a desert safari in Doha, and *many* expat community meetups at local bars and restaurants. https://www.internations.org

American Citizens Abroad

Located in Washington D.C., American Citizens Abroad has over 40 years of experience in educating, advocating and informing both the US Government and US Citizens living and working overseas on issues of concern to the overseas U.S. citizen community. ACA advocates for expats in the areas of taxation, FATCA & FBAR compliance, banking, voting, citizenship, Social Security, and Medicare and healthcare.

For $70 a year ($55 if age 65 or over) you can access ACA's network of resources, including information on FBAR, FATCA, revocation of U.S. passport due to IRS tax debt, advice about banking problems, and a directory of income tax preparers who specialize in expatriate taxation. Membership will also qualify you to join the U.S. State Department Federal Credit Union. https://www.americansabroad.org

Meetup Groups

There are Meetup groups all over the world, for many different interests. Whether you are a retiree, a digital nomad, or expat working abroad for a company, there likely is a Meetup group near you for U.S. expats.

For example, there are about 20 Meetup groups in Bangkok, Thailand which focus on interests such as cycling, walking, running, language learning, day trips, photography, scuba diving, coffee & a movie, or entrepreneurs interested in creating a new startup business. https://www.meetup.com/

Facebook Groups
There are almost as many Facebook groups as there are people. If you're interested in a particular location, check and see if there's an expat Facebook group for it; odds are, there are one or more groups. https://www.facebook.com/

Local Online Bulletin Boards
Many times, a location that has a number of expats will have a locally operated bulletin board (in English) that provides information to the expat community. Examples are Gringo Post (Cuenca, Ecuador) and GTO List (Guanajuato, Mexico). Check and see if there is such an online bulletin board for the area in which you are interested.

Mexperience
As its name suggests, this website focuses on Mexico as a destination for U.S. citizens. Located in Playa del Carmen, Mexperience offers a free newsletter and a number of e-books, such as *Living and Retirement in Mexico 2022* (free to download). The company offers assistance with applying for residency as well. https://www.mexperience.com

American Society of Jalisco
In Guadalajara, Mexico is the American Society of Jalisco with a lovely house and grounds, an English language library and DVD lending library. The membership leans more towards retired persons or those interested in moving to the Guadalajara/Lake Chapala area. https://www.facebook.com/groups/1208469089227179/about

Guadalajara Reporter (Mexico) – online English language newspaper for expats in the Guadalajara area. https://theguadalajarareporter.net/

Lake Chapala Society (Mexico)
In the Lake Chapala area, the Lake Chapala Society from its almost-one-full-square-block) headquarters offers its members Spanish language

classes, activities such as iPad classes, TED lecture series, weekly showings of films, an English library of over 26,000 books and over 4,000 DVDs, as well as a mail service to the U.S. and support for newcomers. They even have regular shopping trips by bus to Costco and Home Depot in Guadalajara. Annual membership in 2022 is MXN 830 (about USD $40), with a discount for those age 79 and over. If you're visiting for just one month, a 30-day membership is MXN 290 or about $15. https://lakechapalasociety.com/public/

Mr. Money Mustache – How to Live Frugally in the U.S.
This blog, started by Canadian computer scientist Pete Adeney (who now lives in Colorado), documents his journey of living frugally while improving his quality of life. Mr. MM has many valuable tips on how to take the scissors to your living expenses and invest the savings for future financial independence.

Now living in Colorado, Mr. MM said "no more" to being a wage slave and treasures his freedom. Start saving those pennies so that you too can become an expat. https://www.mrmoneymustache.com/

Being Frugal.net
Founded in 2007 by a homeschooling mom, Being Frugal.net is a blog about how to save money in many different aspects of everyday life. "A learning place for family lifestyle, finances and frugality." http://www.beingfrugal.net/

U.S. Income Tax Return Preparers Who Specialize in Expat Returns (Chapter 13)

If you decide that the H&R Block Expat Edition of their tax preparation software is not for you, or you need more personal attention in doing your income taxes, I would suggest using someone who specializes in U.S. expat returns, as it is an area that requires specific knowledge that the typical tax return preparer might not deal with every day.

There are U.S. expat return preparers who do nothing but expat returns; some are based in foreign countries and can be more economical than using one of the high-priced international accounting firms.

Investigate for yourself the firm's qualifications. What are the qualifications and experience levels of its return preparers? Be sure to inquire about the firm's IT security practices and data encryption – how will they avoid being hacked? How they will handle written correspondence with the IRS? Does the firm have access to an online tax library for its preparers to consult?

> *Below are some possibilities for expat tax return preparers; being listed below is not an endorsement and **I have no firsthand knowledge** of any of the following firms' quality or fees. All claim to specialize in the expat taxation area, including filing delinquent income tax returns or FBARs. All operate online and will file your return electronically.*

- **Bright! Tax** – bills itself as the leading online U.S. expat tax services provider, employs only full-time American CPAs who work year-round. https://brighttax.com

- **Greenback Expat Tax Services** – has clients in 217 countries and territories, team of CPAs and enrolled agents in ten different time zones. Also prepares Canadian and UK income tax returns. https://www.greenbacktaxservices.com/

- **Online Taxman** – owner Vicenzo Villamena is based in New York City and has an online team with physical offices in New York,

  Hong Kong and Medellin, Colombia. They handle all U.S. expat taxation matters and controversies. https://onlinetaxman.com/

- **ExpatTax.com** – American CPAs and enrolled agents who specialized in expat professionals, digital nomads, educators and self-employed/small business owners anywhere in the world. Offices in Hong Kong, Shanghai, Tokyo, Bangkok and Vancouver, Canada. https://expattax.com

- **My Expat Taxes** – Europe-based software startup, offers a do-it-yourself online base plan, or with add-on professional review, or a personal accountant who will do everything from beginning to end. https://www.myexpattaxes.com

- **Taxes for Expats** – online firm of CPAs, attorneys and enrolled agents who handle all U.S. tax matters for expats residing in any country worldwide. Has a custom app for iOS and Android smart phones that enables you to log into your account at any time. 20% discount for clients who file three or more years' returns at one time. https://www.taxesforexpats.com

- **Pinnacle Accounting Inc.** – based in Ohio; owner Jake Mitrovic is an enrolled agent whose U.S. local accounting firm that specializes in expat taxes. He has a free newsletter than you can sign up for as well. https://www.expatriate-taxes.com

- **Expat Tax Online** – owner Andrew J. Landin is a former Ernst & Young and PriceWaterhouseCoopers tax manager now based in Australia. https://www.expattaxonline.com

About the Author

Ann Fourt had an early spirit for adventure and exploration when at the age of three she got her first tricycle and took off down the street. No one thought much of it until the police brought her home, having found her pedaling the tricycle a mile away.

A retired tax CPA, internal auditor and fraud examiner, Ann speaks German and Spanish and has lived in Germany, Mexico and Ecuador. She currently lives in Cuenca, Ecuador.

If you enjoyed this book, please go to Amazon.com and leave a review. A year's worth of hard work went into writing this book and she hopes you got valuable information from it.

INDEX

Index

Index

Made in the USA
Monee, IL
11 June 2024

59752136R00164